A
Landscape
History of Japan

A
Landscape
History of Japan

Edited by

Akihiro KINDA

Kyoto University Press

Caption for cover photos:

FRONT: Digital areal photo of Kyoto (Virtual Kyoto, Geography Department, Ritsumeikan University).

BACK: Tonami dispersed settlement area in Toyama prefecture in 2009.

Copyright © 2010 Kyoto University Press

Copyedited by: Editage (a division of Cactus Communications Pvt. Ltd.)
www.editage.jp
Typeset and designed by: Cactus Japan K.K.
www.cactus.co.jp

Printed in Japan

Kyoto University Press
Kyodai-Kaikan (Kyoto University Hall)
15-9 Yoshida-Kawara-cho, Sakyo-ku
Kyoto-city 606-8305
Japan
www.kyoto-up.or.jp

ISBN 978-4-87698-792-4 (Paper)

Contents

Introduction of the editor and authors vii

Preface ix

PART 1 Aims and methodology

CHAPTER 1 Methodology of Japanese landscape history:
A contextual approach 3
Akihiro KINDA

CHAPTER 2 Formation and transformation
of administrative districts 21
Akihiro KINDA

PART 2 Urban landscapes

CHAPTER 3 National and provincial capitals in ancient Japan 37
Akihiro KINDA

CHAPTER 4 Medieval towns 65
Aki YAMAMURA

CHAPTER 5 Capitals and towns in early modern times 89
Aki YAMAMURA

PART 3 Rural landscapes

CHAPTER 6 Ancient and medieval rural settlement 115
Akihiro KINDA

CHAPTER 7 The early modern rural landscape 137
Taisaku KOMEIE

CHAPTER 8 Modernization of the countryside 163
Taisaku KOMEIE

PART 4 Landscape, materials and representation

CHAPTER 9   Landscapes and maps   189
                Akihiro KINDA and Kazuhiro UESUGI
CHAPTER 10   Landscapes in literature and painting   223
                Taisaku KOMEIE
CHAPTER 11   Monumental landscape   243
                Kazuhiro UESUGI

PART 5 Cultural landscapes

CHAPTER 12   Characteristics of the Japanese landscape history   267
                Akihiro KINDA

Subject index   275
Author index   283

Introduction of the editor and authors

Akihiro KINDA, D. Litt. (*Kyoto*)
President, National Institutes for the Humanities (Japan).
Professor Emeritus, Kyoto University.
Some traditions and methodologies of Japanese historical geography, *Journal of Historical Geography 23-1*, 1997.
The concept of 'townships' in Britain and the British colonies in the seventeenth and eighteenth centuries, *Journal of Historical Geography 27-2*, 2001.

Taisaku KOMEIE, Ph.D. (*Kyoto*)
Associate Professor of Geography, Kyoto University.
His main research interests are historical geography of mountain villages and environmental history of forest both in Japan and Korea.
Chu-kinsei Sanson no Keikan to Kouzou (Landscape and Structure in Medieval and Early Modern Highland Japan).

Aki YAMAMURA, Ph.D. (*Kyoto*)
Associate Professor of Geography, Aichi Prefectural University.
Her main research interest is historical geography of medieval and early-modern towns in Japan.
Chusei Toshi no Kukan Kozo (The Spatial Structure of Medieval Towns in Japan).

Kazuhiro UESUGI, Ph.D. (*Kyoto*)
Lecturer in Historical Geography, Kyoto Prefectural University.
His main research interest is geographical knowledge in early modern Japan and commemoration of wars.
Edo Chishiki-jin to Chizu (Maps and knowledge: Intellectual Culture in the 18th century Japan).

Preface

When I was a graduate student at Kyoto University in the 1970s, the most popular method for reconstructing past landscapes was based on the concept of thick cross sections in Japan. This method had been insisted on by Professor Kenjiro Fujioka, a mentor of mine, ever since I was an undergraduate student at the university, although some of his senior disciples such as Professor Kenryo Ashikaga wanted and tried to implement methods of more rigid cross sections. As for me, I tried to analyze the process of changing rural landscapes as precisely as possible as part of my MA thesis that was completed in 1971. Since the landscape had become a central theme in my work, I too had to think about the nature and implications of such a concept.

A few years later, I came across Professor H.C. Darby's concept of thin cross sections in the second edition of his work *A New Historical Geography of England* published in 1973; it took me a few more years, however, to realize that the method proposed in the second edition was radically different from that employed in the first. Much later, in the 1990s, when I read Professor Darby's article (1983) on cross sections in *Transaction of the Institute of British Geographers 8*, it was a surprise for me that Darby was still engaged in deliberating on the choice of methods. He wrote that while he had adopted the method of thin cross sections, he had considered the thick cross section method as a viable alternative when he had begun to edit the second edition.

I thought that we had better create another method as a possible third way of dealing with the reconstruction of landscapes. The reason for this will be mentioned in the first chapter of this book. Thus, a new contextual approach to landscape history is what we have adopted in this book.

I have mainly been interested in the ancient and medieval landscapes and worked closely on these subjects in this book. Some of my interests have, of course, been stimulated by the mentors I have had since I was an undergraduate student. I have been initiated into the art of old maps by Professor Takeo Oda, learnt methods related to the morphology of 'land and settlement' with reference to German geography under Professor Ichro Suizu, and developed an interest in the past landscapes under the guidance of Professor Fujioka.

The other authors of this book include Dr. Taisaku Komeie, who is interested in rural landscapes and various materials including literatures and paintings from the early modern and modern times, Dr. Aki Yamamura, who is an authority on the urban landscapes since the medieval times, and Dr. Kazuhiro Uesugi, whose area of specialization involves materials such as early modern maps and representations of landscapes including monuments. I was privileged to supervise the works of each of these talented individuals at Kyoto University, from their undergraduate levels through to their respective PhDs. They have contributed effectively to this book, each in their area of specialty.

This book is published by a Grant-in-Aid for Publication of Scientific Research Results from the Japan Society for the Promotion.

I do hope that this book contributes something to the subject of historical geography and paves the way, if only a little, to a more comprehensive understanding of Japanese landscape history.

December 2009
At the end of the year, the Fourteenth International Conference of Historical Geographers was held in Kyoto, Japan.

Akihiro KINDA
President, National (Japan)
Institutes for the Humanities

PART 1

Aims and methodology

CHAPTER 1

Methodology of Japanese landscape history: A contextual approach

Akihiro KINDA

Introduction: Japanese historical periods

Japanese historical geography had its own history of descriptions in several traditional themes; during the first half of the twentieth century, while some of these traditional inquiries continued, Japanese historical geography was influenced by developments in western countries. Following the end of World War II, much attention was directed to the development of "thick" cross-sections in the 1950s and 1960s; since the 1970s, Japanese historical geography has been characterized by the progress of empirical investigations that have employed integrated methods, new techniques and data, and new methodologies. In describing the landscape history of Japan, this chapter will refer to selective topics that have attracted the attention of scholars: urban form and function, morphology and the cadastral land system, and rural settlement and land-use. It also needs to be noted that for Japanese historical geographers the term "prehistoric" refers to the period up to the sixth century; the "ancient" period generally refers to the seventh century through to 1185; the "medieval" period extends from 1185 until the mid-sixteenth century; finally, the "early-modern" period is considered to have lasted from the mid-sixteenth century until the year 1868, when the "modern" period is reckoned to have begun.

Identifying places and reconstructing past geographies

Interest in the historical–geographical matters of Japan in the ancient and medieval periods was centered on the political and administrative systems of the day, since such knowledge was necessary for aristocrats to govern effectively. Each aristocratic family compiled precedents for laws and ceremonies into a manual during the medieval period, when they shared political power with the newly emerging warrior classes, and were in charge of providing detailed knowledge of procedures and ceremonies at the imperial court. One such manual, *Syugaisyo* was written at the end of the thirteenth century in the form of a manuscript book in three volumes. This manuscript book was revised the following century, and published in the seventeenth century. It had complete accounts of the capital,

4 A Landscape History of Japan

the political regions and land systems, and had had a considerable influence not only on the aristocrats in the medieval period but also on intellectuals much later, including modern scholars[1]. The contents of such manuals inevitably included some comparisons with China, which was from where political systems and ideas were introduced into Japan and implemented after being modified. For later topographies, written in many provinces during the eighteenth and nineteenth centuries, the ancient and medieval administrative units such as the provinces, counties, *go* (a kind of British *hundred*) and manor were important. The locations of administrative centers, palaces, deserted temples and shrines, ancient highways, abandoned castles, and the former courses of rivers were also interpreted, drawing upon the earliest descriptions in the topographies and chronicles of the eighth and ninth centuries[2]. Such historical–geographical scholarship—well established in Japan much before the adoption of the modern scientific thinking of the Western countries—was powerful and popular enough to have been compiled into an eight volume dictionary of names of historical places in 1900–1909. Two new series of huge dictionaries have been published since 1978, with 1,000 to 1,500 pages making up each volume for each of the prefectures[3].

Until the beginning of the twentieth century, there had been two clearly distinguishable traditions in Japanese historical geography: one focused on the very close links between history and geography in both Japan and China; the other focused on very ancient places and their descriptions in primary sources. In 1907, when the first professor of geography in Japan, T. Ogawa, was appointed at the Department of History, Kyoto University, it marked the beginning of the development of modern historical geography, with a substantive research agenda that included studies of the plans of ancient capital cities, the origins of settlement patterns, changing processes and systems of urbanization and transportation, historical metrologies, and comparative studies with China[4]. Nearly all studies provided interpretative descriptions of changing landscapes. It seemed that historical geography was regarded as a field that undertook the tracing of the antecedents of present-day geography[5].

S. Komaki, in a paper read at the I.G.U. Congress in Warsaw in 1936 and in a book published in 1937, adopted the methodologies of H. Mackinder, O. Schluter, S. Passarge and A. Hettner and defined prehistoric and historical geography as a science of space, not of time. He emphasized that the principal objective of historical geography was the reconstruction of the cross-section of a place in a particular period in the past; Komaki consolidated the basic methodology of modern historical geography[6]. His approach was effective in differentiating historical geography from other schools of geography that ignored historical processes. An identification of ancient rural landscapes by J. Yonekura in 1932 that applied A. Meizten's genetic method[7] and relied upon the characteristic shapes of nucleated villages and the regular grid patterns of their paddy fields, provided a possible interpretation of ancient administrative units of rural areas and a practical model for subsequent research. Yonekura also recognized the origin of the systematic land system and the accompanying grid patterns known as the *jori* as having lain in the practices of the seventh century; he also reconstructed the shape of the provincial capital "Ohmi-kokufu" as a tetragon-shaped town with grid street patterns[8]. Both of Yonekura's postulates were also accepted not only in historical geography but also in associated disciplines.

Although both Komaki's cross-sectional approach with respect to prehistoric geography and Yonekura's reconstructions of ancient landscapes provided only static understandings of past geographies, they did expand the intellectual horizon of their time, and their methodologies went on to become "new" traditions. The latter maintained the "old" tradition of having close links with history and with the subject of China in addition to carrying descriptions of very ancient places despite its "modern" features.

The concept of "thick" cross-sections and retrospective interpretation

The progress of Japanese historical geography has been based primarily on the nature of the methodology applied. Komaki's conception of the cross-section, as the reconstruction of a particular static past, was redefined by K. Fujioka in 1955 to mean "the history of regional change," an approach which traces regional change through time[9]. Although this method seems to be basically similar to H. Darby's theory of successive cross-sections, Fujioka's definition of a cross-section was, in fact, clearly "thick," and was similar to a narrative method considered but not adopted by Darby as an alternative to the intercalation of "horizontal cross-sections" and "vertical themes" which he employed in his *A New Historical Geography of England*[10].

The use of "thick" cross-sections made it possible to incorporate the results of studies in archaeology and history as well as in contemporary geography, and made it possible to evade, partly, the incompleteness of documentary sources when it came to reconstructing "thin" cross-sections. Fujioka propounded the idea of "archaeological geography," a subject woven around archaeological data and relic landscapes; it was an idea that was realized in the form of a series of publications entitled *Lectures on Archaeological Geography* in 1984–1989[11]. Fujioka's method could also embrace related factors to describe changes in, for instance, economies, ideologies and physical environments in different period, and could apply, to historians' ideological explanations such as in the case of Marxist interpretations. Considerable research was undertaken by Fujioka and his pupils, resulting in five volumes entitled *A General Historical Geography of Japan* published in 1975 and 1977. These volumes presented five cross-sections for each region of Japan in the prehistoric, ancient, medieval, early-modern and modern periods[12], thus differing from Darby's approach, in his new 1973 edition, of several "thin" cross-sections and interlinked narrative accounts[13].

Fujioka always considered relics of past landscapes and the continuing role of the past in the present-day geography of a region; his thinking was so strongly retrospective[14] that he sometimes applied his method of historical geography to contemporary urban geographical inquiries[15]. He undertook many studies of provincial capitals in ancient Japan to reveal the general tetragonal planning and its local variations in addition to conducting comparative research on ancient Japanese and Roman road patterns[16]. His methodology and practical survey in the field became so widely-accepted that Japanese historical geography was re-established as a sub discipline. Many empirical inquiries have employed Fujioka's method to analyze subjects such as prehistoric regions[17], ancient imperial and pro-vincial capitals, ancient county seats, river and sea ports, ancient grid patterns of the field (*jori*), ancient roads and relay posts, and early-modern castle towns[18].

Researches on topics pertaining to the early-modern and modern Japan had slightly different areas of emphasis from Fujioka's work because of the many documentary sources available for those periods. While such researches were also basically dependent on the "thick" cross-section method, their reconstructions and descriptions were much more detailed and more clearly dated. Agricultural systems, rural development, demography, land reclamation, irrigation systems, shapes and structures of towns and rural settlements, land ownership and admin-istration under the feudal system, and the location and changing patterns of mar-ket towns and transportation systems were all popular themes[19].

The reconstruction of past physical environments has been a major theme since Komaki's early work on prehistoric regions, and such studies have extended to cover the historical period as well. Past climates, vegetation and sea levels as well as geo-morphological features have come to be included in the discussion[20].

Ever since its institution as a subject, Japanese historical geography has, in all associated research, had the landscape as one its underlying focus areas. The Japanese word *keikan*, which has become popular as a technical term not only in geography but also in other disciplines—instead of the word *fukei* which implies a visual and perceptual landscape—is a translation from the German *Landschaft*. This means that "landscape" in Japanese geography has been more of a regional or spatial concept, rather than a visual concept[21], and has often been used to convey a meaning similar to the word "region." The spatial plan or morphology of land-scape had been the most important factor in many geographical works; this has led to some confusion when discussions have been held with scholars employing the English meaning of landscape, especially those from the W. Hoskins' school in England[22] and C. Sauer's school of cultural geography[23].

The "thick" cross-section theory has therefore been combined with the aerial concept of landscape, and treated as regions would be approached. In a "thick" context such as this, the interpretation of regional change can be flexible and suf-ficiently narrative to incorporate "the vital spark of history"[24].

Integrated analysis

Since the late 1960s, empirical research on the orthodox cross-sectional framework has made considerable progress not only in terms of quantity but also in terms of quality. Most methodologies developed in the Western countries were introduced or re-examined in the 1970s, such as those in the works of a history of geographical thought[25] and of a collection of introductory essays on sixteen geographers that included August Meitzen, the oldest, and Alan Baker, the youngest[26]. Some of the major themes can briefly be mentioned here; the following chapters explain these in more detail.

The *jori* grid pattern, consisting of squares with sides of approximately 109 meters, had boundaries that were usually in the form of narrow paths and ditches in cadaster or real feature, within which there were typically ten rectangular subdivisions; this was the basic unit of paddy cultivation and was widely distributed on the alluvial plains of Japan until the transformations brought about by land reform and urbanization took effect. This has been surveyed in many regions and examined as a key relict feature; the *jori* grid pattern is thought to be indicative of the changing patterns of spatial organization in ancient Japan. The discovery of straight boundaries of provinces and counties, some following the *jori* grid patterns and others not, made it possible to study the planning of regions as it had been in the past[27]. Within the *jori* grid patterns, almost all arable lands were once thought of as paddies, and non-annually-cultivated lands were considered as expressions of the rotation systems of the day, such as those associated with European medieval villages; both interpretations, however, were merely inferred or arrived at by analogy, and have been proved groundless[28]. In fact, 15–50 per cent of arable land in ancient Japan was actually dry field, and many fields were cultivated only once every few years because of the shortage of irrigation water or because of some other physical or social environmental limitation[29]. During the medieval and early-modern periods, agricultural improvement took the form of more intensive farming with the introduction of double cropping and commercial crops without effecting any drastic changes in the shapes of fields[30]. Very detailed reconstructions of land utilization in early modern Japan were carried out for various villages, which led to discussions on the land use system and socio-economic changes in those rural areas. Strong control on the rice and cotton crop rotation of villages, on the effective usage of limited irrigation capacities, and on adjustments in response to flood hazards, are now known to have been in place[31].

The progress in research on castle towns, which were predominantly formed in the late medieval and early-modern periods in Japan, is also noteworthy. A castle town generally comprised several major components: a castle, warrior/bureaucrat quarters, merchant/craftsman quarters, temple districts, narrow streets and three or more moats. Comparative studies of castle towns within Japan and those in historical towns overseas have been carried out in addition to reconstructions of individual castle towns that had no square or "*Markt*" and no city walls[32]. K. Yamori categorized castle towns into five morphological types: (i) scattered distribution of the town components on and around a castle located on a hill; (ii) concentrated distribution of components around a castle located on a lower mound or at a similar level to the town, surrounded by outer moats or physical obstacles as fortification; (iii) split location of merchant/craftsman quarters on both sides of outer moats around a castle, and warrior/bureaucrat quarters with temple districts inside the moats, and along main roads outside the moats; (iv) segregated location of merchant/craftsman quarters outside outer moats; (v) any of types (ii)-(iv) with the castle being used just as an administrative centre. These five types represented the development of town planning through time in that order, and reflected socio-economic, structural and functional changes of the towns and of their feudal regions; type (ii), it may be noted, was the typical castle town with some variations constituting a few sub-types[33].

The critical evaluation of historical texts is becoming common and the increasing availability of new source materials has made it possible to produce fuller reconstructions and explanations of past geographies. Title deeds from the ancient and medieval periods—recorded land transactions, exchanges, inheritances and donations—have survived but these are too few and fragmented for any detailed research in historical geography. However, a systematic analysis of such deeds has shown that the rural landscape consisted of homesteads and hamlets, and that there were few villages from the eighth to the twelfth century. Nucleation and village formation began in the twelfth century under the management of some manors, but was not fully implemented until the end of the thirteenth century[34]. Title deeds and taxation records have also been used to inquire into the locations and functional areas of ancient administrative units[35]. Studies of diaries and commentaries on agriculture written by intelligent farmers have yielded explanations with regard to regional differences of crops, crop combinations, fertilizers and agricultural calendars in the late medieval and early-modern Japan[36]. While old maps were extremely useful materials for reconstruction, their potential as information has been considerably expanded by careful textual critiques[37].

The morphological analysis of relic landscapes and land divisions has been considerably improved by the accumulation of data and the interpretation of 1: 2,500 maps and air photographs. Ancient straight roads were presumed in maps by T. Kishi[38] and K. Ashikaga[39] in 1970: many relics of such roads have since been identified, not only on maps but also in the course of archaeological excavation[40]. The city plan of an ancient capital "Kunikyo"[41] and plans of medieval market towns[42] were also reconstructed by using this technique, based on the analyses of land dividing patterns and micro-geomorphology. Irrigation ponds with rectangular shapes and villages following *jori* grid patterns were interpreted as having been constructed in the ancient period, but the rectangular shapes have since been proved to have been formed later to fit preceding grid patterns[43].

Such integrated empirical analysis has a number of distinctive possibilities: the first can be called a "direct approach" to a particular phenomenon at a particular time by using multiple source materials of the period; the second is text analysis, similar to studies undertaken by historians, but emphasizing the spatial perspective; the third is morphological analysis using improved techniques and data; and the fourth involves a combination of the abovementioned methods.

As a result of integrated analyses, reconstructions of the past and studies of the processes of change have become more sophisticated. Traditional "thick" cross-sections themselves are no longer seen as effective frameworks for reconstructing past landscapes and explaining landscape changes. Detailed analyses of each component and process, and of the nature and direction of change in a particular place and time, are considered to be essential. It is necessary to study each landscape component in detail and, whenever possible, situate narrative interpretations of them within the "thick" cross-sections or in interposed narrative accounts between "thin" cross-sections. Although such analysis can provide a vital picture of landscape components and of the relations between them, entire landscapes cannot be reconstructed in this way. The danger inherent in this integrated methodology is that it tends to produce detailed descriptions of only certain components in a particular period and place.

Such methodologies, on the other hand, have extended the scope of historical geography to include topics such as commodity flows, pilgrimages, disasters and entertainment in medieval and early-modern Japan, depending on new possibilities provided by the source materials available. Village documents have been used effectively to analyze medieval markets and their spheres of activity. This shows that there was not yet an ordered hierarchical structure such as a central place system in spite of the wide circulation of money and the wide network of commodity flows between the lords, including those who represented the bigger temples in Kyoto and Nara and their local manors[44]. The account books of merchants and traders in early-modern Japan have shown that a national transportation system centered in Osaka and Edo (Tokyo) was well-established and that even fish manure was delivered over very long distances, as were rice, wine, cloth and paper[45]. The "hotel" registers of a religious settlement testify that across the nation, at each place of lodging, catchment areas for pilgrims were maintained[46]. Temple registers, well known as records of demography, have been used for analyzing the damages and injuries inflicted by floods, famines, pests and the eruption of volcanoes upon the local populations (differentiated by age, sex, occupation and place of residence)[47]. Tourist guide books, published and commonly used in early-modern Kyoto, have also provided a valuable insight into the structure of the city at that time, indicating the locations, sizes and productions of theatre, which were often invited to perform in the temple grounds in order to raise donations[48].

Comparative studies have also been combined with integrated analyses. While it is known that the ancient capital cities in Japan were modeled after Chinese towns, a majority of the early historical studies focused only on unearthing the origins of city planning and few managed any comparative analyses; this was partly due to the absence of a political relationship between China and Japan. Now, field surveys have produced new data[49], and a systematic comparison of shapes and sizes has been undertaken in order to identify both the differences and the similarities between the ancient cities of China and Japan[50]. Japanese ancient capital cities have been shown to have had a numerically standardized place-identifying system, and the capital city itself and each unit or "bo" in their grid-pattern plans is marked by an absence of walls; these are two characteristic differences between the Japanese and the Chinese cities of the period[51].

Progress in techniques and data

A dramatic increase in data has resulted from a slew of archaeological excavations. Only a few sites of settlement in historical times had been excavated before the late-1960s, which did not permit comparison with results achieved from studies in historical geography and history. Huge amounts of data have been compiled since then. Many sites have been found under paddy and dry fields outside villages, and it is from such sites that it has been confirmed that the rural landscape in medieval times was made up of homesteads and hamlets, and nucleation, as already demonstrated by studies in historical geography; today, however, the picture is much more vivid and varied.

Progress in archaeology has been supported by such technical developments as pollen, plant-opal and micro-geo-morphological analyses. Pollen diagrams are effective in constructing pictures of past vegetation: increases in pine pollen, identified several times, are indicative of development brought about by human activity such as shifting cultivation in paddy fields in the prehistorical and historical times, or timber cutting for the pottery and iron works industries; in certain cases, increases in pine pollen could be because of a growing population. An increase in mugwort pollen is known to be indicative of a comparatively drier environment as a result of climatic change, or of a changing relative location in relation to a displaced river channel, or a change in sea level[52]. Plant-opal analysis has revealed more directly the existence of rice cultivation, and of paddy desertion and invasion by Japanese pampas grass[53]. Micro-geo-morphological analysis has become much more detailed, relating classifications of deposits with archaeological findings, and has made it possible to determine the distribution of paddies in a particular period and place in a well-researched area[54]. These analyses have provided good reconstructions of past environments; they have tended to provide explanations of the relationship between human activities and physical environments from an ecological point-of-view, with which historical geographers need to be more familiar.

Numerous manuscript materials have been transcribed and edited. There have been publications of municipal, prefectural and national historical records, many of which include a volume or part of a volume that portrays old maps and cadastral surveys, often compiled by historical geographers. Municipal and prefectural histories also contain historical maps and distribution maps, produced by historical geographers, of archaeological sites and of the *jori* grid patterns of the area. Two prefectures have published very detailed volumes of local place names, village boundaries, old river channels and *jori* grid patterns: each contains more than one hundred sheets of 1: 5,000 maps[55]. All of them are supporting integrated analyses of historical geography and some present research results at the same time.

Cadastral maps have been prepared for each village and town in Japan. They were generally compiled at least twice in the late-nineteenth century and they provide considerable potential for historical-geographical inquiries despite their inaccuracies as maps. The means of producing them and their varying qualities have been so well examined[56] that cadastral maps have become the most effective source materials for morphological analyses and a retrogressive approach[57]. The difficult task of comparing them with current maps or air photographs is under-way in many municipalities.

A huge amount of historical data is now being compiled, such as "A Data Base of Medieval Manors" and "A Regional Data Base for the Southwest Islands." Quantitative analysis is still not used much in historical geography, but it has been applied to the diffusion of pilgrimages[58], and to the migration distances for mar-riage-fields, using temple records in early-modern Japan. The latter has shown, for example, that there was a large migration area with a radius of approximately 25 kilometers centered on Osaka, with other smaller areas adjoined to it[59].

Behavioral and perceptual approaches

Studies of the changing landscapes increasingly emphasize decision-making processes and adopt a behavioral approach to historical analyses. For example, the massive engineering works of a powerful sovereign, Hideyoshi Toyotomi, at the end of the sixteenth century involved the construction of a palace and a castle town, changing the course of a large river and of road networks, reforming the structure of Kyoto from the traditional capital city to a kind of castle town, and demolishing preceding castle towns and transportation networks in the Kyoto area. These changes have been interpreted by K. Ashikaga in terms of Hideyo-shi's behavior and regional planning[60]. Another example is provided by a study of the development of intensive farming in a rural area: the lowering and flatten-ing of paddy fields to make them wider and to improve irrigation, constructing irrigation ponds to enable better water management, and introducing profitable crops. Such improvements have been explained, in part, in terms of the popular culture of villagers[61].

The concept of "imagined worlds of the past"[62] has also had an impact upon Japanese historical geographers. The idea of "perceived worlds of the past"[63] has now become so common among them that many of the integrated analyses have approached past geographies, changing landscapes, relict features and geographi-cal change as components of perceived worlds. Attempts have been made to intro-duce such new methodologies into Japanese historical geography: one among them was a commentary on the new approaches, including perceptual, behavioral, idealist and phenomenological/humanistic approaches, with some examples of their applications[64]; another was a collection of papers, employing new meth-odologies, translated into Japanese[65]. Some papers using perceptual approaches have presented research results whereas others have simply offered guidance on the application of their approach. For example, villagers in mountainous areas in early-modern Japan had territorial perceptions which encompassed their village or hamlet, its surrounding fields, and the nearby slopes which were used as com-mon land; the outer mountains were generally regarded as useless. Such territorial perceptions varied regionally, reflecting different physical environments and socio-economic conditions. Many new settlements developed only just beyond the basic unit of settlement containing the village/hamlet and the fields, not only because of the limited space for new settlements but also because of the territorial perceptions of villagers[66]. Medieval market towns were also often located on the feudal boundary, in a dry river bed or in temple grounds, because such places were recognized as comparatively free from feudal authority and from the areas used by farmers in the course of their daily lives. Such points have been made in many studies. Studies of human territoriality, such as those on the formation of settlement territories in mountainous regions and relationships between counties and the spatial fields of particular shrines[67], are growing in number in Japan as they are in Western countries[68].

According to the semiologic method, historical geographers must endeavor to understand the messages inherent in symbolic landscapes. Semiologic and semantic approaches were introduced by M. Senda as a way of understanding perceived spaces in ancient Japan by finding symbolically significant spaces through circular and square images. The circle was identified at the central locations of palaces in the capitals throughout the empire; the circle was also used as a symbol for trees, courts, and marketplaces. The square, meanwhile, was recognized in terms of the tetragonal shapes and grid street patterns in the imperial and provincial capitals in addition to the *jori* grid pattern. A circle representing heaven and a square representing the firmament are shown on the *mandara* or *shri-yantra* designs, which were considered to be maps of the world[69]. I. Suizu pointed out that medieval legends and tales had a social significance that was unique to the landscape, and that they were connected with a profound structure, which was neither real nor Euclidean geometry but was related to topological space, in which medieval people actually lived[70]. Such approaches have expanded our understanding of landscape.

The cartographic study of maps depicted or drawn in the Medieval or Ancient Period has, in particular, benefited from the increasing data and improving methods. Two editions, *Cosmology of Pictorial Maps* on Medieval maps[71] and *Manorial Maps in Ancient Japan* on Ancient maps[72], are cases in point; the details will be provided in chapter 4.

These new methodologies are significant because they have freed the historical geographer from the source-bound nature of the reconstruction of cross-sections. They do, nonetheless, conform to the tradition of "thick" cross-sections in Japanese historical geography. All perceptual, semantic, semiotic and topological understandings of the space are contextual rather than static. On the other hand, it is difficult if not impossible to demonstrate beyond doubt that the explanation or understanding provided is the only, correct one. If the only reason why any understanding is correct is that it "fits the facts"[73], historical geographers using these methods need to look for more convincing explanations.

Such analyses of old maps have produced good results. A large number of pictorial maps were produced and used in ancient and medieval Japan, and many printed maps were published and manuscripts were drawn in early-modern Japan. These have inherent inaccuracies, including selective emphasis, omission and abbreviation, and are sometimes entirely imaginary constructs. The features drawn on some pictorial maps of small areas have been classified into point, area and linear elements, and identified as landmarks, vegetation and traffic routes[74]. Heavily emphasized features in river maps have been interpreted as indicating perceived impediments to navigation[75]. Strange inscriptions and drawings on the borders of maps of Japan in medieval and early-modern times are seen as expressions of spatial cognition[76]. Such perceptual representations on old maps are not difficult to follow by historical geographers because any source material itself is already recognized as a representation. Therefore, the understanding of a historical geographer might be possible to revise or correct by others analyzing same maps. However, it is a fact at present that every old map does not always have cosmological significance as a whole, and does not always have similar symbolic significance. Old maps, of course, have various functions, and play much more than a symbolic role[77].

Contextual approach

Historical geography in Japan today appears to be splitting into three approaches: integrated analysis based on empirical inquiry; specific analysis based on technological progress and data processing; and the contextual, perceptual and behavioral perspectives. In practice, the three are progressing simultaneously, as well as interacting with each other. The traditional "thick" cross-section uses data from the materials of history and archaeology; historical-geographical techniques for reconstructing past landscapes have become popular among the practitioners of these disciplines, and historical geographers cooperate on survey projects on archaeological sites and in the process of publishing municipal histories. Historical geography in Japan has been healthy enough to export its skills and results to neighboring disciplines, and sometimes to carry out its own projects and mobilizing those disciplines unto the fulfillment of such projects. Historical geography has become an interdisciplinary sub-field of geography, although that spawns a tendency to lose some scope of its own.

Recounting the progress of historical geography within such an interaction expresses some unique experiences in terms of the nature of the past landscapes of Japan. Some cultural landscapes or elements of Japanese historical geography have been more or less preserved since their origin, and others have vanished or been transformed; the time periods corresponding to such formation or transformation have however been different in each case. An example of the former is the "jori" grid pattern, and an example of the latter is the ancient provincial capital; both of these subjects have benefited from studies by historical geographers, and both are important topics in this book.

Such progress requires historical geographers to think about past landscapes and the perceptions of them in their time by relying more on the detailed and integrated analyses and the interaction of methods, although historical geographers tend to form an understanding of a landscape in the past from those in the present or from some clear examples of other places and times[78]. Thus historical geography in Japan today is progressing, in part because of its multiplying methods and concepts and in part because of its growing inter-disciplinary links, revealing a dialectical process.

Here, in this book, we shall employ a contextual approach to describe a landscape history of Japan[79]. Landscape history in this book is a method that is used to study the cultural landscapes in each period and the transformations undergone by them; it is a method that depends on integrated and elaborate analyses and multiple data-based depictions of factors related to landscapes. (see Figure 1.1)

The contextual approach entails the following research angles and procedures:

1. The features and situations of each factor of the landscape in each period should be analyzed and depicted as accurately as possible.
2. An important working process is to search both the functional and historical ecology and the vectors for transformation of factors.
3. Such processes prevent the clouding of recognition of the facts and the lack of dynamics in the method of the "thick" cross-section.
4. These processes also ensure that facts are not overlooked and that there is not insufficient recognition of facts in the "thin" cross-section method.

Searching each factor of the landscape individually, the contextual approach, on the other hand, tends to split into the segmental recognition of factors of the

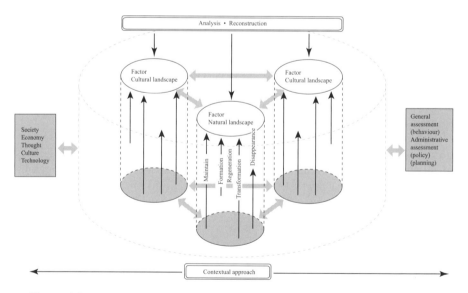

Figure 1.1: Historical biology of landscape factors and perspective of the analysis.
Source: Akihiro KINDA.

landscape. This tendency is recovered by analyses and the integration of the contexts between facts determined reciprocally. In other words, this contextual approach is a research angle that works with the relationships between political, social, cultural, natural and other factors. This contextual approach is, in a manner, the third school of research methods besides those based on "thin" and "thick" cross-sections.

Attitude to cultural landscape: A conclusion

The lands lived on by humankind and the cultural landscapes thus formed change ceaselessly. Every factor of the cultural landscapes can be traced through various processes. Some factors may continue to exist and others might suffer severe changes. Some might be very old and others might be very new. Some may have disappeared.

Traditional landscapes are usually synchronized with or are harmonious with their environments. Although it takes time to attain harmony, the landscape is always evolving, on its way to a harmonious state at any given time. Furthermore, we have to consider that harmony itself is a perceived phenomenon. The most important factor might be the thoughts of the people on the landscapes that they live within.

H. C. Darby completed the method of drawing changing landscapes as thin cross sections in 1973. K. Fujioka, on the other hand, who belonged to the same generation as Darby, insisted on the method of the thick cross sections, which Darby had once thought was as an alternative way of thinking.

With regard to the actual condition of the landscape factors, as already mentioned, we have to trace each landscape factor as precisely as possible. Finally, and importantly, we must consider the contextual and contemporary factors.

Notes

Selected publications are cited as their latest book versions. Publications in Japanese are indicated thus: [J].

1. A. Kinda, *An Historical-geographical Study of the Jori Plan and Rural Landscapes* (Tokyo 1985) 14–17 [J].
2. U. Tsujita, *Geography in Early-modern Japan* (Kyoto 1971) [J].
3. T. Yoshida (Ed.), *Dictionary of Place Names in Great Japan* 8 Vols. (Tokyo 1900–1909) [J]; S. Itshi et al. (eds.), *Gazetteer of Historical Place Names in Japan* 50 Vols. (Tokyo 1979–1996) [J]; R. Takeuchi *et al.* (eds.), *Kadokawa Dictionary of Japanese Place Names* 51 Vols. (Tokyo 1978–1990) [J]; the latter two series are edited as one or two volumes for each of the 47 prefectures, which are the highest units of local government, and are, in many cases, consisted of one or two ancient provincial areas.

4. T. Ogawa, *Historical Geography of China* 2 Vols. (Tokyo 1928, 1929) [J].
5. G. Ishibashi, Changing processes of ports, *Chigaku Ronso* 3 (1910) 1–31 [J]; K. Uchida, Historical considerations in geographical studies, *Chiri Kyoiku* 2 (1925) 105–10, 225–28, 524–28 [J].
6. S. Komaki, *A Study of Prehistoric Geography* (Kyoto 1937) 41–105 [J].
7. J. Yonekura, Jori sytem as a rural planning, *Chiri Ronso* 1 (1932) 307–52 [J].
8. J. Yonekura, *Rural and Urban Settlements in East Asia* (Tokyo 1960) [J].
9. K. Fujioka, *A Study on Prehistoric Region and Urban Areas* (Kyoto 1995) 42–67 [J].
10. H.C. Darby, Historical geography in Britain, 1920–1980: continuity and change, *Transactions I.B.G.* 8 (1983) 421–428, [on p. 423].
11. K. Fujioka (Ed.), *Lectures on Archaeological Geography* 5 Vols. (Tokyo 1984–1989) [J].
12. K. Fujioka (Ed.), *A General Historical Geography of Japan* 5 Vols. (Tokyo 1975–1977) [J].
13. H.C. Darby (Ed.), *A New Historical Geography of England* (Cambridge 1973).
14. A.R.H. Baker, A note on the retrospective and the retrogressive approaches in historical geography, *Erdkunde* 22 (1968) 233–34.
15. K. Fujioka, *An Historical-geographical Study on Contemporary Cities* (Tokyo 1977) [J].
16. K. Fujioka, *An Historical-geographical Study on Cities and Traffic Routes* (Tokyo 1960) [J].
17. T. Ono, *A Study of Japanese Prehistoric Geography* (Tokyo 1986) [J] ; M. Date, *Formation and Diffusion of Japanese Ancient Cultural Regions* (Tokyo 1991) [J]; K. Ashikaga, *A Study of Japanese Ancient Geography* (Tokyo 1985) [J]; K. Fujioka, *Provincial Capital* (Tokyo 1969) [J]; R. Kinoshita, *Provincial Capital: Changing Process* (Tokyo 1988) [J]; K. Ashikaga, An historical-geographical study of ancient county seats, *Rekishichirigaku Kiyou* 5 (1963) 105–36 [J]; M. Senda, *The Ruins of Ancient Harbours* (Tokyo 1974) [J]; T. Tanioka, *A Geography of Plain* (Tokyo 1963) [J]; T. Tanioka, *Development of Plain* (Tokyo 1964) [J]; H. Watanabe, *A Study of the Jori System* (Osaka 1968) [J]; T. Mizuno, *An Historical-geographical Study of the Jori System* (Tokyo 1971) [J]; M. Hattori, *An Historical-geographical Study on the Ritsuryo State* (Tokyo 1983) [J].
18. K. Fujioka (ed.), *Traffic Routes in Ancient Japan* 5 Vols. (Tokyo 1978–1979) [J]; K. Ashikaga (1985) *op.cit.*; R. Kinoshita, Results and problems of recent studies of ancient Japanese roads, *The Human Geography* 40 (1988) 336–54 [J]; K. Yamori, *A Study of City Plans* (Tokyo 1970) [J]; K. Yamori, *Castle Towns* (Tokyo 1972) [J].
19. T. Kikuchi, *Development of Reclaimed Settlement* 2 Vols. (Tokyo 1958) [J]; Y. Nakajima, *Market Towns* (Tokyo 1964) [J]; Y. Asaka (ed.), *Historical Geography in Japan* (Tokyo 1966) [J]; M. Kikuchi, *An Historical-geographical Study of the Early-modern Village* (Tokyo 1968) [J]; T. Kitamura, *An Historical Study of Japanese Irrigation Systems* (Tokyo 1970) [J]; K. Yamori,

Regional Structure in Early-modern Japan (Tokyo 1970) [J]; K. Uchida, *A Geographical Study of Rural Demography in Early-modern Japan* (Tokyo 1971) [J]; T. Kitamura, *Historical Case Studies of Japanese Irrigation Systems* (Tokyo 1973) [J]; G. Tomioka, *Trade Route of Salt and River Boat* (Tokyo 1977) [J]; Y. Sueo, *An Historical Geography on the Development and Utilization of Hydraulic Power* (Tokyo 1980) [J]; H. Yamazumi, *An Historical Geography of the Early-modern Village* (Kyoto 1982) [J]; T. Fukuda, *Early-modern Reclaimed Settlements and their Origins* (Tokyo 1986) [J]; T. Mizoguchi, Labour migration in Kai Province during the Tokugawa era *The Human Geography* 33 (1981) 485–506 [J].

20. H. Iseki, The sea-level about 2,000 B.P. around Japan, *Nagoyadaigaku Bungakubu Ronshu* 62 (1974) 155–76 [J]; Y.Kagose, *Lowlands: development and change* (Tokyo 1972) [J]; M. Kusaka, *Physical Environments in Historical Times* (Tokyo 1980) [J]; H. Iseki, *Alluvial Plain* (Tokyo 1983) [J].

21. S. Komaki, *op.cit.*; I. Suizu, *Life Space of Social Groups* (Tokyo 1969) 387–446 [J].

22. M. Williams, Historical geography and the concept of landscape, *Journal of Historical Geography* 15 (1989) 92–104.

23. K. Yamori, *Old Maps and Landscapes* (Tokyo 1984) 3–32 [J].

24. D. Whittlesey, The horizon of geography, *Annals of the Association of the American Geographers* 35 (1945) 1–36.

25. I. Suizu, *Pioneers in the Modern Geography* (Kyoto 1974) [J].

26. K. Fujioka and M. Hattori (Eds.), *Statues in Historical Geography* (Tokyo 1978) [J].

27. T. Tanioka (1963) *op.cit.* 71–102, 138–55; M.Hattori, *op.cit.* 382–422.

28. S. Takashige, *Cultivated Land and Village of Ancient and Medieval Village* (Tokyo 1875) 157–70 [J].

29. A. Kinda (1985) *op.cit.* 241–306; A. Kinda, The *jori* plan in ancient and medieval Japan, *Geographical Review of Japan Ser. B* 59 (1986) 1–20.

30. A. Kinda (1985) *op.cit.* 307–38; A. Kinda, *Micro-geomorphology and Medieval Settlement* (Tokyo 1993) 224–45 [J].

31. T. Ukita, Land use in Nara Basin in the Tokugawa Shogunate, *Geographical Review of Japan* 30 (1957) 927–46 [J] ; T. Ukita, Cotton production in Japan before industrialization, in A.R.H. Baker and M. Billinge (eds.), *Period and Place: Research Methods in Historical Geography* (Cambridge 1982) 180–186.

32. K. Fujioka, *An Introduction for Japanese Historical Geography* (Tokyo 1962) [J]; T. Matsumoto, *An Historical-geographical Study of Castle Towns* (Tokyo 1967) [J].

33. K. Yamori (1970) *op.cit.* 247–85.

34. A. Kinda (1985) *op.cit.* 339–443.

35. Y. Tomatsuri, Geographical approach to the relationship between "go" and irrigation in ancient Japan *Geographical Review of Japan* 46 (1973) 533–49 [J].

36. S. Arizono, *A Geographical Study of Early-modern Commentaries on Agriculture* (Tokyo 1986) [J].

37. H. Kawamura, *A Study of Provincial Maps Ordered by Tokugawa Government* (Tokyo 1984) [J]; Research group on pictorial maps of Katsuragawa (ed.), *Cosmology of Pictorial Maps* 2 Vols. (Kyoto 1988, 1989) [J]; A. Kinda *et al.* (eds.), *Maps of Ancient Manors in Japan* (Tokyo 1996) [J].

38. T. Kishi, An history of old roads, in T. Kishi and K. Tsuboi (Eds.), *Ancient Japan,* Vol. 5 (Tokyo 1970) 93–107 [J].

39. K. Ashikaga (1985) *op.cit.* 249–60.

40. R. Kinoshita (1988) *op.cit.*

41. K. Ashikaga (1985) *op.cit.* 59–111.

42. K. Kobayashi, *A Study of Sengoku Castle Towns* (Tokyo 1985) 19–208 [J].

43. A. Kinda (1993) *op.cit.* 131–60.

44. H. Fujita, Markets and their trading commodities in the medieval rural region, in Dept. of Geogr. Kyoto Univ. (ed.), *Space, Landscape, Image* (Kyoto 1983) 122–34 [J]; H. Fujita, The function of rural markets in medieval Japan from the view point of flow system, *The Human Geography* 38 (1986) 316–34 [J].

45. E. Furuta, *Regional Patterns of Manure Flow in the Early-modern Period* (Tokyo 1996) [J].

46. T. Iwahana, *An Historical-geographical Study on the Faith of Dewasanzan* (Tokyo 1992) [J].

47. M. Kikuchi, *Disasters of Japan in Historical Times* (Tokyo 1980) [J].

48. H. Yamachika, Formation of theatre districts in precincts of temples and shrines in Kyoto during the late Edo period *The Human Geography* 43 (1991) 439–59 [J].

49. M. Akiyama, Urbanization in Shanhei in the nineteenth century, in The committee for the commemoration of the retirement of Professor Fujioka (ed.), *Studies in Urban and Historical Geography* Vol. 2 (Tokyo 1978) 99–108 [J]; T. Kishi (ed.), *Ruins of Ancient Capitals in China* (Tokyo 1982) [J]; K. Hayashi, A characteristic of local towns in early-modern China, in Dept. of Geor. Kyoto Univ. (Ed.), *op.cit.* 135–59 [J]; M. Senda (Ed.), *Pan-China Sea Culture and Japan* (Kyoto 1990) [J].

50. S. Takahashi, *Japanese Ancient Cities* (Tokyo 1995) [J].

51. A. Kinda (1985) *op.cit.* 77–125.

52. Y. Yasuda, Prehistoric environment in Japan: palynological approach, *The Science Reports of Tohoku University* 28 (1978) 117–281; Y. Yasuda, *An Introduction of Environmental Archaeology* (Tokyo 1980) [J]; M. Takahashi, *Environmental Archaeology of the Plain* (Tokyo 2003) [J].

53. S. Toyama, The theory of *Jomon* agriculture and paleobotanical study *The Human Geography* 37 (1985) 407–21 [J]; S. Toyama, *Reconstruction of the Environment of Archaeological Sites* (Tokyo 2006) [J].

54. M. Takahashi, Geo-environment and land use in the recent alluvial plains after the end of the ancient period *The Historical Geography* 167 (1994) 1–15 [J]; M. Takahashi, Ancient manorial maps and the physical environment, in A. Kinda *et al.* (Eds.), *op.cit.* 115–28 [J].

55. Kashihara Archaeological Research Institute (ed.), *Reconstruction of the Jori Plan in Yamato Province* (Nara 1980) [J]; A. Kinda (Ed.), *Reconstruction of the Jori Plan: History of Fukui Prefecture Material Series* Vol. 16B (Fukui 1992) [J].
56. T. Kuwabara, *Cadastral Maps* (Tokyo 1976) [J]; J. Sato, *Cadastral Maps in the Early Meiji Era* (Tokyo 1983) [J].
57. A.R.H. Baker (1968) *op.cit.*
58. Y. Sugiura, Spatial diffusion of "Okagemairi" in 1771 *Geographical Review of Japan* 51 (1978) 621–42 [J].
59. H. Kawaguchi, The sphere of intermarriage beyond the administrative boundaries in the early-modern period *The Historical Geography* 124 (1984) 17–28 [J].
60. K. Ashikaga, *Historical Geography of Medieval and Early-modern Cities* (Kyoto 1984) 111–32 [J].
61. A. Kinda (1993) *op.cit.* 224–52.
62. H.C. Prince, Real, imagined, and abstract worlds of the past *Progress in Geography* 3 (1971) 1–86.
63. A.R.H. Baker (1972) *op.cit.*
64. T. Kikuchi, *Methodologies of Historical Geography* (Tokyo 1977) [J].
65. M. Senda, *Geography Beyond Maps* (Kyoto 1981) [J].
66. H. Uehara, A study of the spatial structure of rural society at the southern foot of the Mt.Yatsugatake in the Edo period, *The Human Geography* 37 (1985) 485–512 [J].
67. T. Hori, The reorganization of the "Ise Shingun": an explanation of territoriality in the eighth and ninth century of Japan, *Shirin* 78 (1995) 97–137 [J]; T. Komeie, Physical boundaries and medieval territories of mountain settlements in western Japan, *The Human Geography* 48(1996) 48–68 [J].
68. G. Kearns, Historical geography, *Progress in Human Geography* 15 (1991) 47–56.
69. M.Senda, Perceived space in ancient Japan, in A.R.H. Baker and M. Billinge (Eds.), *op.cit.* 212–19; M. Senda, *Historical-geographical Studies of Ancient Japan* (Tokyo 1991) [J].
70. I. Suizu, *Profound Structure of Landscape* (Kyoto 1987) [J].
71. Research group on pictorial maps of Katsuragawa, *op.cit.*
72. A. Kinda, Ancient Manorial Maps and Landscape (Tokyo 1998) [J].
73. R.G. Collingwood and J.N.L. Myres, *Roman Britain and the English Settlement* (Oxford 1936) 134.
74. Research group of pictorial maps of Katsuragawa, *op.cit.* 48–109.
75. A. Onodera, *A Study on the Early-modern Maps of Rivers* (Tokyo 1991).
76. T. Ohji, Maps of Japan and the world, in Y. Arano *et al.* (Eds.), *Japanese History in Asia* Vol. 5 (1993) 27–51 [J].
77. A. Kinda, Pictorial maps, maps and historical studies, in N. Asao *et al.* (Eds.), *Iwanami Lectures: Japanese History, Supplementary Series* Vol. 3 (1995) 307–26 [J]; S. Minamide, Ancient and medieval manorial maps, in Kinda *et al.* (Ed.) *op.cit.*
78. A. Kinda, *Landscape of Ancient Japan* (Tokyo 1993) [J].
79. A. Kinda, *Inquiry into ancient landscape history* (Tokyo 2002) [J].

CHAPTER 2

Formation and transformation of administrative districts

Akihiro KINDA

Evolution of ancient spatial organizations

The Japanese islands are located at the eastern fringes of the Eurasian continent. Traditional Japanese cultures have been variously influenced by the continental cultures. For example, during the *yayoi* period, activities such as the cultivation of rice paddies and the manufacturing of bronze tools were adopted from the tenth century BC; a similar inherited practice was the ritual of burying mirrors with dead bodies inside great tombs called *kohun* in the later centuries. Such influence was also observed in the manufacturing of iron tools in the third century AD. The ancient kingdom known as the *Yamato-chyotei*, which extended to cover an area equivalent to the present national size, had been established with the unification or conquest of regional kingdoms. The kingdom had transformed into an imperial state by the first half of the seventh century; it accommodated palaces, and had a bureaucratic system wherein policies related to land planning were formulated. By the sixth century, Buddhism had reached the state via the continental countries and had soon gained a following; it was practiced alongside the traditional Shintoism.

The second half of the seventh century saw the rise of several formal systems such as *ritsuryo*—an administrative and penal code—under the strong influences of China. These systems became the basis of traditional Japanese culture and were also applied to a few modern cultural landscapes such as the modern administrative districts, the prefectures. Japanese culture was, in general, strongly influenced not only by Chinese characters and the Buddhist religion but also by political systems derived either directly from China or indirectly from the Korean kingdoms. The basic code *ritsuryo* was fully implemented by 701 AD and it became the basis of ancient Japan; by then, the provincial system had also been inserted. By 824 AD, 68 provinces were established, which comprised territories of former regional kingdoms or were created by the political or artificial division of these kingdoms. Each province normally consisted of several counties, which had delineated boundaries and included several *ri*, which were later termed as *go*; these consisted of 50 large families that were taxed and placed under a measure of control. The *ri* was not distinct spatial units, but units of local administration. The number of counties increased to 555 in the 720s. (see Figure 2.1)

The ancient state organized provinces into eight regional divisions consisting of Kinai and seven *do*, or road districts: these were Tokai-do, Tozan-do, Hokuriku-do, Sanyo-do, Sanin-do, Nankai-do and Saikai-do. Kinai, which consisted of five provinces, was where the imperial capitals and their environs for performing their special roles were located. Kinai and the seven *do* went on to become very basic regional units in Japan. By the beginning of the eighth century, the royal highway system had been established in each road district to connect each provincial capital to the imperial capital. The highways were constructed as straight roads through each road district and were lined with postal stations, which housed horses and packhorse men that were used for mailing documents and for providing horses to designated official travelers. The widths of the highways were between 6 to 12 meters, with ditches on both sides. Sanyo-do was the highest class highway system—around 12 meters wide and with 20 horses at each postal station. The highways also provided access to tax bearers.

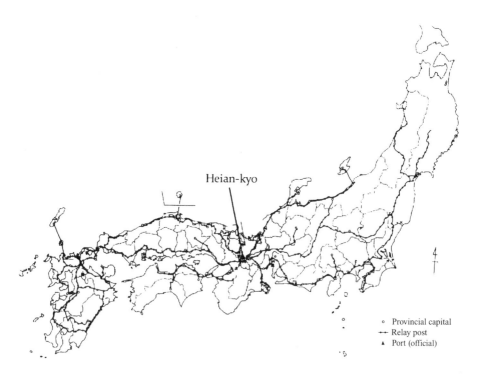

Figure 2.1: Administrative districts and imperial highways in the late 8th and 9th centuries.
Source: Akihiro KINDA.

Water transportation was also used in the ancient times. It was especially important for heavy goods like rice, which was the basic product in cultivation as well as the principal driver of the economy and the tax systems; silk and linen were also valuable terms of exchange; all this despite the fact that coins had been issued by the state and were in circulation. The state organized its water transportation system to cater to the capital Heian-kyo from the provinces along the Japan Sea and the Setouch Inland Sea. Lake Biwa was also important for transporting such goods from the provinces along Japan Sea.

Urban landscape in ancient times

In the Yamato Dynasty of the sixth century, each king or queen generally ruled directly from his or her own palace. Bureaucratic regimes had not yet been institutionalized. However, the administrative system quickly changed to a regulated one, based on the codes of the contemporaneous China—"Sui" or "Tang." The imperial capital, Fujiwara-kyo, was constructed with urban planning at the end of the seventh century; the second imperial capital, Heijo-kyo, was built later in 710. During the Heijo-kyo period, other capitals such as Kuni-kyo were in use temporarily and the sub-capital, Naniwa-kyo, was founded. The imperial capital was transferred to Nagaoka-kyo in 784 and from this location transferred again to Heian-kyo in 794. The construction plans of ancient Japanese capitals were generally based on a grid street pattern and an overall rectangular area. It is notable that old capitals were generally demolished and their functions and materials moved to the new ones.

Each province had an administrative capital, *kokufu*, which consisted of various facilities including a court, several groups of wooden buildings for ceremonies and administration, storehouses, workshops and residences for the governor, deputy governors and officials. The main administrative facilities were miniatures of those at the imperial capital, although the *kokufu* did not have continuous built-up areas; these towns rather had loosely centered clusters of functions. The governor also commanded the provincial army and held religious services in the province. The provincial government managed village registers and land registrations, cadastral mappings, taxation, repair and construction of roads and canals, reclamation of waste lands, mining iron and other minerals, and manufacturing iron and other tools. Everything was reported to the central government. While rice was the main tax, and was stored and used in various ways by the local governments, except for certain designated provinces, most submitted taxes in other forms as well: large volumes of silk and other special products were sent to the capital.

There was also a regional capital called "Dazaifu," which administered several provinces in south-western Japan. In the north-eastern part of Japan, on the contrary, there were several military bases, equipped with administrative functions, which had rectangular fortifications.

Provincial landscapes in ancient times

The cadastral system based on the *jori* plan was established in the middle of the eighth century. The *jori* plan was a uniform system that indicated locations by a numbering method which was based on the areal unit of *cho* (approximately 1.2 hectares, 109 meters in length on each side) and the grid pattern. This basic section was called *bo* in the eighth century and *tsubo* during and after the ninth century. A square consisting of 36 basic sections was called a *ri*; it formed a square measuring 654 meters on each side. A linear arrangement of the *ri* was usually called a *jo* and a combination of the two led to the coining of the term *jori*. The *jori* system of numbering locations was uniformly adopted in each unit of the counties in every province. The main function of the *jori* plan was the allocation and registration of land; all arable lands taxed or managed by the government were indicated in the *jori* plan, although these were often parts of the basic land sections.

In ancient times, the settlement patterns were generally dispersed; in other cases, people chose to live forming hamlets. People over six years of age were allocated arable lands—0.2 hectares for males and two thirds of that area for females. But these allocations were not always near their dwellings. There were occasions when people had to cultivate paddies in remote locations by staying in temporal cottages; there were also cases when owners had to let lands to other people.

The most popular type of building in ancient Japan, in both urban and rural areas, was made of wood; it had pillars, which were embedded directly in the ground, and covered by thatched or board roofs. Pit houses, however, were still popular in north-eastern Japan. Many prestigious buildings such as the palaces and mansions were roofed with fine, sliced, cypress board not only in the political or cultural centers but also in rural areas.

The number of Buddhist temples in the Chinese or Korean styles increased quickly. They were big buildings constructed on foundation stones, with tile roofs and painted frames, and by 692, a total of 545 temples were built, including temples that were attached to palaces.

Under this influence, some of important governmental buildings became to be constructed on foundation stones with tile roofs.

Transformation of the political and economic structure in the medieval times

The administrative system of the central government underwent a gradual decline from the tenth century onward owing to regional conditions. The political power of the manor lords, on the other hand, was generally strengthened and the warriors' status also heightened in and after the 12th century. Many provinces came to have a more independent administrative unit from the tenth century onward because of the weakened power of the central government. Some of provincial political and administrative powers were moved to the manor. Then, the first warrior government was established under the formal appointments by the Emperor in Kamakura, about 350 kilometers to the east of Heian-kyo; the east and west political centers actually competed with each other from 1192 to 1333. After the fall of the Kamakura government, both the warrior government, now called the "Muromachi," and the imperial government existed side by side within *Kyo* (now the name of Heian-kyo, later Kyoto), but they were still competition, despite their partial and rather complicated amalgamation.

Apart from *Kyo*, the province functioned formally as a local administrative unit of the imperial government until around the fifteenth century. From the end of the twelfth century, however, provincial constables were appointed by the warrior government in Kamakura and their powers gradually encroached on the provincial governments.

The systems of maintaining royal highways and centralizing taxes, both focused on the capital, were almost broken, although many bigger manor lords collected and brought annual tributes or taxes to *Kyo*, where they lived. Alongside those changes, the regional economies developed and a monetary standard became popular. Lower administrative units established in ancient times—the counties and the *go* in the provinces—no longer retained their functions. The manor replaced them; the manors were governed both by officials and a military estate steward, the former being appointed by the manor lords and the latter by the warrior government.

Kyo was still the biggest city and was the political, cultural and industrial center throughout the ancient and medieval times. However, the built-up area came to be concentrated in the eastern capital from around the eleventh century. The north-eastern part of the original capital area and its nearest suburbs were especially favored. Many major streets in the capital expanded into the suburbs and beyond. There was also the development of villas in nearby resort areas like Uji and Saga. The city structure changed gradually because of changes in the political structure and the administrative units like the *bo*, which was surrounded by major streets and consisted of 36 sections. During the medieval times, town communities became actual administrative units. These communities were formed by the dwellings on both sides of a street. Their size was similar to that of a section, but their boundaries were different from those of sections. This type of community subsequently became popular as the basic unit of cities and towns, and continues, especially in Kyoto, to be so until today.

Other cities and towns developed considerably. Kamakura, one of the twin political centers, became a very dense built-up city in a small valley in 13th and 14th centuries. Some provincial capitals declined because of changes in the role of the provincial governments. Newly appointed provincial constables wielded great political powers and became military governors during the course of the fourteenth century; some of them constructed towns around or near their residences or castles.

In rural areas, 15–50 per cent of the arable land was actually dry field within the *jori* grid patterns of ancient Japan and many fields were cultivated only once every few years because of the shortage of irrigation water or because of some other physical or social environmental limitation. During medieval times, agricultural improvement took on the form of more intensive farming with double cropping or commercial crops in the same field pattern without any drastic change in the shape of fields. Reclamation resulted in many diluvial terraces with ponds for artificial irrigation in addition to the drainage of shallow marshes. This meant considerable expansion and improvement of agricultural landscapes.

In ancient times, the most popular settlement patterns were dispersed homesteads and hamlets. There were few villages from the eighth century to the twelfth century. The village formation movement began in the twelfth century under the management of certain manors, and was completed in some regions by the end of the fourteenth century, and by the end of the sixteenth century in the alluvial plains of south-western Japan. Nearly all manors lost their communal and economic functions and were placed by the village communities in their respective regions.

Spatial organization and landscapes in early modern times

In the middle of the sixteenth century, the Portuguese and Spanish came to Japan, bringing trade, guns and Christianity with them. Japanese merchants also made voyages to Eastern and South-East Asia. A number of ports like Sakai and Hakata became prosperous international trade centers not only as mother ports for Japanese ships but also as international ports that welcomed both Asian and European ships. Some of these had self-governing systems apart from the control of the regional military lords, the *daimyo*. Sakai, for example, became the biggest international-trading and gun-producing center.

The *daimyo*, some of who originated as provincial constables, simultaneously controlled both people and the economy within their territories because the second warrior government—the "Muromach" government—had lost power. The spatial organization of the nation that had hitherto been focused on the political centers now underwent a complete changed: fragmentation and decentralization was rampant throughout Japan, although Kyo, where the Emperor and aristocrats played out their ceremonial and political roles, was still the biggest city.

Some *daimyo* and powerful warriors of the time accepted Christianity or accorded permission to Christians to preach within their territories. Seminaries and churches, established in Azuchi, Kyo and other major towns, might have been very new and conspicuous buildings at that time in Japan. In such circumstances, the castles were turned into building complexes having fashionable symbolic towers as the main buildings; since the second half of the sixteenth century, various residential towns were built around these building complexes. Of the innovations begotten from the Western world, the most important was the gun, which changed not only the nature of the army—from regiments of mounted warriors to gun-carrying infantry divisions—but also the structure of the castles.

After short hegemonies of Nobunaga Oda and Hideyoshi Toyotomi, the Tokugawa government was established at the beginning of the seventeenth century. After displaying an initial welcoming attitude toward the guns, the developed economies, and the religion of the West, the new government prohibited both Christianity and international free trade. Christians survived by pretending to be Buddhists, and international contact and trade was restricted to the port of Nagasaki, and between limited countries—the Netherlands, China and Korea.

Strengthening their political as well as military power, the regional military lords constructed not only castles and residences but also built towns for merchants and craftsmen. The early type of castle town included warrior residences, market places and temples scattered around a castle located on a hill. The preferred location of the castles gradually shifted to lower hills or mounds as more of these castle towns were built. Merchant/craftsman quarters developed around the castle in a typical castle town. Castle towns were generally surrounded by outer moats or other fortifications, including natural features. There were some variations and transformations in such patterns. It is notable that temple districts were often parts of the fortification. Kyo, too, was transformed by Hideyoshi Toyotomi in the 1580s into a castle town that housed his huge palace and castle, adjoining temple districts, and surrounding fortification.

A great number of castle towns were constructed as military, political and economic centers. Each *daimyo*, many of who were regional military lords or higher warriors/bureaucrats in the house of the Tokugawas, kept a castle town in his territory, called a *han*. There were approximately 200 functioning castle towns in the period between the second half of the seventeenth century and the Meiji Restoration in 1868. Some of them were located at former provincial capitals or provincial constables' residences, but many were established at new locations to spawn military, political and economic centers in their surrounding areas.

Market towns and port towns, both along rivers and by the sea, developed considerably. A typical market town usually held a fair at a market place three to six times per month. Many peddlers could travel to these market places because the market days were scheduled conveniently in each region. Permanent shops became popular too besides the markets that operated on weekly or other bases. Farmers brought rice and other products to such local towns to pay their taxes or for selling purposes. The territory of a *daimyo* was effectively a closed system not only to facilitate better control but also as a way of integrating the social and economic activities of the people within the territory. At a more grassroots level, the village as an administrative unit was strictly controlled and taxed. Villagers were often obliged to lead miserable lives and were liable to suffer various disasters. The former provinces were often merely units for grouping these smaller territories; in certain cases, however, counties were actual administrative units within the territories controlled by the powerful *daimyo* and the Tokugawas.

Consolidation and change in spatial organization

The regional unit was based on *han* areas under the Tokugawa Government. Within a *han*, the village or the town was the local administrative unit. Consequently, the regional hierarchy generally consisted of four levels—the province, the county, the village or the town, and the sub-division within the village or town in addition to the minor places. The *jori* indication system from the ancient times and the manor system from the medieval times were both no longer actually used, although the *jori* grid patterns were still popular components of rural landscapes, especially in south-western Japan, and many areas of manors were succeeded by a village area or areas of several villages, where relatively developed region.

From the beginning of the seventeenth century, Edo (Tokyo at present) developed rapidly and became the biggest castle town and the capital of the Tokugawa Government. Its population reached one million, approximately a half of which were warriors/bureaucrats and their families, the other half, common people including merchants and craftsmen. Osaka, which had been established as a castle town, also developed to become the second biggest city and the biggest trading centre accommodating approximately half a million people. Kyo retained its status as the third biggest city of Japan with around half the population of Osaka, and remained the capital of the Emperor and the traditional cultural/industrial center.

A new national highway system was established with post towns, which focused on Edo, while some followed the earlier royal-highway system. (see Figure 2.2). All *daimyo* had to travel between Edo and their territories along the highway, accompanied by many of their warriors and bureaucrats, once every one or two years. Coastal navigation routes also developed considerably, forming a network

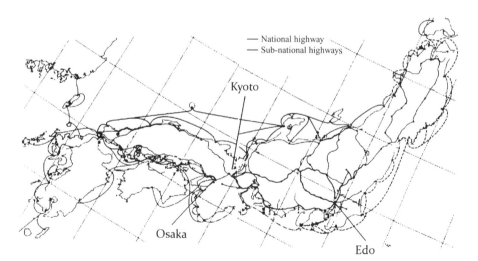

Figure 2.2: Highway and water transport networks in early modern times.
Source: Akihiro KINDA.

of many ports with a primary focus on Osaka and Edo. Trades of rice, cloths, rice wine and many other products were concentrated around Osaka and Edo. Despite this dual focus in spatial-organization, regional economies and cultures continued to mature in Japan during 16–18th centuries, albeit perhaps in a slow and rather dull manner. The rural and urban landscapes along the highway from Nagasaki to Edo via Osaka and Kyo, and the streets of Edo were paid glowing tributes by European resident officers in their various reports and diaries as being very harmonic and clean.

Reformation of spatial organization and the landscape under the strong influence of western culture and economics

In 1868, the Tokugawa government was defeated and a new government took over under the Emperor, who moved his seat from Kyo (Kyoto) to Tokyo (the erstwhile Edo, means east Kyo). International trade began again at several major ports and new relationships with America, the Netherlands, Russia, Britain, France, and other European countries were established. In 1889, a modern constitution, which was based on German models, was enacted.

The new local government replaced the *han* with the prefecture and consolidated the administrative structure, including those in Hokkaido; this took a few decades. Thus, some of the consolidated prefectures were based on the pre-existing

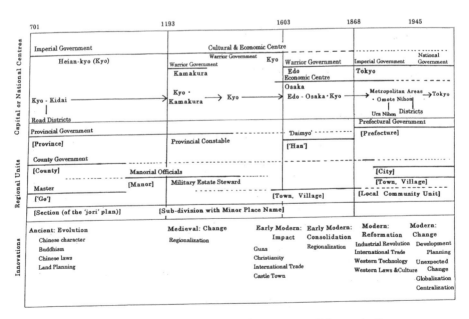

Figure 2.3: Change and reformation of the Japanese spatial organization.
Source: Akihiro KINDA.

provincial areas which were changed in minor ways; the road districts, however, were not revived as administrative units.

Within the prefecture, various local administrative units appeared one after another; some were conceived as reformations of the villages, others as agglomerates of the villages or as the revival of the counties. In 1889, the cities, towns and villages were ordained as the basic local administrative units; these had, generally, larger areas and populations than those of the previous villages and towns, and were placed under the supervision of the prefectural government. Counties again were conceived as ceremonial units, only for grouping towns and villages.

The regional hierarchy now had five levels—(i) the prefecture, (ii) the city or the county (many traditional counties were a cluster of towns and villages), (iii) the newly agglomerated town or village, (iv) the local community unit (based on a former town or village, within a city or a town or a village), (v) the subdivisions, associated minor places within a local community unit. There were not a big difference between the levels (ii) and (iii) in terms of their regional hierarchy. Although agglomeration of the local governments continued at a fast clip, this system has remained unchanged at a basic until today.

Socio-economic change and the industrial revolution

Many political and administrative systems have now been introduced from Western countries, cultures, technologies and sciences. These include the constitution and the university system, both based on German models at the beginning. The most severe impacts on the socio-economic structure have been brought about by the industrial revolution and by increasing the volume of international trade. The import of high-quality cotton, for example, has meant that cotton cultivation has disappeared in Japan. It was once one of the most profitable crops. In contrast, the silk industry, including cocoon production, has become an important exporting industry.

At the beginning of the 20th century, strong leadership by the central government brought about the industrial revolution, which was based on the strong performances of the textile industries of the period as they used imported European technologies to good effect. Textiles soon became the main export products. Iron and machine industries attained the same levels a few years later, but various machines and chemical products continued to be imported until World War II. Electric power replaced water mills and many hydraulic power stations were constructed, which changed the lives of the villagers even in mountainous regions. Railways were constructed between various towns, including numerous minor towns. Since electricity generation had started with imported generating stations, 50 megahertz became a standard in western Japan, and 60 megahertz in the east.

There were very few paved roads in Japan because nearly all transportation was on foot. Horses were popular to ferry people and loads across distances. Oxcarts were an exception; they were used in ancient Heian-kyo by noblemen, and also for heavy goods in the slopes around Kyo in the medieval times. There was generally no tradition of the drawn carriage in Japan until the late nineteenth century. Streets and roads, even highways, had usually very soft surfaces which were suitable for pedestrians, and were often narrow and curved. Those characteristics were very different from the Western highways, and they had to be improved for carriages at first and for cars a little later. This had needed a long time.

Confusion of the landscape

Traditional houses were constructed of wood with clay walls and had wooden doors and windows, both of which often consisted of paper screens. Among roof materials were tiles, straws and boards, varying from place to place or depending on social status. One or two storied houses were popular, except in certain mountainous regions, and were usually made harmonious with the landscape through social or administrative control. However, brick buildings with glass windows and other western style buildings, most of them incomplete imitations, began to be constructed at the end of the nineteenth century and quickly spread from major cities to towns and even to rural areas. Furthermore, concrete and tinplate, and many other kinds of building materials were put in use, especially after World War II. As a result, the traditional landscapes were disturbed, and variously confused landscapes appeared.

Such confusion spread and became more and more serious. One of the main reasons was the change in the life style from the traditional living rooms—people sitting on the "tatami" mats—to the western style rooms that used chairs. This brought a drastic change not only into business/industry buildings but also into ordinary houses. Japanese people often accepted such change without serious contradiction. This might be because of the traditional Japanese thinking that regarded a new building as desirable to commence a new stage of life or to welcome an important guest. The case for using renewal buildings is exemplified in the ritual of re-building the Ise Shrine once every twenty years. The mixture of Japanese and Western styles might produce new styles, but confusion is often the result, and this is likely to continue for a little while. For example, many of the traditional style houses or shops in Kyoto, which were built approximately a hundred years ago, are in need of fundamental repair or re-building; many of the building owners, however, are unable to spend much money for repairs and may therefore choose new style buildings. Furthermore, a regulation enacted in 1950 forbids the re-building of traditional wooden homes owing to the danger of fires, and advocates western style homes instead.

Industrialization and the urbanization have greatly encroached upon rural areas causing landscape confusion everywhere in Japan. Land consolidation in rural areas was carried out in the first half of this century and again, for more mechanization, since the late 1960s. Industrialization has been effective in improving and agglomerating paddies to make for a better rural economy. Land consolidation originally involved the mechanization of agriculture so as to save labor which could then be used in manufacturing industries. The result could well be the destruction of the sustainable economies of rural areas and the end, quite possibly, of the traditional landscape of terrace paddies that are dependent on very labor-intensive cultivation.

There has been neither any effective policy nor any comprehensive agreement across the sections of society to maintain or renew the rural and urban landscapes of Japan. While there have been some examples of initiatives to preserve historical or natural landscapes, they have been restricted to a few areas only. Since 2006, there has been one solitary movement to raise awareness of the importance of the traditional landscape; this led to certain new laws for preserving the cultural landscapes. However, there is clearly too little being done.

Expected and unexpected change in both spatial organization and the landscape

Industrialization led to the formation of four major industrial regions before World War II: in and around Tokyo, Nagoya, Osaka, and in northern Kyushu. This process revealed, at the same time, a new regional gap between the Japan Sea coastal region and the Pacific coastal region, which arose from the differences in the processes of industrialization. The Japan Sea coastal region was often called Ura-Nihon (Back Japan)—it had an undesirable image because of much snow and industrial backwardness. The Pacific coastal region, in contrast, was called Omote-Nihon (Front Japan)—it had a bright image because of winter sunshine and a developed industry.

Immediately after World War II, there was an urgent political/economic need to preserve the exhausted country, to develop natural resources and to improve the infrastructure for the manufacturing industry. The Comprehensive National Development Act was enacted in 1950 and the National Income Doubling Plan was instituted in 1960. The Comprehensive National Development Plan (CNDP), which tried to develop several new industrial areas—in addition to the four major ones—as new industrial cities and special areas for industrial consolidation, was started in 1962.

However, many of these were concentrated in the Pacific-Setouchi coastal belt, similar to Front Japan, and the regional gap was not reduced. People moved to metropolitan areas in Pacific-Setouchi coastal belt, and outside this area, the net migration flows became negative. The drift of population away from the countryside, especially from the mountainous regions, revealed many depopulated areas, where rural communities could not be maintained. There became often deserted villages. On the other hand, metropolitan areas like Tokyo and Osaka were overpopulated and were expanding outwards so that both rural and urban landscapes were fragmented and the improvement of social infrastructure often delayed.

A new CNDP began in 1969 and CNDP III in 1973, both aimed to achieve well-balanced development in the country. However the regional structure remained unchanged. The scheme for producing many regional units, each of which had a medium size city like the German regional centre, was part of CNDP III, but the trend towards larger metropolitan areas continued. CNDP IV in 1987 expanded on its earlier concept to visualize a dispersed multi-nuclear structure for the country; CNDP V in 1997 introduced the idea of multi-country axes. Both of these plans had tried and are still trying to form other nerve-centers of regional life and economy besides Tokyo MA.

The centralization of the net migration flows has always focused on metropolitan areas; the focus on Tokyo, especially, has never abated. Several metropolitan areas, including Tokyo MA and Osaka MA, continue to grow, but the ratio of the increase in Tokyo MA is much higher than that in other metropolitan areas. Economic activity, especially the kind associated with the tertiary sector, has been concentrated in Tokyo MA; the erstwhile twin-centered structure, that used to focus on Tokyo and Osaka, has shifted almost entirely to a Tokyo centered structure.

The urban system in Japan is now hierarchically aligned under Tokyo MA, although Osaka MA still retains the status of the second national centre and has its own hierarchical dominance over adjoining regions. Seven major regional units, centered in Sapporo, Sendai, Tokyo, Nagoya, Osaka, Hiroshima and Fukuoka, lie under Tokyo MA; these centers function as regional capitals. New railway systems (Shinkansen or the bull train), new motor way networks and domestic airlines support this spatial organization, alongside the administrative and controlling systems of both the national government and the various enterprises.

The traditional spatial organizations, at the national level, with a multi-centered structure consisted of Tokyo, Osaka and Kyoto. The system, at present, is changing to a single-focus structure based around Tokyo, although the nation is still administratively organized on a prefectural or provincial level. This changing spatial organization is now faced with the global economy and culture, and must adapt adequately. Such circumstances may strengthen the changes in the hierarchical structure of the spatial organization process as well as exacerbate the confusion of landscapes.

PART 2

Urban landscapes

CHAPTER 3

National and provincial capitals in ancient Japan

Akihiro KINDA

Cultural and political relationships within eastern Asia

The characters in the Japanese culture are based on those imported from China. Even Buddhism reached Japan via China and Korea by the sixth century. In this process, the Chinese versions of Buddhist scriptures were also transmitted to Japan. The construction of the first Buddhist temple, Asuka-dera, began in 588. The number of Buddhist temples rapidly increased under the official support of or the practical use by powerful clan families and royal princes, inevitably accompanied by some political struggles in the early stages. In 624, there were 46 temples, and this number increased to 545 in 692[1]. The second-earliest national chronicle, *Kojiki*, describing the history from the beginning to the 620s, was edited in 712, and *Nihon-syoki*, describing events until 697, edited in 720 and, were written in Japanese using Chinese characters; the earliest issues were burnt in the seventh century. This method of using Chinese characters became standard for writing Japanese in ancient Japan. The *hiragana* and *katakana* characters, both created in Japan for adjusting to spoken Japanese, were added in the ninth century, although the former initially became popular among women in the subsequent centuries.

The Japanese kingdoms in the Japanese islands had maintained political relationships with the Chinese dynasties in the Asian continent since the third century. The Yamato dynasty, which had unified Japan since the fifth century, sent several special envoys at the beginning of the sixth century to the Sui dynasty, which was ruling China since 589, to establish a closer relationship as an independent kingdom and to introduce Chinese culture in Japan. The Japanese culture was, in general, strongly influenced by the Chinese characters and Buddhism. It was also influenced directly by the political systems of China or indirectly and in different ways via the Korean kingdoms such as Koguryo, Silla, and Paekche. The Korean kingdoms competed with each other in the Korean peninsula at the time. After overthrowing the Sui dynasty in 618 and ruling the whole of China in 628, the Tang dynasty expanded the Chinese Empire by occasioning changes in the administrative and military systems. Many neighboring kingdoms, including the Korean ones, were obliged to reform their own governing systems in order to cope with the powerful Tang Empire or to accept the nominal status as a possession of the Empire[2]. This geopolitical situation was even recognized by the Yamato dynasty, although it sent special envoys to the Tang Empire. Political struggles between powerful clan families and royal princes in the Yamato dynasty became acute under the volatile situation, and the most powerful clan family perished in a coup d'etat called the Great Reform in 645. Subsequently, various reformations in the central and local administrative systems, in the official and social ranks of both the powerful clans and the general public, and through the enactment of penal and administrative laws were brought into effect, although these developments had not been completed by 701.

A close relationship developed between the Yamato dynasty and the Paekche kingdom, especially after the fall of the Kaya kingdoms, one of which had formed a strategic alliance with the Yamato dynasty, in the southern Korean peninsula in the mid-sixth century. The Yamato and Paekche kingdoms were confronted by Silla, which had the backing of the Tang Empire. The troops from both sides fought at the mouth of the Kum River in 663, and the allied forces of Yamato and Paekche were defeated. This brought about the collapse of Paekche, and many people, including high-ranking officials, sought refuge in Japan. The Yamato dynasty grew quite concerned about the possibility of a Tang invasion of Japan and expedited its efforts to reform the administration system and to construct a defense system. In 667, the royal palace was relocated from the east end of Osaka Bay to the southwest of Lake Biwa located inland, probably because of the poor defense the original location offered and of the attention to the northeast area of the Japan Islands[3], as well as to activate the government (see Figure 3.1). After the death of the emperor, who led the political process of the Great Reform, his son and his young brother fought to succeed to the throne, and a new chapter in the history of the dynasty began with the young brother succeeding in 672. He became the new emperor and relocated the royal palace back to Yamato, and the reformation of the systems and the enactment of laws progressed considerably.

The dynasty maintained a close relationship with Silla, although the latter was an old enemy along with the Tang Empire. The systems prevalent in Tang and Silla served as alternative models of the reformation and newly enacted laws from time to time; however, the Japanese systems adopted some mixed approaches or those with considerable modifications. It is believed that the first administrative codes were enacted in 668, and the first penal and the second administrative codes, in 689. After these forerunners, the penal and administrative codes called *Taiho-ritsuryo* were fully introduced in 701; these codes were similar to those prevalent in Tang, albeit with considerable modifications, and they became the standard system, although some minor changes were introduced in 718 and a little later[4]. The Yamato dynasty formed an ancient empire in the second half of the seventh century, equipped with its own penal and administrative codes based on those of the Tang Empire.

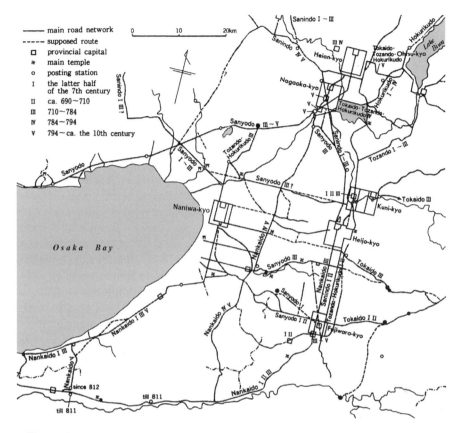

Figure 3.1: Imperial palaces, capitals and highways in the capital district from the late 7th to 10th centuries.
Source: Akihiro KINDA, depending on K. Ashikaga.

The ancient kingdom and the regional unit

The administrative system of the Yamato dynasty at the end of the sixth century and the beginning of the seventh century was based on both the direct control of the people and the direct management of the land . It is believed that groups of people obeyed and served under a specific powerful clan family at the time. The Yamato dynasty ruled such powerful clan families, many of which had formed small kingdoms, and assigned them with specific responsibilities in the dynasty's administrative system in the fifth and sixth centuries. The king of the dynasty had his own subjects as well as other clan families, because his ancestors were also powerful clan families that hailed from the southern part of the region, which later formed the province of Yamato in central Japan. The land was directly managed by a type of manor belonging to the king; the land was used for cultivating rice paddies, which formed the economic backbone of the kingdom. This system is thought to have originated in the sixth century. The lands originated either from the paddies directly reclaimed by the dynasty or from the lands offered to the dynasty by the clan families. This system of directly managed land distributed on the basis of political divisions by the dynasty became popular in many regions of prior kingdoms in the first half of the seventh century[5].

In the mid-seventh century, after the Great Reform, the direct public administration system underwent a change and was now based on citizenship with rights and duties. In around 670, a village registry system was implemented and carried out once every six years. Paddies were allocated to the people, who paid taxes and served in both the military and the guards. Territories of the erstwhile kingdoms of clan families were reorganized into new local administration units, *ri* consisting of around 50 large families and county which supervised *ri* within the county. The county was a spatial unit with a boundary, and the *ri* was not a rigid special one but a local public administration unit. The name of *ri* was changed to *go* when the county system was formally implemented in 701. Some of the large families did not comprise of actual family members but were formal units for receiving paddies, paying taxes, and sharing duties. Powerful clan families could retain control as administrators of these new units. The number of counties increased in the second half of the seventh century[6]. The administrative organization of the county was consolidated, and there were 555 counties (*gun*) in the 720s. Each county comprised around two to twenty *ri* or *go*.

The provincial system was also introduced in the second half of the seventh century and was almost fully implemented in 701. There were 58 provinces and three provincial islands in 701, and 66 provinces and two islands in 824—some created out of the territories of prior regional kingdoms and others formed by the political or artificial subdivision of these territories[7]. The number of counties in each province varied, with the minimum being 2 and the maximum being 35. Some aristocrats and bureaucrats in the Yamato dynasty were appointed as the governors and higher-ranking officers of the province, although members of the local powerful clan families were appointed as officers of the county. All the officers of the counties and *ri* fell under the jurisdiction of the governor of the province. The governor also commanded the provincial army and held religious services in the province. The governors' offices managed the village registers and land registrations as well as cadastral maps, taxes, repairs or constructions of roads and canals, the reclaiming of wastelands, mining of iron sands and other minerals, and the manufacture of iron and other tools. All activities were reported to the central government, and some taxes and special products were sent to the capital.

From a king's royal palace to the imperial capital

The king or queen of the Yamato dynasty generally administered the palace in which he or she resided. Many kings had palaces in the southeastern corner of the Nara Basin in the sixth century. However, emperors or queens in the seventh century relocated their royal palaces within the area or to other areas. The royal palace during 630 and 636, for example, followed an early government plan before the enactment of the first administrative codes. This plan consisted of two main combined sections of facilities surrounded by walls and a few attached buildings. The northern section had a main building for the king's dwelling, and the southern section had a court for ceremonies with east and west office buildings on both sides; the buildings were used for official work by the heads of the clan families[8].

The national chronicle *Nihon-shoki*, edited in 720, describes a "capital", Asuka-*kyo*, in detail in and after 676. The southeastern corner of Nara Basin contained several distinguished buildings, including royal palaces. Besides the royal palaces, there were other palaces of royal princes and some huge residences of powerful clan families as well as several bigger temples. Some scholars have tried to find the early urban planning for the entire area, but have met with limited success, and discussions are still in progress. However, it might be reasonable to be used the term "capital" by later bureaucrats, from their points of view, who lived and worked in the second imperial capital, Heijo-*kyo*, in 720, when the chronicle was edited.

The ancient capital can be defined as a city or town that contains not only royal palaces but also government facilities and dwellings for the general public as well as noble men. The construction of the first imperial capital according to this definition was planned probably before 680 and the actual construction partly began in 684 at the latest[9]. However, plans to transfer the capital were put on hold until 694 because of either the emperor's illness or other reasons. This new capital, called Fujiwara-*kyo*, was in use from that year until 710. The construction and use of Fujiwara-*kyo* as a capital was contemporaneous with the formulation and enactment of the second and third administrative codes. Fujiwara-*kyo* was thought to be a capital modeled on the Chinese capital, in keeping with the codes of the same period, which were based on the Chinese ones[10].

Fujiwara-*kyo* was planned to be restructured into a rectangular-shaped city with grid street patterns. The most influential reconstruction is the rectangular capital area 2,120 meters wide from east to west and 3,180 meters long from north to south. This area was divided into 265-meter sections called *bo*, and the imperial palace occupied 16 sections at the center. Each *bo* had a name, similar to Chinese capital cities; twenty principals, one for each east-west belt of *bo,* were appointed by the city government. The government of the capital had a full-fledged ministry and the same status as ministries of the provincial governments[11]. The location of such a plan—a rectangular shape for a city—was thought to be regulated by straight main roads existing prior to the construction of the capital. However, recent archaeological excavations have found some ruins of streets and facilities outside the reconstructed capital plan. A few models of the plan for a capital, some of which indicate a larger capital area, have been presented. Although there are still some ongoing discussions, each of new ideas presents that Fujiwara-*kyo* might have been four times the previously estimated area and twice as long on both sides[12]. (see Figure 3.2).

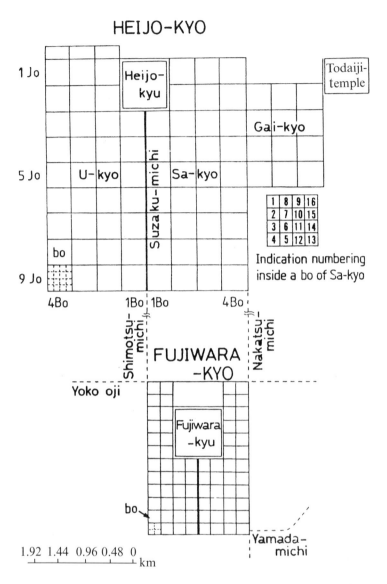

Figure 3.2: Outline of Heijo-*kyo* and Fujiwara-*kyo* plans.
Source: KISHI, 1988.

The construction of the second imperial capital, Heijo-*kyo*, began to be constructed in 708 in the northern part of the Nara Basin, and the emperor took up residence there in 710. Heijo-*kyo* continued to serve as the capital until 784, although other capitals were also used intermittently and a subcapital was founded in 734. The plan of Heijo-*kyo* consisted of a rectangle about 4.5 kilometers long and about 4 kilometers wide from east to west, but had areas stretching to the east and to the northwest. The capital's area was divided into east and west by a 74-meter-wide main street. Each part comprised nine belts called *jo*, one of which consisted of four *bo,* which was subdivided into sixteen sections. Each *bo* was divided by 24-meter-wide major streets and each section was divided by minor streets. A *bo* usually had an area of 500 meters square, but not every *bo* was equal in area. The area of a section was also a little less than the standard 120 meter square. Such differences in area were because of the width of both major and minor streets, which often cut off sections[13]. The east and west capital cities were separately controlled by the local government of each capital city; thus, Heijo-*kyo* had two capital city governments, with nine principals, each of which was appointed at each *jo* numbered from one to nine.

The imperial palace district, which comprised the imperial palace and quarters of the ministries and other governmental facilities, was located in the north-central part of the main rectangle. The main part of the district was the imperial palace, which was divided into three main quarters—the emperor's private palace, the main building for special ceremonies, and a court surrounded by many long buildings. These long buildings were the government headquarters for usual bureaucratic sanctions by both the emperor and higher-ranking bureaucrats, although the detailed plans of the district changed with the intermittent transformations of the political process . It is noteworthy that many temples were constructed in Heijo-*kyo,* and some of them were moved from the former capital or somewhere close to the former palaces, and that the Todaiji temple, established as the principal temple of the provincial ones, was constructed just outside the northeast corner of the capital in 745. A marketplace was established in the southern part of each *kyo* and was managed by the market supervisor. The general public was allocated housing lot on the basis of at least one sixteenth of one section (about 900 square meters) for a family, although the size of the housing lots varied according to the official ranks. The standard area of a house for the general public ranged between 35 and 53 square meters with a few attached cottages, but the noblemen had bigger and more buildings. Noblemen were generally allocated an entire section and biggest example occupied four sections.

While the general public, who lived and worked in the capital, could pay taxes within the capital, and many of those who lived in the provinces made annual visits to the capital to pay taxes or provide services directly to the central government. The total population of Heijo-*kyo* is presumed to be around 100,000, and it is believed that this number increased when some major constructions like that of the Todaiji temple were being carried out.

City planning of Heian-*kyo*

The imperial capital was relocated in 784 and then again to Heian-*kyo* in 794. Heian-*kyo* was the last ancient capital. The city plan of Heian-*kyo* is shown in Figure 3.6.

At a glance, this plan looks similar to the main rectangular area of Heijo-*kyo* as well as of the subsequent capitals, but on a closer look, Heian-*kyo* appears to be considerably different from the other capitals despite their basic similarities, namely, the rectangular shape, the grid street pattern, and the size of the area[14].

Heian-*kyo* was planned as a perfect rectangle 5.2 kilometers long and 4.5 kilometers wide, located between two rivers on the alluvial fan in the northern part of the Kyoto Basin. The capital was divided into the east and west capital cities by an 84-meter-wide main street; just like in Heijo-*kyo*, both cities were independently governed by their respective governments. Each capital city consisted of nine east-west belts called *jo*, which were controlled by a principal, one of which contained four *bo* of 121 meters squire. Each *jo* as well as *bo* was separated by major streets between 24 and 51 meter wide, except for the main street. Each *bo* was subdivided into sixteen sections called *cho* by 12-meter-wide minor streets. Such a planning was fully implemented in Heian-*kyo*. Consequently, every section had an area of 121 meter square, because, unlike in Heijo-*kyo*, the width of the street was separately determined on the basis of the area of section.

The imperial palace district was located at the north-central part of the capital area, in which facilities similar to Heijo-*kyo* were established. The private palace of the emperor in Heian-*kyo*, however, was constructed as a separate structure surrounded by walls; in fact, it was located further from other facilities as compared to Heijo-*kyo*. As in Heijo-*kyo*, two marketplaces were established and managed by the market supervisors, but unlike Heijo-*kyo*, only two temples were established in Heian-*kyo*. The manner of allocating housing lots in the capital was nearly the same as in Heijo-*kyo*.

The *jo* were numbered from one to nine from the northern end to the southern end; this numbering system was also implemented for major streets running from east to west along the belts of *bo*. The *bo* were also numbered from one along the main street at the center to four at the east or west ends. Sections in each *bo* were numbered again from one to sixteen. Consequently, each section was systematically indicated, for example, "7-*cho* (section), 5-*jo* 2-*bo*, *Sa-kyo* (east capital)" (written in reverse in Japanese). This numerical system for indicating places was thought to have been established in Heijo-*kyo* before it was in Heian-*kyo*, but a recent study on this system has established that it had not yet been implemented in Heijo-*kyo*. It should be noted that the Chinese capital cities in the eighth and ninth centuries did not have such numerical indication systems, but each *bo* had a particular name. The Japanese numerical system for city planning was originally established in Heian-*kyo* or a little before that to suit special conditions, although it was a modified version of the system adopted in Chinese capitals[15].

The most important differences between the ancient capital cities in Japan and China lay in the function and structure of *bo*. First, a Japanese principal of an administrative unit was appointed at each *jo*, which consisted of four *bo*; however, in China, a principal controlled each *bo*. This means that the Japanese *bo* was neither a social unit nor an administrative one, and it differed from the Chinese *bo*. Second, the Japanese *bo* was either enclosed only by a thin, decorative wall or separated only by narrow ditches, although each Chinese *bo*, which housed a community, were surrounded by fortified walls. In Japan, the walls of the *bo* as well of the entire capital were, generally speaking, more thin and decorative than those in China.

Structure and transformation of Heian-*kyo*

When Heian-*kyo* was built in the northern part of the Kyoto Basin, located in a province across the border of two counties, several *go* were incorporated into the capital and many paddies were urbanized. Many common farmers who were allocated paddies are thought to have been evicted from the capital and were allocated paddies in other areas. One major shrine in each county, where the capital located, received special donations from the government and became the principal shrine of both the capital and the citizens, including royal families and aristocrats. Following Chinese culture, the mountains and rivers surrounding the capital were considered to be the gods of cardinal points. Major works were carried out for constructing riverbanks to prevent floods, especially along two big rivers at the east and west of the capital. The riverbeds were far wider than the current ones, and many locations on the riverbed adjoining the capital were generally used for pastures and funerary purposes until 842 when such utilization was limited to particular places.

The population of Heian-*kyo*, similar to that of Heijo-*kyo*, was around 100,000. Almost 90% comprised the general public and the rest consisted of the royal and aristocrat families, higher-ranking bureaucrats, and their servants. The government facilities were limited to the imperial palace district and the surrounding areas, and many residences of noblemen and higher-ranking bureaucrats were also located close to those areas. Figure 3.6 shows the sections in which some buildings or markets are thought to have existed according to archaeological and documentary evidences. Except for many sections in the southwest part, the buildings or facilities were widely distributed in the ninth and tenth centuries, but in the eleventh and twelfth centuries, they were mainly concentrated in the east capital. It is notable that the west capital was quite vacant and the residential districts expanded to both the northern and eastern suburbs outside the original capital area. In particular, the northeast part of the original capital area and its nearest suburbs were the most preferred and most expensive residential districts for aristocrats and higher-ranking bureaucrats, as indicated by a contemporary diary of an aristocrat, because the imperial palace was moved from the original location to this part at the beginning of the eleventh century after the palace was burnt down. In the case of the eastern suburbs across the Kamo River running from the original capital to the east bank, many big temples were established in the second half of the eleventh century and new aristocrats and warriors got residences here in the twelfth century[16].

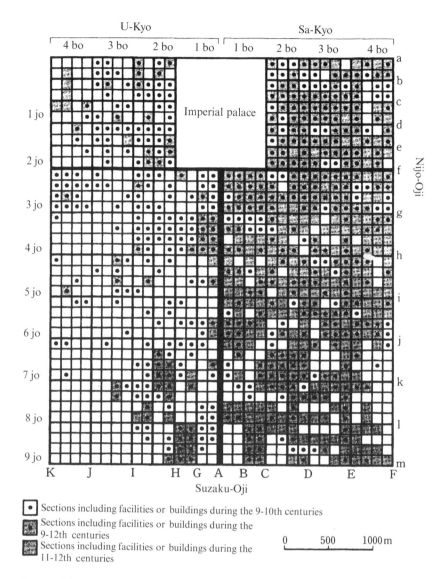

Figure 3.3: Facilities and buildings in Heian-*kyo*. A~k and a~m are corresponding to those in Figure 3.4.
Source: Akihiro KINDA.

Figure 3.4 shows the surface remains of the grid streets of Heian-*kyo* as land divisions extracted from by the large-scale maps of 1922.

This pattern reflects the changing structure of the capital as described above. The grid street patterns were well maintained in the east capital city but the series

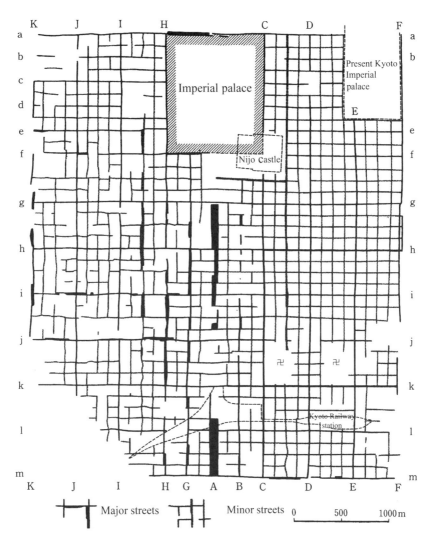

Figure 3.4: Remains of the street pattern of Heian-*kyo*. A~k and a~m are corresponding to those in Figure 3.3.
Source: Akihiro KINDA.

of grid patterns was not continuous in the west capital city, although the width was, partly, rather well kept. The southwest corner of the capital had no remains of the grid pattern. A document reported that in addition to the imperial palace district and government districts, there were approximately 580 urbanized sections in 828, but about 400 sections have not yet been identified. According to another document, there were around 300 sections cultivated agriculturally in the west capital in 1086. Findings reveal vacant sections and many areas with no surface remains of the grid patterns (as shown in Figure 3.3); this can be attributed to the changing structure of the capital.

Heian-*kyo* and the former capitals were the center of the imperial highways and the destination of various products from all provinces. The imperial highways with relay posts to five directions were started formally from the main gate at the southern end of the main street, although many major streets in the capital stretched into suburbs and further with the urbanization and development of villas in nearby resort areas. The marketplaces in each capital city had access to the water transportation network by means of the artificial canal, which was constructed in each capital city. The marketplaces were further connected with the Inland Sea or Lake Biwa through this network of canals and rivers. These transportation networks were maintained with minor modifications in the ancient and medieval times, even after the government's national transportation system became insufficient in the tenth century. Heian-*kyo* could boast important infrastructure, and in the eleventh century, it became the biggest home city of the manorial lords and also the biggest handicraft centre[17].

Function and location of a regional capital, Dazaifu

Among many local administrative centers, Dazaifu was the most eminent regional capital in ancient Japan. Mention of several predecessors of Dazaifu, with slightly different names, were found in *Nihon-shoki* in the seventh century from 609. The fortifications of the city were first constructed in 664. It was consolidated in 702 as a regional capital and a satellite city of the imperial capital where a national ministry was located. Dazaifu originally had a minister and several deputies under him. All of them and many directors under them were appointed in the imperial capital and assumed responsibilities in Dazaifu. Dazaifu was located to the far west of the imperial capital but was the largest ministry of the central government, consisting of 33 sections or directors. Each section or director had a certain number of bureaucrats and servants. The latter assisted directors and cultivated the paddies of both the ministry and bureaucrats; these paddies were distributed according to the status of each group. The central ministry in charge of foreign affairs and defense was located in Dazaifu because of its location close to the border of continental countries. Main facilities of Dazaifu were located upstream of a river approximately 15 kilometers inland from the Port of Hakata, at which the state guesthouse was located, faced the South China Sea.

In 664, soon after the defeat of the allied forces of Yamato and Paekche at the hands of the Tang and Silla dynasties, huge straight banks with moats, called *Mizuki*, were constructed as fortifications in the valleys surrounding Dazaifu. The longest one in the northwest of the central hall quarter, located a little downstream of a river, is still preserved, although several parts were dug out to construct roads and railways. The bank was approximately 13 meters high and 1.2 kilometers long. The width of the earthen walls at its base was originally 75 meters and had moats 60 meters wide and 4 meters deep attached on the northern side, specifically, outside the wall. This *Mizuki* originally had the east and west gates open to main roads between the central hall quarter and the Port of Hakata. Six shorter *Mizuki* were constructed for defending against attacks at other small valleys of the northwest side and a few more *Mizuki* were constructed to defend the southern valleys.

In the subsequent year, two mountain castles were constructed in the northern mountains and in the southwestern mountains of the central hall quarter of Dazaifu under the superintendence of former high-ranking officials of Paekche. A mountain castle, Ohno-jo, constructed on a north mountain of Dazaifu, had many warehouses distributed on the flat top of the mountain 410 meters high and was surrounded by stone and earthen walls with four gates. More than 70 buildings were constructed, all of them with pillar base stones. The total length of the wall was 6.2 kilometers. Little information is available on the other mountain castle but it seems to have had a similar plan. This style of mountain castles is thought to have been introduced from Korea, and the typical case like Ohno-jo was constructed under the directions of Korean refugees.

Many mountain castles were constructed in the northern part of the road district including Dazaifu and in the other road disticts along the Inland Sea between Dazaifu and the capital district. These were also similar Korean-style mountain castles, but their origins are not clear. According to some legends, the mountain-top shrines were surrounded by religious facilities. These regions were thought to be quite vulnerable to attacks by foreign naval forces at the time. However, many of these mountain castles fell to ruin probably in the ninth century or a little later.

Another important function of Dazaifu as a regional capital was to supervise nine provincial governments within the road district. Many orders were delivered to those provinces from or through Dazaifu, and some goods paid as taxes, which were usually sent to the imperial capital, were sent to Dazaifu by provincial governments. For these purposes, Dazaifu was planned to have a network of highways in the road district[18].

Plan and structure of Dazaifu

Dazaifu was described as a "remote imperial capital" in a famous poem by a provincial governor and as "a big city throughout the world" in an official report issued by Dazaifu itself—both written in the eighth century. Modern historians and historical geographers have given due consideration to these descriptions. Although the former was a perceptive description, it led to the reconstruction of Dazaifu as a smaller version of the imperial capital. The most famous idea was a tetragonal shape with a grid street pattern with intervals of 108 or 109 meters. The authors of this idea thought that this plan was established in the second half of the seventh century and continued until medieval times.

Archaeological excavations in the last few decades have revealed that early government buildings in the central hall quarter existed partly in the second half of the seventh century and that the plan of the central hall quarter drastically changed at the beginning of the eighth century and again in the mid-tenth century. The former plan had neither a symmetrical plan nor magnificent buildings like the latter ones, although archaeological data are still insufficient for conclusive findings. The second plan had a completely symmetrical layout of the buildings with tiled roofs and pillar base stones in the square court with a length of approximately 115 meters. The court is surrounded by corridors, and it has rectangular courts, surrounded by earthen walls with tiled roofs, at its north and south sides. The layout of the third plan was basically similar to the second, but it consisted of a few more buildings and more magnificent buildings. This means that the function and organization changed, and the third plan must have been formulated by the most powerful government, unlike the early reconstruction described above.

A historical-geographical research found that the grid pattern reconstructed on the basis of relics found in the ground as well as some archaeological data like pass and ditch patterns and the morphology of paddies did not have intervals of 108 or 109 meters as estimated previously but intervals of approximately 100 meters (see Figure 3.5). All historical records of land from the tenth to the twelfth centuries show that the maximum area of land was approximately one hectare; this indicates that the grid pattern had intervals of 100 meters. Furthermore, they show that a place indication system based on this grid pattern was established in the mid-tenth century. It was also found that Dazaifu got a full-fledged government comprising more higher-ranking officials in the tenth and eleventh centuries.

The development of Dazaifu can be summarized into three stages. In the first stage, the early organization of Dazaifu was founded in the beginning of the seventh century and the location seems to have been in the same place as the second and third Dazaifu. In the mid-660s, new fortifications, *Mizuki*, and two Korean-style mountain castles were constructed; however, not much information is available on other government facilities in this stage.

Dazaifu entered the second stage at the beginning of the eighth century. The organization was consolidated into a ministry containing 33 sections for the regional capital of a road district. A new layout for government buildings was implemented in the central hall quarter, and other government office quarters were constructed in the surrounding area. Furthermore, a 34-meter-wide main street was constructed southward from the main gate of the central hall quarter. Several quarters of facilities such as residences for ministers and their deputies were located along this main street. In addition, the largest temple in the road district, Kanzeon-ji, was located, and there was also a north-south street running from the main south gate of the temple. A provincial capital, a military base, and other major temples were established in and around Dazaifu, although detailed information on these structures has not been found. It is believed that many *Mizuki* and two mountain castles have been maintained. The mountain castle was once a part of the organization in the second stage and then became an independent department.

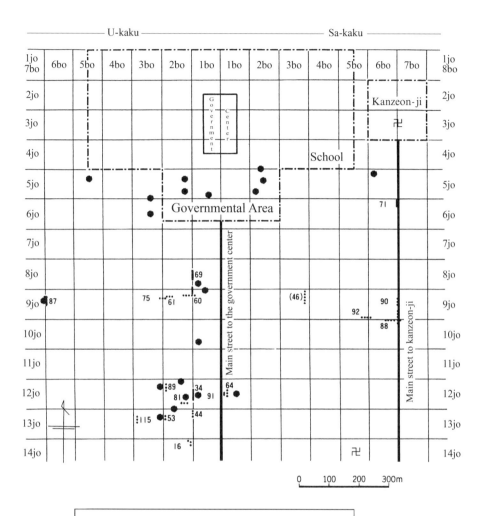

Figure 3.5: Plan and remains of Dazaifu.
Source: Akihiro KINDA.

A state guesthouse, *Korokan*, was constructed as a section of Dazaifu near the mouth of a river running from the central hall quarter of the city. A national highway connected the central hall quarter and *Korokan* through the west gate of the longest *Mizuki*. In the second stage of Dazaifu's construction, a cluster system of the facilities was planned, where each facility formed a quarter surrounded by earthen walls with tiled roofs. These quarters were called *kaku* as described in historical sources, including famous poems written by an honorable minister who was relegated from the post of a prime minister in the first half of the tenth century.

Dazaifu's landscape was characterized by some large, decorative buildings in the central hall quarter and many government buildings in the surrounding quarters, along with the Kanzeon-ji temple, but it consisted of many other clustered facilities of various functions connected by straight streets or roads[19].

Change in the city planning and structure of Dazaifu

Almost all buildings in Dazaifu were burnt down in a rebellion in 941, following which the third stage of the city's development began. It had a grid street pattern with intervals of approximately 100 meters and a rectangular area approximately 2.4 kilometers long and 2.2 kilometers wide (shown in Figure 3.1). It was during this stage that the place indication system, according to which each section of this grid pattern was numbered, was introduced. It is believed that this system was introduced in Dazaifu after it was in the imperial capital, Heian-*kyo*, but it received special recognition by the higher- ranking officials of Dazaifu.

It is assumed that such a major change was funded by the local government, and not the central government. The latter consisted of officials, including deputy ministers, who had settled down in and around Dazaifu and who became local powerful families in that period. They seemed to regard Dazaifu as a capital like Heian-*kyo*. They probably hoped that the newly reconstructed Dazaifu, with its elaborate city plan and majestic landscape comprising buildings, replaced and supplemented the administrative power of the central government, which had been weakened at that time. They possibly felt that a more magnificent Dazaifu was necessary to maintain or strengthen their own political and administrative powers in the Saikai-do district. Dazaifu came to have more higher-ranking officials than it did in the eighth century, as well as more independent authorities in many departments. Such an organization also seems to have been effective for performing their political and administrative power within the Saikai-do district.

The administration, record office, military, education, and several other departments at the third stage became well organized under a chief director and the deputies of the respective departments; moreover, they became more independent than the departments at the second stage of Dazaifu, which had the largest ministry of the state in the eighth century. The number of departments in the eleventh century, as identified by various sources, was 20, although their compositions were not exactly known. The independence of some of the departments led to conflicts among them or with the Kanzeon-ji temple on the ownership and boundaries of their lands. A typical example would be the conflict between the military department and the Kanzeon-ji temple because of the expansionism of the military and the ambiguousness of the boundaries of the land with regard to the new grid pattern system. These disputes continued after the establishment of a new system, because which partly reused previous streets or ditches. The trend of departments becoming independent authorities might be another reason why they needed a systematic land indication and grid pattern system for clearly establishing the boundaries of lands[20].

Function and location of provincial capitals

The provincial government was an administrative center where higher-ranking officials, including the governor and his deputies, officials, and servants, were in charge, although their numbers varied with the size of provinces. The number of higher-ranking officials ranged between 5 and 9, and the total number of regular staff members and official servants was between 367 and 865 in the first half of the eighth century. The governors were responsible for not only the administration but also the military, justice, and all governance-related matters within the province. The governor also performed religious services of the shrines in his province. Most higher-ranking-officials were appointed among second-class noblemen and higher-ranking bureaucrats in the imperial capital and spent a few years in service in the provinces.

The administrative center of a province, called *Kokufu,* served as the provincial capital, which boasted various facilities, including a central hall quarter and several clusters of wooden buildings for ceremonies, administration, as storehouses, and as workshops, as well as residences for the governor, deputy governors, and officials. The plan of the central hall quarter was basically similar to that of Dazaifu, but with local variations and on a smaller scale. It is believed that *Kokufu* served as an urban area consisting of those facilities. Since governors supervised the collection of taxes and managed their storage and transportation—some of the taxes were sent to the imperial capitals—the provincial capital occupied, generally speaking, the most convenient location in that it had access to the national highway system and the water transportation network. The most important function of the national highway system, as explained in chapter 4, was to connect each provincial capital to the imperial capital. Many governors and officials used this highway system to reach the imperial capital, carry annual reports from the provincial capital, set out for their official duties, and return home. They were provided with conveyance expenses, but a large number of laborers and the draft pressed into service in the imperial capital or in military bases were obliged to carry their own tools and food. Many people transported paper, linen and silk as taxes to the imperial capital by themselves.

Some provincial capitals were located in a county at the center of a province and many others in an area rather close to the imperial capital. Both these locations are thought to have been convenient for administering the entire province or to maintain a closer relationship with the imperial capital[21].

Concerning the physical characteristics of the location, it is notable that many facilities of the provincial capital were constructed on the diluvial terrace. Such a location was relatively safe from floods and free from humidity. The latter was especially important for warehouses, and such a location was mandated by a state government order in the eighth century. Some provincial capitals were, however, constructed on the alluvial plain. Documents and archaeological excavations have revealed that these locations often suffered from floods in spite of the presence of slightly higher mounds that served as natural levees.

Basic plan and change in the structure of provincial capitals

The plans of provincial capitals were, just like those of Dazaifu, considered to be smaller versions of the imperial capital with grid street patterns and a rectangular area. A length of eight *cho* (approximately 872 meters) was considered a standard, although it is believed that the sizes varied with the size of the province. However, the morphology and structure of provincial capitals, as revealed by interdisciplinary research works, differ from these earlier tetragonal models. As can be seen from Figure 3.6, the newly found typologies of provincial capitals are neither tetragonal in shape nor do they have grid street patterns within the area.

The central facility of the provincial capital was a central hall quarter surrounded by earthen walls with tiled roofs; this layout is similar to that of Dazaifu but with local variations, and it is smaller in size and with fewer buildings. Almost all the buildings in the provincial capitals were constructed with wood and had board roofs, but in the mid-eighth century or a little later, many of the buildings in the central hall quarter were replaced with more decorative ones that were constructed on foundation stones and with tiled roofs. There seem to be three models—A, B, and C—of the plan for provincial capitals, as shown in Figure 3.6. Model A had a straight main street running southward from the main gate of the central hall of the provincial capital, and model B had a main street running from east to west. Many clusters of wooden buildings surrounded by fences or earthen walls with tiled roofs were distributed along the main streets or their branches in both models. In addition to a central hall, a provincial capital typically contained several clusters of governors' residences, warehouses, workshops, temples, and a marketplace, some of which were often located at a certain distance from the central hall quarter. Other facilities like a provincial army base, a county seat, and a relay post of the national highway system were sometimes located near the central hall quarter. In model C, there is a large quarter, including a central hall quarter and other administrative buildings, surrounded by fences or earthen walls with tiled roofs. This type also had some clusters of the facilities located outside the central quarter.

As already mentioned, the provincial capitals were often located on the diluvial terrace, which was eroded by many small valleys and had jagged features. This might be one of the reasons why the facilities were distributed as clusters. These clusters, however, were not always adjacent to each other and were often scattered

Diorama of the Izumo provincial capital, with permission from Shimane prefecture (Type A)

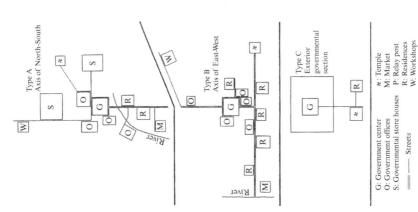

Type A
Axis of North-South

Type B
Axis of East-West

Type C
Exterior governmental section

G: Government center
O: Government offices
S: Governmental store houses
━━ Streets

⛩ : Temple
M: Market
P: Relay post
R: Residences
W: Workshops

Figure 3.6: Typology of provincial capitals.
Source: Akihiro KINDA.

even if they were located on flat alluvial plains. Furthermore, some of the facilities like workshops and storehouses were constructed a few kilometers away from
the central hall quarter. Provincial capitals in ancient Japan, irrespective of the
subtype, did not have densely built areas through the entire capital, but had several clusters of nonagricultural facilities loosely scattered.

The administrative systems of the provinces as well as that of Dazaifu were
reorganized in and after the tenth century. The provincial governments became
more independent, although they were still subjected to a guideline under the
orders of the central government and the previous administration system, based
on the administrative codes of 701, was followed. Principal governors were also
appointed by the emperor, but the former preferred to send their deputies to
their provinces instead of carrying out their duties themselves. This tendency was
contemporaneous with another movement where deputy governors and officials
often strengthened their political, economic, and administrative powers in the
provinces. Many of them settled down in the province and became local powerful
families. The heads of these families were appointed as provincial officials, whose
numbers increased and often included former county officials in and after the
tenth century.

In the course of these changes, provincial capitals tended to acquire different
patterns. Some provincial capitals, just like Dazaifu, gradually came to have a
rectangular shape or were planned thus by governmental officials. In other cases,
some central halls in the province were rebuilt rather poorly as compared to their
previous versions or they fell to ruin during the tenth and eleventh centuries. The
residences of deputy governors often served as the main facilities of provincial
administration and ceremonies at the time.

From the eleventh century onward, manorial lords often claimed to control
the entire area under the manor without any intervention from the provincial government. Despite opposition from the provincial government, in the twelfth or
thirteenth century, the manor became, generally speaking, an administrative unit
controlled directly by the lord of the manor, many of which were lived/located
in or near Heian-*kyo*. The provincial governments were obliged to restructure
the administrative organization of the county and *go* under the jurisdiction of
the provincial governors. As a result, the area that fell under the jurisprudence
of the provincial governors decreased. The provincial governments completely
lost their military power in the 1180s and their administrative power in due time.
The warrior class, which originally comprised the guardsmen of the aristocrats,
emerged as the new administrative and military power[22].

County seats and other main facilities in the province

In the second half of the seventh century, the county was originally established
as the domain of a powerful local clan, and the county chief was presumably the

head of clan. After the new local administration system consisting of province, county and *go* was established in the eighth century, the county chief and his deputies were selected among local powerful families, unlike the system for selecting provincial governors. Their residences were located within the county, and although they already held power, it seems that they wanted to be appointed as district supervisors to maintain their power in the eighth century.

It is believed that the facilities of the county seats were neither large in number nor did they have a complicated organization. The main facilities comprised a central hall of the county and storehouses, but sometimes, there were a few attached facilities for district supervisors and accommodation buildings for the provincial governor's patrol. The central hall district of the county seat was often planned as a rectangular arrangement of the buildings, similar to the provincial plan, but smaller in scale. The rectangle had a length of 60 to 150 meters. However, because the rice given as tax was usually stored and used, and had to be renewed on a yearly basis within the county, the number of storehouses located outside this central hall was 10, 20, or more.

Some of the county seats were found along the national highway, even though they were not required to be located close to it. The center of the county possibly provided a convenient location from where the county government could perform its functions, since it was not only the geographical center of the county but also a nodal point for roads or the water transportation network, or the traditional center of the clan territory.

Many county seats established in the eighth century fell into ruin by the tenth century, when both the structure of the provincial government and the plan of the provincial capital changed. Some functions were taken over by the provincial government, and the counties and manors were reorganized as administrative units. Many powerful families obtained positions in the provincial government[23].

Besides provincial capitals and county seats, some nonagricultural facilities were founded in rural areas in ancient Japan. The location of workshops like those of pottery and ironworks depended on the availability of raw materials, and warehouses for rice were also distributed somewhere outside the provincial capital and county seat. The manor houses and attached storehouses were usually smaller and fewer than the county seats. Many of these structures were strategically located close to the water transportation networks for the convenience of the lords of manors and each location presumably had a place to dock along the closest river.

A village leader was also appointed in each *go,* the lowest administrative unit. He often relayed orders from the provincial and county governments to the people in the *go,* and even village leaders sometimes issued some documents and reports. Some archaeological excavations reveal smaller rectangular facilities and accompanying buildings outside both the provincial capital and county seats. These might be examples of the office of the village leader. The composition of the village government, however, is not yet known[24].

The importance of ports in ancient times is evidenced by the fact that the central government noted principal ports, the journey duration, and the standard transportation expenses from each province to Heian-*kyo* at the beginning of the tenth century. Rice and timber for building were the main goods transported through the water network. Moreover, some documents and official records have been found with the names of the ports listed in them[25].

The most conspicuous facility in ancient Japan, not only around the royal palaces and in the imperial capitals but also in the provincial area, must have been a Buddhist temple. A Buddhist temple complex generally consisted of a few big wooden buildings, including the pagoda, constructed on foundation stones and having tiled roofs. The exterior of the temple buildings were often painted bright red and green, although traditional shrines and residential buildings were originally not painted. Therefore, Buddhist temples made very remarkable structures, and a total of 545 temples were built by the end of the seventh century.

The Horyuji temple (see Figure 3.7), a UNESCO World Heritage Site and the oldest wooden building in the world, is an example of such a Buddhist building. The original constructions were burnt down in 670, but the second ones, which can be seen at present, were constructed soon thereafter. The temple was founded by a crown prince and was one of the first class temples in the size. Five-storied pagoda and the main building were surrounded by rectangular earthen wall with tiled roofs. More than ten other similar large temples were constructed around the districts of royal palaces at the time. Many other temples built in the course of a century from the mid-seventh century were slightly smaller, but large and magnificent nonetheless. Many Buddhist temples were founded by local clans in the provincial district as well as in the surrounding districts of royal palaces. In many counties, a few ruins of those temples, including one nearby the county seat, were found. Some temples attached to the county seats seem to have been constructed by local clans occupying the positions of district supervisors. Other clans seem to have constructed their own temples in their home territories, and several or more temples have been found within each county in this case.

Besides those very old temples established independently, in 741, the emperor ordered the construction of two Buddhist temples in each province, one for male priests and the other for female priests and both subsidized by the province; the constructions of both were almost completed by the 770s. Those temples were provincial and many of them were either located along national highways or close to the provincial capital area. The Todai-ji temple was established as a state temple as well as the headquarter of provincial temples. Those major temples were officially subsidized by the state, and because of the different subsidy plans, the number of these temples increased rapidly from the mid-ninth century.

The provinces of Mutsu and Dewa—the latter was established a little later— formed the northern frontier of Honsyu Island. The provincial government of Mutsu was established in the principal plain in the southeastern part of the region, which was located close to the entrance of the area from the imperial

Figure 3.7: Horyuji temple since the 7th century (a UNESCO world cultural heritage). (Photo by Manabu Watanabe).

capital. In the first quarter of the eighth century, the administrative center of the frontier moved to Taga-jo, which was also located in the southern part of the province and in the principal plain within the province, and it served as the center in both provinces[26].

Taga-jo and other military bases

Taga-jo was a provincial capital and the principal military base of the state army from where they could control the area, where people partially accepted the *ritsuryo* code. The army and provincial government were originally not separated. Since the military base was moved to the north from Taga-jo in 802, Taga-jo became just a provincial capital without a military base. However, Mutsu was the largest province, comprising 36 counties in the second half of the ninth century, and its capital was larger than a typical provincial capital. Taga-jo could be considered similar to a regional capital like Dazaifu.

According to archaeological data, the central hall quarter of Taga-jo was constructed in the second half of the eighth century and remained until the mid-tenth century. The first buildings with pillars embedded directly in the ground were enclosed in a rectangle (120 meters from east to west and 150 meters from north to south) of earthen walls with tiled roofs. The plan of the second central hall, built in the second half of the eighth century, was almost the same as the first one, but all the buildings were replaced with those with tiled roofs and pillar base stones. All buildings were replaced with decorative ones, and the southern part of the court was paved with pebbles. The second constructions were burnt down, after which reconstruction began at the end of the eighth century, with minor changes made to the buildings and a new pavement with hewn stones added. In the second half of the ninth century, they were rebuilt and used until the mid-tenth century.

The most characteristic facilities of Taga-jo were the outer earthen walls with tiled roofs around the central hall quarter located on a diluvial terrace. The terrace and hilly area surrounded by the outer wall forms an irregular area of approximately 70 hectares. The outer walls and the central hall quarter were rebuilt. Some other facilities were located within the outer walls. It is believed that a special organization combining the administrative center and military functions was required to implement this large, elaborate plan for Taga-jo.

Furthermore, many facilities, including roads and large residences, were found by archaeological excavations in the south and southwest parts outside the outer walls. The 12-meter-wide west-east road ran parallel to the southern part of the outer walls. Its east end was a temple attached to Taga-jo; the temple was constructed with the same tiles as the central hall buildings. Another main road was considered as a southward extension of the main parade through the southern main gate of the outer walls. The two main roads were not at a right angle with each other, but it is thought that some other partly excavated parallel roads formed a diamond-shaped grid. These facilities located outside the outer walls, with the exception of the temple at the east end of the road, were mainly constructed in the ninth and tenth centuries.

These facts indicate that most principal facilities of Taga-jo were probably maintained after the relocation of the military and that residences and streets were constructed outside the outer walls during the ninth and tenth centuries. The various facilities of Taga-jo were distributed in a very large area, which was slightly smaller than the total area of Dazaifu when it was planned as a rectangular city in the tenth century. It is believed that even in Taga-jo, the principal facilities were clustered within the outer walls in the eighth century. The basic plan of this area was not changed, but many other facilities were added in the ninth century, similar to the changes made to the structure of Taga-jo. Taga-jo lost its military function, but its administrative functions as well as the number of officials must have increased rapidly to govern the large area and population of the provinces, which consisted of 36 counties at the end of ninth century.

In the mid-seventh century, the earliest two military bases in the northeast frontier were constructed along the Sea of Japan in an effort to consolidate the ancient state. The details of their location and facilities are not yet fully known, but they are thought to be located in the present-day city of Niigata. Ten other military bases were constructed further north in the eighth century, although some of their ruins have not yet been found.

Taga-jo was the military headquarter in the eighth century, but at the beginning of the ninth century, after the big rebellion was suppressed, the headquarter moved to Shiwa-jo, approximately 150 kilometers north of Taga-jo, as shown in Figure 3.8.

Figure 3.8: Shiwa-jo (military base in the early 9th century: reconstructed by Morioka City Board of Education, with permission of the Board).

Shiwa-jo was located on the alluvial plain, and the northern part of the area was eroded by a river. However, it had a rectangular fortification of 930 meters wide. Similar to Taga-jo, the total area was approximately 70 hectares. The layout of the facilities differed from that of Taga-jo; it had a more regular tetragonal plan as compared to that of Taga-jo.

Shiwa-jo was hit by a flood, and it was a reason to move to be reconstructed in 813. Shiwa-jo had a rectangular plan similar to type C of the provincial capital (Figure 3), although some corners were not at right angles and were irregularly shaped. In the eighth century, other smaller military bases were constructed, many of them had typical rectangular fortifications. It should be noted that in the eighth and ninth centuries regional capitals like Dazaifu and Taga-jo and the provincial capitals did not have a typical rectangular plan, but the military bases did[27].

Such governmental facilities, along with temples, were distinguished as landscape factors.

Notes

1. M. Mohri, Flower of Buddhism, in Tsuboi and Hirano eds., *New Edition; Ancient Japan 6*, (Tokyo, 1991).
2. A. Kinda, *Research on the Landscape History of Ancient Japan*, pp. 43–70, (Tokyo, 2002).
3. Kinda, *ibid.*
4. T. Yoshida, Japan in the eighth century, in *Series of Iwanami's Lecture, Japanese History 4.* (Tokyo, 1994).
5. M. Kamata, *Study on the Public under the 'Ritsuryo'*, pp. 5–52, (Tokyo, 2001).
6. W. Ikebe, *Investigation into names of the County, 'Go', 'Ri' and Relay Post in 'Wamyosho'*, pp. 20–137, (Tokyo, 1891).
7. E. Ishigami, Discussion on the Ritusryo State, in Tsuboi and Hirano eds., *New Edition; Ancient Japan 1*, (Tokyo, 1993).
8. H. Kano, Evolution of Yamato dynasty, in Tsuboi and Hirano eds., *New Edition; Ancient Japan 5.* (Tokyo, 1992).
9. T. Kishi, *Study on the Royal Palaces and Capitals in Ancient Japan*, pp. 5–28, (Tokyo, 1988).
10. T. Kishi, *ibid.*
11. T. Kishi (1988), *op.cit.* pp. 435–462.
12. T. Ozawa, *Study on the Structure of the Royal Palace and Capital in Ancient Japan*, pp. 239–264, (Tokyo, 2003).
13. H. Hayashibe, *Study on the Formation of Ancient Palaces and Capitals*, 292 p., (Tokyo, 2001).
14. A. Kinda, *An Historical-geographical Study of Jori Plan and the Rural Landscape*, pp. 77–125, (Tokyo, 1985).
15. Kinda, *ibid.*

16. Kinda (2002), *op.cit.* pp. 98–111.
17. A. Kinda, Heian-*kyo*, in Kinda ed., *Heian-kyo/Kyoto,* (Kyoto, 2007).
18. T. Kagamiyama., Study of Capital City, Dazaifu, (Tokyo, 1968), T. Kishi, Dazaifu and the capital-city system, in Kyushu History Museum ed., *Collection of Essays on the Old Culture of Dazaifu* (Tokyo, 1983), A. Kinda, *Landscapes of Ancient Japan*, pp. 185–188, (Tokyo, 1993).
19. Kinda (1993), *op.cit.* pp. 188–224.
20. R. Takeuchi ed., *Historical Records of Dazaifu, Vol. 1–13*, (Fukuoka, 1964–1986), T. Kishi, *Study on the Ancient Japanese Capitals*, p. 281, (Tokyo, 1988), Kinda (1993), *op.cit.* pp. 224–242.
21. K. Fujioka, *Kokufu*, (Tokyo, 1969), R. Kinoshita, *Kokufu*, (Tokyo, 1988), A. Kinda (1993), *op.cit.* pp. 243–249.
22. Kinda (2002), *op.cit.* pp. 124–225.
23. H. Sasayama, Change of the ancient state, in Tsuboi and Hirano eds. (1993), op.cit.
24. M. Sato, Administralion and people, in Tsuboi and Hirano eds. (1993), op.cit.
25. T. Sakaehara, *Study on Economic History of Ancient Transportation in Japan*, pp. 275–317, (Tokyo, 1992).
26. A. Shindo, Province of Mutsu, in Society of the Japanese Archaeology ed., *Provincial Capitals*, (Mie, 1996).
27. Morioka city Board of Education ed. *Shiwa-Jo,* pp. 46–51.

CHAPTER 4

Medieval towns

Aki YAMAMURA

Medieval capital; Kyoto

From the later part of the 11th century to the later part of the 12th century, the ex-emperors who were the fathers of the ruling emperors retained the real political power. Some large ex-emperors' palaces were moved out of the ancient Heian-kyo to its suburbs, Toba, Shirakawa and Hojujidono. The powerful warriors, the Taira clan, supporting the ex-emperor also located their home base at suburb, Rokuhara. Kamakura government, which was established by the Minamoto clan, confiscated the estates there (Figure 4.1).

Shirakawa, one of the suburbs, was situated on the east extension of the Nijo street, the east-west axe of the Heian-kyo at that time. Shirakawa was located on the sloping terrain of the alluvial fan. The ex-emperor created terraces, and went on to build the Hossho-ji temple, with its 9-storey tower, on the highest level of the fan (Uemura 1999). A tower of such proportions had never been constructed in Heian-kyo until then. The landscape of Hossho-ji represented the power wielded by the ex-emperor in those days. Hossho-ji, which had been planned as the ex-emperor's private temple, was also used by the public during national Buddhist ceremonies. Ex-emperors commonly demonstrated the legitimacy of their political power by flaunting their acceptance by Buddhist authority. After the construction of the Hossho-ji temple, successive emperors and one of their wives built five other large private temples, one after another, during the next 70 years. These temples stood on the lower terraces and were thus, symbolically, in deference to the Hossho-ji. On the lowest terrace, palaces were constructed along the Nijo street for the ex-emperor to attend the ceremonies at the Hossho-ji. Later, warehouses, private houses of worship, temporal residences for close aides of the ex-emperor, and priests' houses were built in Shirakawa.

While the suburbs had been constructed in the early medieval times, the ancient urban center, the east-side of Heian-kyo, had also undergone development. It was simply called Kyo or Kyochu. In Kyo, the residences of the aristocrats lined both sides of the Nijo street, which was extended to form the main street of Shirakawa as well (Yamamura 2007). Some residences belonging to powerful aristocrats and the imperial family were concentrated above Nijo street. On the other hand,

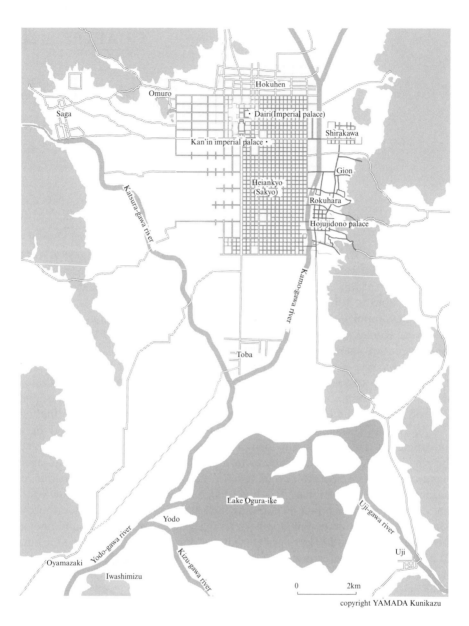

Figure 4.1: The spatial structure of early medieval Kyoto, 11–13th century.
The original map was made by Prof. Yamada, Kunikazu (Doshisya Women's Colledge of Liberal Arts).

many small houses belonging to craftsmen and merchants were located along the Machi-street, which was one of the north–south streets of Kyo. Those houses were mixed with the residences of the aristocrats and warriors (Kiuchi 1977). The commercial aspect of Machi street was enhanced progressively through the medieval times. In particular, the intersections of Machi street and two east-west streets, the Sanjo and the Shijo streets, were developed as prime downtown territory (Akiyama and Nakamura 1975).

In the southern parts of Kyo, the powerful warriors and their servants, and the aristocrats had gone on to build large residential quarters around Rokujo street by the middle of the 12th century. At that time, the small houses of the craftsmen and merchants were concentrated along Machi street, and especially around the intersection of the Machi and Shichijo streets (Shichijo-Machi, Hachijoin-cho) (Noguchi 1988). These towns had consisted of several blacksmiths' manufacturing workshops that produced a range of products that included swords, Buddhist statues and coins. Moneylenders also had thrived in the area around Shichijo-Machi. In those medieval times, the same stretch of land would accommodate graveyards and craftsmen's workshops as well as afford space for the houses of rich merchants. In this way, towns were formed in early medieval Kyo that consisted of merchants and craftsmen dealing in the same fields of business.

As a result, some suburbs got urbanized rapidly while still having close relationships with Kyo in the early medieval times (Inoue 1989). Other towns like Saga and Kitano were built around powerful temples and shrines, which were located in suburbs of Kyo. Kyo, with its palaces, towns, and residences (of warriors and aristocrats) functioned as the hub of the network of these satellite towns (Yamada 1998). As a whole, the spatial structure of Kyoto is regarded to have been decentralized but complex. Such medieval structure was quite different from the one that had existed in the ancient Heian-kyo.

It was not only the spatial structure, but also the spatial pattern of the allotments, streets and blocks in Heian-kyo that had changed in the early medieval times (Figure 4.2). The original allotments in Heian-kyo were along the north-south streets. Since the middle of the ancient times, many allotments began to construct along the east-west streets. These allotments, each a reed-shaped small rectangle, had faced toward all sides of their respective blocks. A series of such allotments along each street made up a town community. This means that, in the 12th century, each block was composed of 4 towns. With the commercial development of each town, two towns facing each other on the two sides of a street would connect to form a territorial community. Such road side towns would become the basic unit of urban society in medieval Kyoto (Akiyama and Nakamura 1975).

In 1333, the Kamakura government was brought down by Ashikaga Takauji. Takauji established a new warriors' government (the Muromachi government), and assumed the title of shogun. The governmental office-cum-residence of the shogun was moved out of Kamakura and located in Kyoto. Thus, Kyoto was re-designated as the capital, where both emperors and warriors would settle, until the end of the 16th century (The Muromachi era).

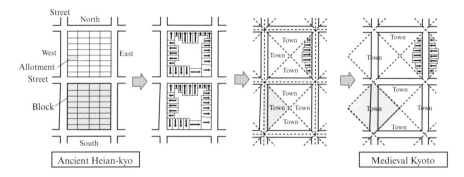

Figure 4.2: The change of the spatial pattern of allotments, streets and towns in Kyoto. Reference: Ashikaga, Ken'ryo (eds.) (1994), *Kyoto Rekishi Atlas* (Historical Atlas Kyoto), Chuokoronsha Inc.

During the Muromachi era, the palace of the emperor was located near the large governmental office toward the north of Kyoto (Figure 4.3). The powerful warriors who were subordinates of the shogun had their residences around the government office (Muromachi-dono). The political functions were concentrated in this area, which was called Kamigyo. On the other hand, a lot of houses belonging to rich merchants and craftsmen were distributed across the south of Kyoto, and especially around Shijo-Machi, an area that had been developed in the early medieval times. This area was overlapped by the residential quarters of a section of people who worshipped the Gion shrine, for peace and the prosperity of their trade. This area, the center of the Kyoto economy was called Shimogyo.

In the late 15th century, the Onin war, which was caused by the conflict arising from the succession of the shogun and expanded to involve government bureaucrats and provincial constables (Syugo), engulfed Japan. Battles raged across downtown Kyoto, including Kamigyo and Shimogyo, and continued unabated for close to 10 years. Downtown Kyoto was burned down and destroyed by these battles. When series of battles in Kyoto had finally run their course, the Muromachi government was unable to restore its powers to their pre-war levels. A weakened central government resulted in frequent wars between the provincial constables who managed their local governments and were ambitious about expanding their territories. The political situation was unstable all around Japan for about a hundred years from late in the 15th century to the end of the 16th century (The Sengoku era).

After the Onin war had ended, the urban areas underwent rapid reconstruction. The landscape of the town was changed. Kamigyo and Shimogyo, where many facilities and houses had been distributed before the war, were brought closer together than they had been before. Moreover, a town wall made of earthwork with moat was built by inhabitants such as merchants and craftsmen in each town. This town wall defended inhabitants keeping the warriors and their battles outside. Inside the wall, the population density rose gradually during the Sengoku era.

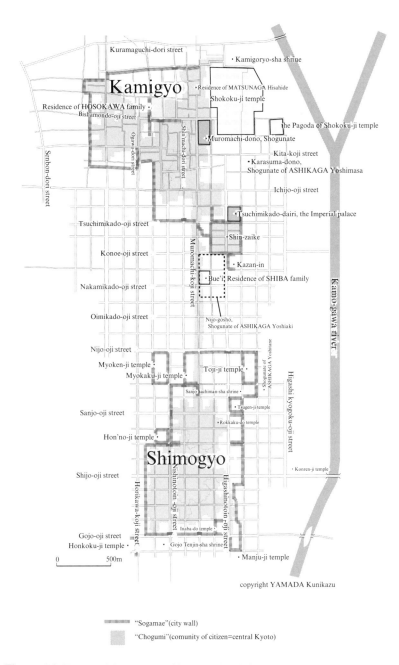

Figure 4.3: The spatial structure of late medieval Kyoto, 16th century.
The original map was made by Prof. Yamada, Kunikazu (Doshisya Women's Colledge of Liberal Arts).

Inside the wall, several territorial communities were associated with each other and promoted the social organization, which had self-rule. The Gion festival in honor of the Gion shrine, which had been stopped during the Onin war, was revived by the inhabitants of Shimogyo. The organization committee for the festival and the luxury floats bore testimony to the economic power and autonomy of the inhabitants of Shimogyo. The double downtowns, Kamigyo and Shimogyo, were connected by the Muromachi street, the main urban axis in this era (Takahashi 1983).

During the late medieval times, the increased population in Kyoto resulted in the effective utilization of the vacant spaces. At this time, many narrow alleys were opened to lead from the ancient streets to the vacant spaces inside the ancient blocks. Such alleys were called Zushi. Zushi were often opened when the vacant lots that had resulted from the large estates of the aristocrats and temples being demolished were redistributed to the inhabitants by the new lords. After the Zushi had been opened, inhabitants along the Zushi formed social communities. The spatial patterns of the Zushi were irregular because they were an offshoot of the needs of life rather than any definite town planning. The distribution of the Zushi was concentrated around the Shijo-Machi area, which had been urbanized in the early medieval times, and the area to the north of the Ichijo street region, which was highly developed in the late medieval times—a trait that indicates that the Zushi was an important device to develop/ rebuild urban spaces. This manner of town development/rebuilding witnessed in the case of Kyoto spread to other medieval local towns. Zushi meant high-density land use in newly developed urban areas of the medieval town (Takahashi 1983).

In the 16th century, many powerful shrines and temples in suburbs of Kyoto had gathered their followers, including rich merchants and craftsmen, around each such site. The largest suburb was Saga, which had many temples around the Tenryu-ji temple, a main street named Suzaku from the days of the ancient Heian-kyo, and a lot of houses that belonged to common people. The urban structure of Kyoto was composed by the network of these satellite towns, Kamigyo and Shimogyo (Yamada 1998).

Kamakura and medieval provincial capitals

In 1192, Minamoto Yoritomo, the head of the most powerful warriors' clan established the Kamakura government. He was given the political status of shogun by the emperor. This was the first government ruled by the warriors' class. Yoritomo set the government office and residence at Kamakura in eastern Japan, far from Kyoto. Until the Kamakura government was brought down in 1333, the capital of the warriors had been separate from the capital of the emperors and aristocracies. There were 2 capitals in Japan from the end of the 12th century to the middle of the 14th century.

Kamakura was situated in an alluvial valley facing the Pacific Ocean (Figure 4.4). The valley was composed of a lot of small valleys; so the shape of Kamakura

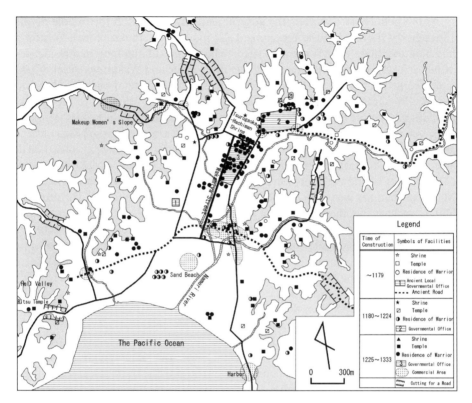

Figure 4.4: Kamakura in the early medieval times.
Source: Aki YAMAMURA.

as a whole was complicated. Before the government was established, two ancient roads had been going through the valley from east to west. Dwellings were located along these east-west roads and at the foot of surrounding hills. Yoritomo, in 1180, built the office of the government along one of these east-west roads. The residences of his followers and some powerful warriors, in addition to several large public temples were located around the office. This spatial pattern had devolved from the remains of the ancient structure. On the other hand, Yoritomo founded a magnificent public shrine, the Tsurugaoka-Hachiman, at the foot of the northern mountains facing the center of the valley. In addition, he built a wide and straight north-south street, the Wakamiya street, as a stone-paved approach to the center of the valley. This series of new projects indicated that Yoritomo might have employed a kind of town planning that was distinct from the existing spatial structures. However, when Yoritomo had lived, the growing population had stayed off the spaces along Wakamiya street for a few decades. Wakamiya street functioned merely as a symbolic approach of the Tsurugaoka-Hachiman rather than an urban axis. The landscape had changed; however, the spatial structure did not change suddenly when the government was established and the population grew.

As the political structure of the government was changed in the middle of the 13th century, the office of the government also moved from the one which Yoritomo had built to a place near Wakamiya street. Many political buildings and residences of powerful followers were concentrated in the area around Wakamiya street, which had become the urban axis of Kamakura. However, the gate of each building did not face Wakamiya street, except for some buildings that belonged to the powerful clans among the warriors. Wakamiya street, however, had not lost its symbolic value yet. Once the road was developed, and urbanization had progressed, narrow alleys (Zushi) connecting Wakamiya street to other major streets were constructed, albeit in irregular patterns. But all of the residences of the warriors did not move in to the vicinity of the Wakamiya street from the small valleys they were originally in. Many new temples were also built in the small valleys or at the foot of surrounding hills. In such valleys, the residences of the warriors were adjacent to temples, graves, and houses of the common people. The mixing of the pre-existing components and the new components made the urban landscape complex and decentralized as a whole in Kamakura during the medieval times (Yamamura 1997).

On the surrounding hills, there were places named, a trifle oddly, as "Hell Valley" and "Makeup Women's Slope." Such names meant that these areas were in the peripheral zone between the real world and another world that housed execution grounds, prostitution, myriad markets, graves and temples. Similar places were found on the sand beach which was some way down Wakamiya street. As urbanization took over, a lot of new houses of warriors and merchants were constructed on the beach. The commercial area, including the burial spaces, had been developed there in the period that spanned from the middle of the 13th century to the 14th century. The commercial activity of this area was related to the harbor on the shore, which had been developed by the Kamakura government and was managed by the Ritsu, a certain sect of the Buddhist order. The Ritsu, which was authorized the right to manage the harbor by the government, set its site on the hill to view the harbor and established the branch temple on the beach to toll the port duties (Minamide 1998). As described above, early medieval Kamakura was surrounded by marginal districts that were removed, somewhat alienated, from the central political space (Ishii 1981).

The ancient government had set up a provincial capital, Kokufu, in each country. In the early medieval times, some of the bureaucrats who stayed in Kokufu became local lords having a strong influence on Kokufu and its surrounding areas. The local lords managed public lands in each country and had a significant influence on the commercial activities between Kyoto and their local regions. Kokufu functioned as the political, economic, religious and cultural center of each region, developing into major local towns. In addition to some offices and residences of the local lords, temples, shrines, warehouses and markets were also built in the medieval Kokufu.

Nagato Kokufu was one of such medieval provincial capitals (Yamamura 2000). Here, facilities such as the residences of local constables and warriors, temples, and shrines were located on the hill; but the pattern of distribution was decentralized in the 14th century (Figure 4.5). Facilities and urban functions were not concentrated along the main street. The direction/pattern of roads/allotments showed that the ancient framework of the structure of Kokufu had been maintained until the 14th century.

A medieval map, the "Shrine Grounds Map of Iminomiya" (Figure 4.6) remains in Nagato Kokufu. The Grounds Map explains how the author, Iminomiya, recognized the landscape of Ngato Kokufu in the political context of the 14th century.

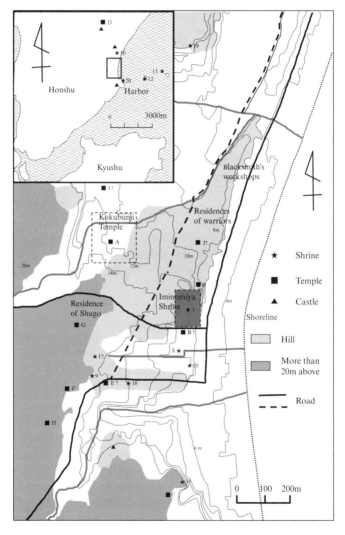

Figure 4.5: Nagato Kokufu in the 14th century.
The alphabets and numbers are corresponded to them in figure 4.6.
Source: Aki YAMAMURA.

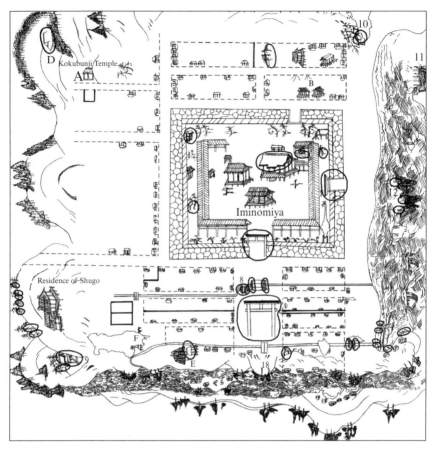

Figure 4.6: "Shrine Grounds Map of Iminomiya" Trace.
Circles are the facilities painted in red, which mean these facilities had close relationship with Iminomiya. The alphabets and numbers are corresponded to them in figure 4.5. The Japanese letters in original map are omitted.
Source: Aki YAMAMURA.

The "Ground map" does not represent the entire real landscape; for example, some of the things that existed at that time do not appear in the map; while some are put emphasis on, others are understated. The Grounds Map was intended to represent Iminomiya's lands and the other facilities and lands to which this shrine was related. Furthermore, the Grounds Map shows that the medieval Kokufu was a squared space surrounded by mountains and the sea; it consisted of the buildings and grounds of the shrine at its center, and related facilities on the fringes. This representation portrays the conceptualization of Iminomiya's territories.

In this way, the real landscape of the early medieval provincial capitals and their imagined landscapes were quite different. While the real landscape was complex and decentralized, the imagined landscape, as conceived by a local lord, had a unified and centralized format, probably because it replicated the ideal format of the ancient capital. That is because specific urban planning had not yet existed or had not fully by the powerful lords in early medieval times. Further, the landscapes were influenced by historical components of pre-existent landscapes and the unstable social movements of the time. The differences between such real and imagined landscapes were found in various Kokufus (Yamamura 2009); it can, therefore, be regarded as one of the characteristics of the early medieval provincial towns in Japan.

Religion and towns

The medieval period was a time when Buddhism, confused with Shinto, had a strong influence on the politics, economy, society and culture of Japan. Almost all of the medieval towns had temples. Medieval temples were centers of not only religious but also commercial, industrial, and cultural activities in the local regions. The most advanced information and techniques at that time were introduced in the local regions by the priests of the temples; these were individuals who had received an advanced education in the capitals or from places overseas. Rich merchants such as money lenders and craftsmen supplied products and money based on the demands of the temples, and operated from around the temples' grounds. That was how the temples came to be the economic and traffic nodes that connected the capitals, local countries, and overseas markets. In particular, in the late medieval times, the markets, the residences of the priests, and the houses-cum-workshops of the merchants and craftsmen were all densely concentrated around the temples. Such densely-populated sections developed into the central towns of the local regions (Niki et al. 2006). The inhabitants of these towns gradually formed social communities as time went by. Some of these communities had the autonomy to manage the organization of their towns under the rule and protection of the temples.

Since ancient times, some temples of the Tendai and Shingon sects had been located in the mountains in silent spaces, ideal for ascetic training. These temples were developed in medieval times and consisted of many related facilities such as main halls, houses of worship, towers, shrines, and shelters in winter; in addition, there were residences for the priests and their families, and stores and markets for the inhabitants. Such temple clusters thrived in the 15th and 16th centuries, when they had the largest territories and populations at the foot of the mountains and along the hillsides. The surrounding territory of these temples, in their time, became large local towns.

Heisenji was one of the largest religious towns in the late medieval times (Figure 4.7). In the beginning of the 16th century, Heisenji had consisted of about 6000 small temples and facilities packed into a space with an east-west length of 1.2 km and north-south span of 1 km; the large parts of Heisenji, however, were demolished in the later part of the 16th century by an attack led by an opposing

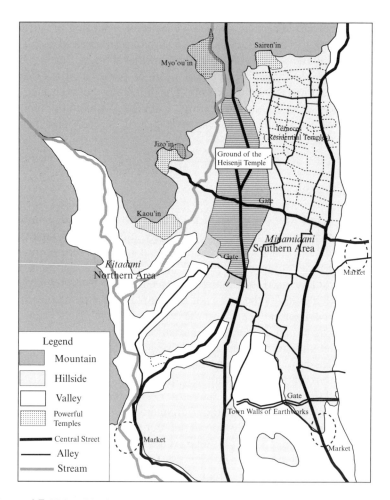

Figure 4.7: Heisenji in the late medieval times.
Reference: Hochin (2003).

sect of the Buddhism. At its peak, Heisenji had many terraces created on the gentle slopes of its hillsides to accommodate its innumerable small temples. At the same time, terraces with square forms were created and distributed regularly over the southern areas of the hillside. There were streets going down the hill that had been built according to the topography of the slope. Many alleys diverged from the streets into the terraces. Some streets and alleys were stone-paved approaches, each with a certain fixed size. The terraces had gates, designed at regular intervals. Stone walls had also been constructed at both sides of the streets. Each terrace was surrounded by mounds or stone hedges. It is possible that Heisenji and its subordinate temples had arranged for each temple to be on a specific site, each decision, meticulous and part of a plan. Some powerful temples were located at the penetralia of the slopes in the north area of the hillsides, and the cluster of terraces designed to accommodate the subordinate temples would lead downward from the dominant temples. However, this layout of streets and terraces was even more meticulous in the south areas of the hillsides. This suggests that the process of creating landscapes differed among areas even within the Heisenji territory. On the peripheries of the Heisenji territory, some markets and commercial towns came up alongside the extensions of the central streets of Heisenji. The territory of the Heisenji was enclosed by surrounding mountains, valleys, and artificial walls (earthworks with huge moats) (Hochin 2003). The layout of streets and terraces, stone-paved paths and stone hedges and huge town walls indicate that the Heisenji had access to an advanced level of engineering technologies and know-how related to town building.

Since the late 15th century, some temples of the Jodo-shin (Ikko) and the Nichiren (Hokke) sects of Buddhism became the social centers in their respective regions. Many towns formed with such temples at their inspirational centre, especially in and around the capital Kyoto. These towns were called the Jinai-machi (temple towns). Generally speaking, these temple towns were located in the plains as opposed to the towns such as Heisenji, which were in the mountains.

Yamashina was distinguishable from other temple towns because its principal temple, owing allegiance to the Jodo-shin (Honganji) sect, was established in 1478 (Figure 4.8). Until it was demolished in 1532, Yamashina was one of the largest temple towns in the country. The Yamashina temple town was surrounded by two circles of walls that were made of heavy earthworks. In the central area within the inner earthwork, the most important facilities such as the central hall, small temples for prayer, and precious statues for safekeeping were located. Outside the central area and within the outer earthworks, less important religious facilities and the residences of priests and inhabitants were set up. Spaces within Yamashina were divided by walls and each unit of space was assigned to priests and behaviors according to their status and level of importance. Such systematic distribution of space was part of a plan to visualize a system of social hierarchy within the Jodo-shin sect. Further, the centralized spatial structure of the huge town walls in Yamashina as well as Heisenji suggest that Yamashina was one of the most advanced towns in the early 16th century Japan. When we consider that the previous medieval towns did not have town walls and that their spatial structures were generally complex and decentralized, Yamashina may be regarded as a groundbreaking town (Niki 2007).

Osaka was developed as the next principal town when the head priest of the Jodo-shin sect moved to the Ishiyama-Honganji in Osaka in 1532. Similar to Yamashina, the central area of Osaka, around the temple, was concentrated with the entire gamut of related facilities and residences. The population of the town is estimated to be between 20,000 and 30,000, making it one of the largest towns at the time. Osaka was also fortified by a wall, guarding the town against the attacks of the feudal lords and appealing as it had cutting edge technology. Osaka was located on a hill, close to the confluence of the Yodo river and the Seto inland sea. There

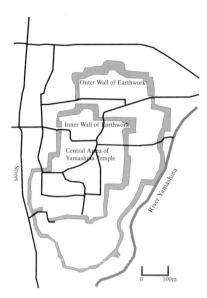

Figure 4.8: Yamashina in the late medieval times.
Reference: Fukushima, Katsuhiko (1998), Jokaku Kenkyu karamita Yamashina Jinaimachi (Yamashina Temple Town From a Perspective of Castle History), Yamashina Honganji Jinaimachi Kenkyukai (eds.), *Sengoku no Tera, Shiro, Machi* (Temple, Castle and Town in the Late Medieval Times), Hozokan.

had been some port towns benefiting from the flow of traffic along the adjacent waterways before the Osaka temple town was set up (Niki 2007). In fact, the urban landscape of Osaka was made up by importing the historical economic functions.

In the 16th century, it was not only the principal temple towns such as Yamashina and Osaka that had town walls which consisted of heavy earthwork and a surrounding moat, many local temple towns had them too. Advanced technology in constructing the town walls was introduced by a group from within the Jodo-shin sect. Most temple towns grew to encompass pre-existent settlements, which had had distinguished urban functions and had been located in the traffic intersections between the water and the roadways. In particular, the temples of the Jodo-shin sect attached importance to the facility of water traffic, and often chose their locations among those pre-existent towns that had harbors along the waterfront. Some temple towns grew to encompass historical urban centers such as ancient ports, shrines, temples of other sects, and erstwhile residences of powerful locals (Fukushima 2000). The streets and blocks in pre-existing towns, which to be fit the relief of the landform, survived in newly approved (Iwanami 1999). In other words, the complex and decentralized spatial structure which most medieval towns had was also found inside the advanced town walls at local temple towns (Niki 2003). The architecture of the town walls appealed to the inhabitants for they saw it as a symbol of their uniqueness and their privilege as a member of the league of temple towns of the Jodo-shin sect (Niki 2007).

Medieval port towns

Recent studies on history and archaeology have emphasized that dynamic water traffic was developed in medieval East Asia, and especially in Japan, which have been surrounded by the sea. Physical distribution and trading using ships that sailed across seas and rivers was active, which resulted in a lot of medieval ports being developed all over Japan. Different sources of powers such as temples, shrines, and warriors moved into these local ports to control and manage them.

Hakata, which was located on the eastern edge of Japan and had been the main gateway to East Asia since the ancient times, developed into the main gate port town that ran the international trade between Japan, Korea, and China. Hakata was situated on a double line of sandbanks, and facing a lagoon (Figure 4.9). The inner sandbank which was called Hakatahama was formed before and was more

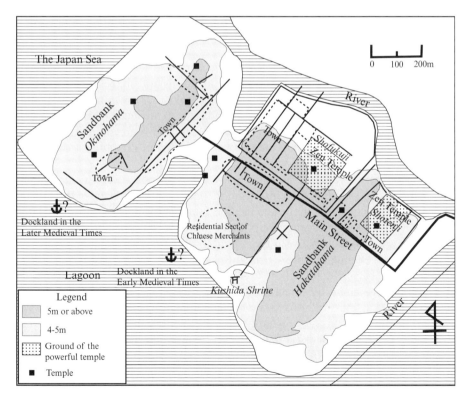

Figure 4.9: Medieval Hakata.
Reference: Miyamoto (1989), Oba (1995, 2004), Zusyu Nihon Toshishi (1993).

stable than the other, Okinohama. Okinohama had grown during the medieval times. A few town blocks had been already made since the ancient times around the Kushida Shrine, which was located in the south-west of Hakatahama. In the early medieval times, the dockland was located on the west side of Hakatahama, facing a lagoon. A residential sect of Chinese trading merchants was formed around the dockland.

In the late 12th century, one of the Buddhist sects, the Zen, erected temples on the east side of Hakatahama by using the financial support of the Chinese merchants. In addition, the street that would become the urban axis of Hakata was laid out alongside the Zen temples in the middle of the 13th century. This street went through a narrow constricted part which had been created by reclaiming the gap between two sandbanks. The towns that formed in front of the temples catered to the temples' demands and lined the main street.

In the beginning of the 14th century, some alleys were constructed across or alongside the main street; these formed the town blocks. But their shapes were not uniform because they were designed to fit the original topography of the sandbanks. The central urbanized area was moved from Hakatahama to Okinohama during the 15th and 16th century. This was why the lagoon had been silted by the soil from rivers during the medieval times and the dock had to be moved to another place which was nearer to the sea. Densely populated areas were built in Okinohama. However, towns in the blocks along the main street were also developed at Hakatahama. Moreover, towns were also formed around the Zen temple grounds in certain blocks, but their directions and shapes were based on the temples and were not uniform with respect to the other towns in Hakatahama. In this way, the process of constructing a landscape in medieval Hakata had been adapted to the changes in the landform; the process had been complex, involving plural urban centers—including many towns in different directions (Miyamoto 1989, Oba 1995, 2004).

As we saw in the case of Hakata, many medieval ports were located along lagoons, coves and sandbanks. This was more remarkable especially in the case of ports facing the Japan Sea in the late medieval times. Obama was one of the largest medieval port towns because the primary route for the distribution of renders and indigenous products between Kyoto and local regions through the Japan Sea passed through Obama (Figure 4.10). Until late in the 15th century, the local central shrine had been situated on the base of the double sandbanks, and the towns had been formed along the street on the inner sandbank, from the shrine to the lagoon. Medieval dockland was located on a lagoon. Since the middle of the 14th century, there had been a lot of temples established by the Zen and the Ji sects that, with the help of the local feudal lord, had been erected on the foot of the mountain. From the end of the 15th century to late in the 16th century, the towns in Obama were expanded along two streets: one was the old street on the inner sandbank, and the other was a street that stretched on the other outer sandbank. In addition, many temples of the Nichiren sect and the Jodo-shin sect were newly erected along the waterfront of the lagoon at that time. Large spaces around the

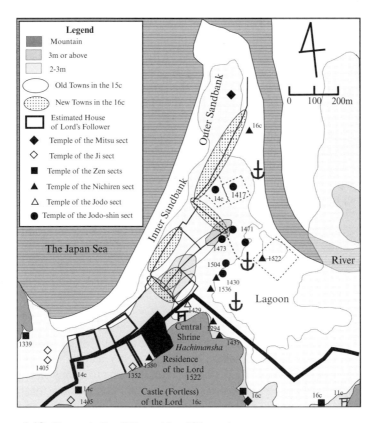

Figure 4.10: Obama in the 15th and the 16th century.
The number indicates the estimated year or period when each temple/house was founded.
Reference: Yamamura, Aki (2010), Muromachi Sengokuki niokeru Minatomachi no Keikan to Bichikei (The Landscape and Landform of Port Towns in the Late Medieval Japan), Niki, Hiroshi and Watanuki, Tomoko (eds.), *Chusei Nihonkai no Ryutsu to Minatomachi* (The Circulation and Port Towns at the Medieval Japan Sea), Seibundo Shuppan in printing.

docks along the waterfront were occupied by these new temples. The local feudal lord built his residence on the foot of the mountain and his fortress on the top of the mountain in the early part of the 16th century. The houses of his followers were also clustered around their lord's residence. However, the fact that none of them were located inside the urban area on the sandbanks and along the waterfront indicates that the warriors could not edge into the economic markets in Obama on their own (Shitanaka 2006). A similar process of changing landscapes was witnessed in other medieval port towns along the Japan Sea.

To summarize, port towns were situated along lagoons and inside sandbanks because temples and shrines were situated there, and service men would gather there to work as merchants or dock laborers in the 14th and 15th centuries. In the

16th century, as distribution of goods became more stable, the populations of port towns grew in tandem. With increasing population density the port towns were made larger by utilizing the remaining area of the sandbanks along the waterfront of the lagoon. Newly coming religious sects, especially the Jodo-shin, established temples and gathered their followers in the port towns, further expanding these towns. The expansion was also helped by the gradual receding of the waterfront, which was caused by the accumulation of river sand and accelerated by the use of invented technology that helped bury the lagoon. The feudal lords, with all their warriors, struggled to control the port towns; they could only construct their offices and residences at locations that were some distance apart from the urban areas of the ports. Thus, medieval port towns were situated only where the natural environment allowed for certain conditions, and their political and economic centers were often religious institutions, and not a secular or a warriors' government. Even in the 16th century, when the technology required to bury a lagoon had been developed, houses of common people and streets could still not be made to line up along the coast.

Medieval castle towns

Since the Onin war in the late 15th century, provincial constables who had been staying near the governmental office in Kyoto started to live in their local territories and never got back to their residences in Kyoto. They had grown to become feudal lords in their local territories by knocking down local warriors and controlling the inhabitants and lands in the adjoining towns and villages. From late in the 15th century to the early 16th century, the provincial constables constructed their residence-cum-offices in their local territories. The estates of the residences often had rectangular shapes and spanned across, approximately, 200 square meters. Most estates comprised guesthouses, daily residences, tea ceremony houses and gardens. Such facilities and their distributional pattern were introduced by the provincial constables based on the practices of the shogun and his close aides in Kyoto. The constables flaunted their authorities to rule the local regions by imitating the Kyoto-style residences of the central government (Ono 1997). Moreover, the landscape of the towns around the residences had much in common. The residences of the deputy provincial constables, temples and guesthouses were located around the constables' residences, spanning smaller rectangular squares. Some houses of the other subordinated warriors were built nearby, but the spatial patterns of these facilities were not uniform. Some straight streets were constructed to connect these facilities, and rectangular town blocks were built around these streets. However, provincial constables had not built their own markets and ports yet. Rather, the local central markets in front of temples and shrines, and the port towns that were in existence much before these new localities were established attended to their needs (Niki 2006). No town walls were built to enclose the area around the provincial residences.

Provincial constables developed as local feudal lords and built numerous castles on top of the mountains for the purpose of defending their territory in the face of attacks led by other local feudal lords. In the beginning of the 16th century, many feudal lords moved their residences to castles at top of the mountains and settled there. As a result, these castles had plural functions not only as fortresses but also as offices and places of daily residence of the feudal lords (Senda 1994). Further, some feudal lords stayed in residences that were located at the feet of the mountains or amidst the flatlands. In such cases, the residences of the provincial constables that had been built before were maintained apart from the castle as an emergency shelter in the mountain. In any case, the innovations, especially in the ways routes and entrances to the castles were constructed, had been remarkable during the 16th century.

Most feudal lords not only built their residences and castles but also constructed urban areas around residences and castles (castle towns). They tried to make their castle towns to akin to the principal towns—the political, economic, and cultural nerve centers of their territories. For this purpose, feudal lords established new markets and towns around their castles/residences or moved the neighboring pre-existent markets and towns into their castle towns. Further, they gathered warriors as followers and housed them around their residences or castles. To summarize, the landscape of the castle towns consisted of three kinds of components, which could be characterized in terms of the social classes, as manifestations of the feudal system. One was the castle or residence of the feudal load; the next were the houses of the warriors who were his followers; finally, there were the markets and merchants' houses-cum-workshops. Historical geographers have estimated the degree of the progress and accomplishment of the feudal system in each castle town in terms of their distributions, locations, sizes and shapes with regard to the three components cited above (Matsumoto 1969, Kobayashi 1985).

Ichijodani was one of the most famous medieval castle towns (Figure 4.11). Many archaeological excavations and researches have shed light on its landscape. Ichijodani was located in a narrow valley. The lord's residence, which had similar spatial components as the one belonging to the shogun in Kyoto, was located in a narrow valley situated at the foot of the mountain. There was a castle as military shelter, which was built behind the residence on top of the mountain. Two excavated areas had houses belonging to the warriors adjacent to the houses-cum-workshops of the craftsmen/merchants and temples. These facilities were thickly concentrated, and it is difficult to ascertain any regularity in the shapes of the streets and blocks of the one of these areas. Some residences of the powerful warriors were scattered over the feet of the surrounding mountain side. Double walls, which were made of earthworks and moats, were constructed at the entrance and exit of the valley (Ono 1997). Outside the wall, at the periphery of the town, the old indigenous market along the river was more developed than that in a valley. The feudal lord could not even by force gather such neighboring markets inside the walls. The landscape of Ichijodani was similar to other castle towns in central Honsyu Island (Niki 2006).

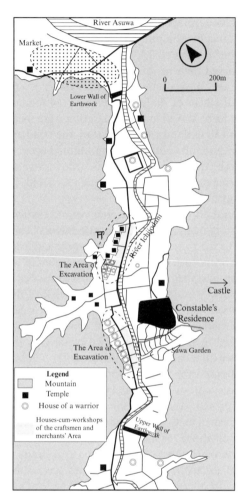

Figure 4.11: Ichijodani in the 16th century.
Reference: Ono, Masatoshi and Suito, Makoto (eds.), (1990), *Jitsuzo no Sengoku Jokamachi* (Clarifying the Castle Town in the Late Medieval Times), Heibonsha Limited, Publishers.

Kojima (1984), a medieval historian, claimed that the dual spatial structure was a remarkable characteristic of medieval castle towns. In other words, two different spaces were combined in these castle towns: one that was ruled by the master-subordinate relationship in the feudal system in the urban center, and the other that was not influenced by the feudal system at its periphery. The latter was the space where many merchants and craftsmen, who were not chained to the land and the lords, enjoyed great political and economic freedom (Amino 1978). As Kojima has claimed, Maekawa (1991) mapped the changing process of the spatial pattern of the castle towns from the end of the 15th century to the end of the 16th century. The map is supposed to show that the feudal lord had gradually been assuming control of the warriors' residences and markets, shaping them into a regular form or arrangement, and separating warriors' residences from markets completely. This model has been seen as the process in which the feudal lord gradually came to wield great power over the medieval society.

However, not all medieval castle towns had the landscapes which could be adopted this model. On the contrary, recent researches have suggested a lot of variety in the landscapes of the local castle towns (Niki 2006).

Bungo-Funai, which developed into one of the largest castle towns in Kyusyu Island, was located on a flatland along a river. The first street which went through the old large-scaled temple had already been built on a natural levee formed by the river in the middle of the 15th century. Until the middle of the 16th century, the feudal lord's square-shaped residence, which was surrounded by the earthworks, stood on the neighboring hill above the lower temple and streets. A new street going down from the residence to the flatland was constructed, and the residences of the warriors are suspected to have existed along this street. Between two streets, another large residence of the lord and some small rectangular estates were packed in. In the middle of the 16th century, the lord added some facilities including storehouses that were built near the residence on the flatlands. Acceptance of Christianity by the feudal lord from the Society of Jesus brought about active international trade with Portugal to the ports of Bungo-Funai. The commercial area near the harbor was attuned to receiving trading ships; the development of the outer harbor at the mouth of the river further enhanced the trading capability of the region. Toward the end of the 16th century, the lord renovated his residence in the flatlands and built the houses of powerful merchants in front of his own. Moreover, the lord changed the locations of some streets and small residences. Such reconstruction indicates that the practice of changing urban landscapes was indulged in by the feudal lords (Tsubone 2006). We can find that the commercial area and the houses of the merchants were built in the center of the town, and not on the periphery, and that international trade brought about a big impact on the landscape of Bungo-Funai. In contrast to the landscape of Ichijodani, Bungo-Funai was not enclosed by a town wall, and opened to the waterfront.

As described above, the landscapes of the medieval castle towns were different from each other, varying along factors such as the extent of the power of a feudal lord, economic functions, historical components in the landscape, and the local contexts that devolved from religions and cultural situations.

Bibliography

Akiyama, Kunizo and Nakakura, Ken (1975), *Kyoto 'Machi' no Kenkyu* (The Study of 'Towns' in Kyoto), Tokyo: Hosei University Press.

Amino, Yoshihiko (1978), *Muen, Kugai, Raku,* Tokyo: Heibonsha.

Fukushima, Katsuhiko (2000), Sengoku Syokuhoki Settsu-Tonda Syuraku to 'Jinai' (Settlement of Settsu-Toda and 'Temple Town' in the Late of Medieval Times), *Jinai-machi Kenkyu,* 5, pp. 1–22.

Hochin, Shin'ichiro (2003), Sengokuki Heisenji no Keikan (The Landscape of Heisenji in Sengoku Era), Ono, Masatoshi et al. (eds.), *Sengoku Jidai no Kokogaku* (The Archaeology of Sengoku Era), Tokyo: Koshi Shoin, pp. 137–148.

Inoue, Mitsuro (1989), Inseiki niokeru Shintoshi no Kaihatsu (The Foundation of the New Towns in Cloister Government Era), Yasuda Motohisa Sensei Tainin Kinen Kanko I'inkai (eds.), *Chusei Nihon no Shoso* (Various Aspects of Medieval Japan), Tokyo: Yoshikawa Kobunkan, pp. 333–365.

Ishii, Susumu (1981), Toshi Kamakura niokeru 'Jigoku' no Fukei (Landscape of 'Hell' in Urban Kamakura), Gokeninsei Kenkyukai (eds.), *Gokeninsei no Kenkyu* (Study on the Feudal Warriors and its System), Tokyo: Yoshikawa Kobunkan, pp. 77–112.

Iwanami, Yuka (1999), Kinsei niokeru Jinai-machi no Keitaiteki Henyou nitsuite (Morphological Change of Temple Towns in Early Modern Times), *Jinai-machi Kenkyu,* 4, pp. 20–42.

Kiuchi, Masahiro (1977), Kamakura Bakufu to Toshi Kyoto (Kamakura Government and Urban Kyoto), *Nihonshi Kenkyu* (Journal of Japanese History), 175, pp. 1–44.

Kobayashi, Kentaro (1985), *Sengoku Jokamachi no Kenkyu* (Study on Castle Towns in Sengoku Era), Tokyo: Taimeido.

Kojima, Michihiro (1984), Sengoku Jokamachi no Kozo (Structure of Castle Towns in Sengoku Era), *Nihonshi Kenkyu* (Journal of Japanese History), 257, pp. 30–59.

Maekawa, Kaname (1991), *Toshi Kokogaku no Kenkyu* (Study on Urban Archaeology), Tokyo: Kashiwa Shobo.

Matsumoto, Toyohisa (1967), *Jokamachi no Rekisichiriteki Kenkyu* (Study on Historical Geography of Castle Towns), Tokyo: Yoshikawa Kobunkan.

Minamide, Shinsuke (1998), Nihon no Kodai Chusei niokeru Minato no Kukan Kosei (Spatial Constitutions of Ports in Ancient and Medieval Times), *Asia Bunkagakka Nenpo* (Annals of the Department of Asian Culture in Otemon University), pp. 139–154.

Miyamoto, Masaaki (1989), Kukan Shiko no Toshishi (Urban History in the View of Spatial Preference), Takahasi, Yasuo and Yoshida, Nobuyuki (eds.), *Nihon Toshishi Nyumon 1; Kukan* (Introduction to the Urban History of Japan vol. 1; Space), Tokyo: Tokyo University Press, pp. 63–83.

——— (2005), Chusei Mianatomachi no Toshikukan to sono Kinseika (Urban Space and its Modernization in Medieval Port Towns), Miyamoto, Masaaki, *Toshikukan no Kinseika* (Modernization of Urban Space), Tokyo: Chuo-Koron Bijutsu Publising, pp. 174–191.

Niki, Hiroshi and Taga-Town Education Committee (eds.) (2006), *Binmanji ha Toshi ka?; Sengoku Omi niokeru Tera to Haka* (Was Binmanji a Town?; Temple and Graves in Sengoku Omi), Hikone: Sun-Rise Publishing.

Niki, Hiroshi (2003), Jinai-machi to Joka-machi; Sengoku Jidai no Toshi no Hatten (Temple town and Castle town; The Development of Towns in Sengoku Era), Arimitsu, Yugaku (eds.), *Sengoku no Chi'iki Kokka* (Regional Nations in Sengoku Era), Tokyo: Yoshikawa Kobunkan, pp. 254–288.

——— (2006), Muromachi Sengoku Jidai no Syakai Kozo to Syugosyo, Jokamachi (Provincial Constables' Quarters, Castle Towns and Social Structure in Muromachi and Sengoku Era), Uchibori, Nobuo et al. (eds.), *Syugosyo to Sengoku Jokamachi* (Provincial Constables' Quarters and Late Medieval Castle Towns), Tokyo: Koshi Publishing, pp. 471–495.

——— (2007), Jinai-machi to Joka-machi; Sengoku Syakai no Tassei to Keisyo (Temple town and Castle town; Achievements and Successions from Sengoku Society), Kaitokudo Kinenkai (eds.), *Osaka, Kinki no Shiro to Machi* (Castles and Towns in Osaka and Kinki region), Osaka; Izumi Publishing, pp. 41–68.

Noguchi, Minoru (1988), Kyoto Shichijo-machi no Chuseiteki Tenkai (Medieval Changes of Shichijo-machi), *Suzaku*, 1, pp. 81–93.

Oba, Yasutoki (1995), Tairiku nihirakareta Toshi, Hakata (Hakata; The Gateway Town Opening to the Continent), Amino, Yoshihiko and Ishii, Susumu (eds.), *Chusei no Fukei wo Yomu 7; Higasi Shinakai wokakomu Chusei Sekai* (Reading the Medieval Landscape vol. 7; Medieval World Surrounding the East China Sea), Tokyo: Shin-Jinbutsuohrai Publishing, pp. 17–52.

——— (2004), Kowan Toshi Hakata no Seiritsu to Hatten (Formation and Development of the Port Town, Hakata), Chusei Toshi Kenkyukai (eds.) *Kowan Toshi to Taigai Koeki* (Port Towns and International Trade), Shin-Jinbutsuohrai Publishing, pp. 9–20.

Ono, Masatoshi (1997), *Sengoku Jokamachi no Kokogaku* (Archaeology on the Castle Town in Sengoku Era), Tokyo: Kodansha.

Senda, Yoshihiro (1994), Syugosyo kara Sengoku Joka he (From Provincial Constables' Quarters to Castle Towns in Sengoku Era), Bunkazaigaku Ronsyu Kankokai (eds.) *Bunkazaigaku Ronsyu*, Nara Daigaku Bungakubu Bunkazaigakka Bunkazai Ronsyu Kankokai, pp. 457–468.

Shitanaka, Takahiro (2006), Wakasakoku Syugosyo to Kowan Toshi Nisizu, Obama (The Provincial Constables' Residence and Port Towns, Nisizu and Obama in Wakasa), Uchibori, Nobuo et al. (eds.), *Syugosyo to Sengoku Jokamachi* (Provincial Constables' Quarters and Late Medieval Castle Towns), Tokyo: Koshi Publishing, pp. 337–348.

Takahashi, Yasuo (1983), *Kyoto Chusei Toshishi Kenkyu* (The Study on the Urban History of Medieval Kyoto), Kyoto: Shibunkaku Publishing.

Tsubone, Shinya (2006), Bungo-Funai no Rekisiteki Tenkai to Tokushitsu (Development and Character of the Bungo-Funai), Uchibori, Nobuo et al. (eds.), *Syugosyo to Sengoku Jokamachi* (Provincial Constables' Quarters and Late Medieval Castle Towns), Tokyo: Koshi Publishing, pp. 387–404.

Uemura, Kazunao (1999), Heian-kyo to Shirakawa (Heian-kyo and Shirakawa), *Jorisei Kodaitoshi Kenkyu* (Annals of Jori System and Ancient Town), 15, pp. 34–68.

Yamada, Kunikazu (1998), Chusei Toshi Kyoto no Henyou (Changes of Medieval Town, Kyoto), Chusei Toshi Kenkyukai (eds.), *Toshi wo Tsukuru* (Making Towns), Tokyo: Shin-Jinbutsuohrai Publishing, pp. 90–122.

Yamamura, Aki (1997), Chusei Kamakura no Toshikukankozo (The Urban Spatial Structure of Medieval Kamakura), *The Shirin* (The Journal of History), 80(2), pp. 42–82.

———— (2000), Nanbokucho-ki Nagato Kokufu no Kozo to sono Ninshiki (The Spatial Structure of Medieval Kokufu: A Provincial Capital and Its Cognition Expressed in a Fourteenth Century Map), *Jinbun Chiri* (Journal of the Human Geography), 52(3), pp. 1–21.

———— (2007), Inseiki Heian-kyo no Toshi Kukan Kozo (The Urban Spatial Structure of Kyo in the 11th Century), Kinda, Akihiro (eds.), *Heian-kyo Kyoto—Toshizu to Toshikozo* (From Heian-kyo to Kyoto; City Maps and Urban Structures), Kyoto: Kyoto University Press, pp. 125–151.

———— (2009), *Spatial Structure of Medieval Towns*, Tokyo: Yoshikawa Kobunkan.

CHAPTER 5

Capitals and towns in early modern times

Aki YAMAMURA

Landscape changes in towns from the medieval to the early modern

At the end of the 16th century, one of the local feudal lords, Oda Nobunaga, rapidly grew in strength and began to expand his territories. He ousted the shogun of the Muromachi government from Kyoto, but before he could take over the entire country, Oda Nobunaga was assassinated by one of his own warriors in 1582. Toyotomi (Hashiba) Hideyoshi, a follower of Oda Nobunaga, succeeded Nobunaga's projects and soon came to dominate all feudal lords and territories in Japan. Since both Nobunaga and Hideyoshi were new rulers who, during their reigns, changed the medieval social systems and were quite distinct in all respects from the other medieval feudal lords, the end of the 16th century is regarded as the beginning of the early modern age. As far as the landscapes of the period are concerned, these rulers constructed many castles and castle towns to accommodate their own headquarters or local branches as they strove to assume greater powers. Previous studies on the castles of this period tell us that these had undergone a dramatic architectural shift from the style of their predecessors; the convoluted moats and high stone walls had given way to towers and elaborate entrances (Nakai 1990, Senda 2000). It was not only the castles but also the castle towns that contributed to a landscape that had several revolutionary components, marking them out as the early modern towns.

Komaki was a new town that Nobunaga had built in 1563. The Komaki castle took its stand on the hill. Many huge stones were built up around the tower keep. Although the methods of stonework were immature, this castle did usher in a new age in engineering technology, considering the fact that few medieval castles had used stone arrangements; they had previously only involved earthworks. The main route was designed to go straight up to the keep, allowing visitors to see the spectacular stones arranged around the keep. These stone arrangements had an intense visual effect, communicating Nobunaga's radical and uncompromising power.

More elements of this evolving landscape were found among the streets and blocks of the Komaki castle town, where several straight streets formed rectangular-shaped blocks (Figure 5.1). A recent archaeological survey states

89

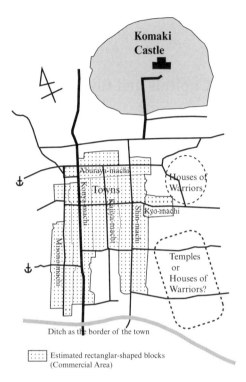

Figure 5.1: Komaki constructed by Oda Nobunaga in 1563.
Reference: Nakajima (2008).

that series of reed-shaped allotments were ordered in some of these blocks. The survey also indicated that the houses of the merchants or craftsmen in each of these allotments opened onto the street (Nakajima 2008). As a result, the houses located on the two sides of a street tied up socially, which contributed to the formation of organized street towns. These parallel straight streets, rectangular-shaped blocks and regular, lined up allotments were spread widely across Komaki (Senda 1989). Such features were not common in any other castle town of that time. The landscape of Komaki town was the most innovative of all castle towns at that time. Maekawa (1991) assumed that the emergence of the sets of rectangular-shaped blocks and reed-shaped allotments, constructed by Nobunaga and Hideyoshi, marked the beginning of the age of advanced castle towns.

However, the innovative town landscape features found in Komaki were not always found in Nobunaga's other castle towns that were constructed after Komaki had been established. Nobunaga's last castle town, Azuchi, constructed in 1576, was famous for its monumental castle. The Azuchi castle had an entire gamut of innovative components—a keep tower, tall stone walls, a golden tiled roof, and large buildings on foundation stones—which would set the standards for the early modern castles. Thus, the engineering techniques employed in the construction of the Azuchi castle were certainly more advanced than those used to build the Komaki castle.

On the other hand, the landscape of Azuchi town was not as modern as that of Komaki (Figure 5.2). The directions of three nearly parallel streets which formed Azuchi's rectangular-shaped blocks were adjusted to conform to the original layout of the medieval times, and the spatial pattern of the blocks was less uniform than the ones in Komaki. Further, Azuchi's streets and blocks covered only the narrow highland and did not extend across the entire area including lowland of the castle town. Such imbalance between the castle and the town was one of the characteristics of the landscape in Azuchi (Kido 2008). Azuchi castle town had incorporated a pre-existent port (Jorakuji) that faced Lake Biwa, which had been

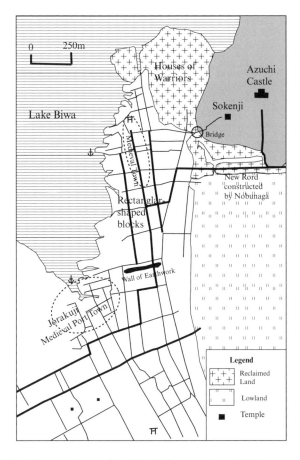

Figure 5.2: Azuchi reconstructed by Oda Nobunaga from 1576.
Reference: Niki (2008).

an important node of water traffic. The way of making landscape in Azuchi castle town following the pre-existed components of landscape was similar to the one of most medieval towns as described in the previous chapter. Thus, the evolution of landscapes from the medieval to the early modern had depended, to an extent, on trial and error, rather than having been achieved linearly and deliberately by the power of Nobunaga (Niki 2008).

After Nobunaga was assassinated, his successor, Toyotomi (Hashiba) Hideyoshi, did not have his headquarters in Azuchi; Kyoto, Fushimi and Osaka were picked instead. In 1583, Hideyoshi began the construction of a castle in Osaka. The location of the castle was the site where the medieval Ishiyama-Honganji temple town had stood, a key junction for water traffic. Hideyoshi began the construction of towns to the west and south of the castle (Figure 5.3). In building the southern town (Hiranomachi), Hideyoshi first constructed

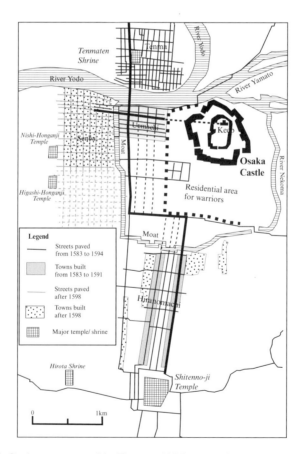

Figure 5.3: Osaka constructed by Toyotomi Hideyoshi after 1583.
Reference: Matsuo (2008).

parallel north-south streets and blocks between the castle and Shitenno-ji, which had been a powerful medieval temple. Hideyoshi simultaneously constructed the street blocks here resembled those found in Azuchi: they were long and thin in a particular direction (i.e., north-south), and they owed their peculiar shape and orientation to a natural condition—the two parallel north-south streets were paved on a long and thin north-south highland. Hideyoshi also built another town, a western town (Uemachi) on an east-west highland. Again, he paved (at least) one street on this highland and constructed several streets orthogonal to this main street. Here too, the blocks which formed the basic unit of the town's community constructed along the streets. These streets blocks were also long and thin in one consistent direction (this time, east-west), and they had this form and orientation because the main street was paved on a long and thin east-west highland. Thus, when the street blocks in both the western and southern Osaka towns were first created, they resembled those found in Azuchi. It can therefore be inferred that Hideyoshi's initial town design for Osaka had inherited elements from Nobunaga's town design of Azuchi (Matsuo 2008). The only new feature that Osaka had at its inception was the coordinated construction of the castle keep and the main street. The keep and the street were created in such a way that the line of the street was directed toward the keep: residents faced the keep as they came through the main street into the center of the castle town, and the ruler, Hideyoshi, could view the entire length of the main street when he looked down upon his town out of the top of his castle keep. This "castle vista plan" would become a feature of the early modern castle towns (Miyamato 2005).

The Osaka castle towns were later expanded beyond their initial conceptions, extending onto the lowlands. Several streets were added parallel to the main streets, the streets orthogonal to the main streets were extended, and new rectangular street blocks and community units were formed. In this way, towns were extended from the highlands to the lowlands, the latter being reclaimed in several places. Such overturning of natural conditions would go on to become a feature of the early modern castle towns. As a result, the shapes of the towns changed from linear to planar (Tamai, 1993). Furthermore, warriors' quarters and merchants' quarters were separated by moats. Such separation of quarters, which symbolized and perpetuated differences of rank, would be another feature of the early modern castle towns. Only at a later stage (around and after Hideyoshi's death) did Osaka take on the character of an early modern castle town.

Hideyoshi also changed the landscape of Kyoto into that of a castle town, but even the reformed town had an early modern flavor right from its inception (Figure 5.4). In 1586, Hideyoshi began to build a palace called "Jurakudai"; it was to be his headquarter. He built it in Uchino, the place where the royal palace had been located in the ancient times, presumably because he wanted people to associate the sanctity and royalty of the place with his rule. Hideyoshi then arranged for feudal lords and their families to live in the residences he had constructed for them around Jurakudai. These families were moved there as hostages (Yokota 2001).

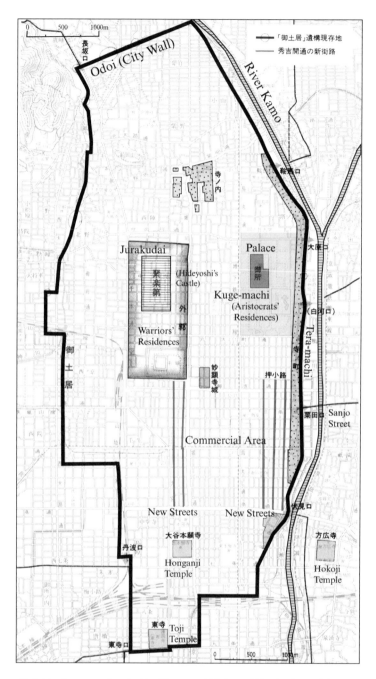

Figure 5.4: Kyoto reconstructed by Toyotomi Hideyoshi in the late of the 16th century. The original map was made by Ashikaga, Ken'ryo (ed.) (1994), *Kyoto Rekishi Atlas* (Historical Atlas Kyoto), Chuokoronsha Inc.

In Hideyoshi's Kyoto, all influential lords and their families were forced to maintain residences, thus producing a warriors' residential quarter.

Hideyoshi divided the square blocks of Kyoto with new north-south streets and created rectangular blocks, the kind of street blocks that had first appeared in the castle town of Komaki when Nobunaga had constructed it. The central parts of the original square blocks which had built in ancient Heian-kyo rarely been utilized. Hideyoshi's road network enabled people to utilize these central parts more easily and promoted the more effective use of the limited town space of Kyoto.

Hideyoshi surrounded Kyoto with earthworks and moats, the length of which was an unprecedented 22.5 km. Several areas of Kyoto had been subdivided by walls in medieval times, but the town as a whole came to be surrounded by a long wall during this period. This town wall (Odoi) was unique in the sense that it was able to encircle an entire town despite being an artificial construct. Until then, a few castle town had been encircled by a complete, artificial town wall. The construction of the town wall was presumably meant to convey Hideyoshi's power and control over his capital Kyoto and the various parties residing there, and that he was the ruler-cum-defender against all potential enemies coming from outside the capital (Niki 2001). Hideyoshi stopped the entry of goods at the gates of Odoi and taxed such goods. People later came to regard the area inside the town wall as the urban area of Kyoto, and the area outside the wall as the rural part of Kyoto.

Hideyoshi, forcefully, moved temples to set them up within the boundaries of the town wall. In medieval times, temples were independent forces, but Hideyoshi put them under his authority and control. These temples were gathered in one quarter that was called "Tera-machi," which was near the rim of the city. Hideyoshi had the temples play the role of shields. A Tera-machi quarter would become a fixture of the early modern castle towns.

Thus, elements of the archetypal landscape of the early modern castle towns figured prominently in Hideyoshi's towns. These elements include the following: (1) the creation of quarters for warriors and their separation from other areas such as the merchants' quarters, (2) the castle vista plan, (3) the erection of walls and moats surrounding a town, (4) the extensive arrangement of straight plural streets and rectangular-shaped town blocks, and (5) the concentration of temples along the periphery of a town.

These features were copied in other newly constructed or remodeled castle towns as Hideyoshi's influence extended to cover all of Japan. The medieval local lords and warriors under Hideyoshi who were sent to foreign lands to manage their local regions were forced to construct or reconstruct castle towns in strict conformity with the typical elements of town planning described above. Most of the new local castle towns of the period were based on the various old medieval centers such as pre-existent castle towns, port towns or temple towns. The lords under the Hideyoshi regime not only constructed a great number of streets, blocks and quarters, they also altered the original routes of many of the medieval streets in their respective towns. Hideyoshi was thus able to dramatically change the landscapes of medieval local towns in the late 16th century. The change was, as it were, from a clutch of decentralized and irregular forms to an integrated and well-arranged set of landscapes.

From the geographical point of view, the locations of the castle towns were often moved or expanded from their settings on the highlands (as planned in the medieval times) to lowland areas such as waterfronts in the early modern times. This was because the lords emphasized the economic functions of the castle towns and situated them in proximity to the highways and waterways threading the lowlands. This indicates that the feudal lords of the early modern times were able to overcome the difficulties in appropriating lowlands, including marshes and waterfronts, for commercial use; this was something that the medieval lords had not been able to accomplish. The landscape changes recorded in Noto-Nanao, one of the medieval port towns facing the Japan Sea that was transformed into a castle town by the late 16th century, illustrate the utilization of the lowlands, a process made possible by the local feudal lords overcoming a host of inhospitable conditions (Yamamura, 2006).

Several rivers had run through Nanao into the sea, and these rivers had had coves in the medieval times (Figure 5.5). The coastline of Nanao was thus uneven and irregular, and quite different from the straight coastline we see today. Nanao had two ports, Tokoroguchi and Fuchu, which used different coves. Each port was located along an important road leading inland. Around both ports, there were powerful shrines, temples and towns. The residences of the medieval feudal lord and his followers were built at the back of those two different port towns.

Toward the late 16th century, the feudal lord built his castle on top of the hill where a powerful shrine had existed (Figure 5.6). The lord moved the shrine to another place far from the port, and built his castle. He also moved the residences of the warriors under him to the foot of the hill. The lord constructed a new town in front of the castle, which included the old port town, Tokoroguchi, as a part of it. The lord created several streets in the new town and gave a few blocks to newly settled merchants and craftsmen. He reclaimed a part of the coves and marshes to concentrate urban functions in these reclaimed lands. The lord marked the border of the town by the rivers, the routes of which he had partly changed. In the 16th century, the lord had thus, to a certain extent, managed to change the landform on the way to establishing a new castle town. He could not, however, reclaim all the coves. In fact, most of the coves survived as marshes, so Fuchu, one of the ports of Nanao, was not assimilated into the new castle town.

At the beginning of the 17th century, the feudal lords were finally able to reclaim most of the coves and marshes (Figure 5.7). The lord moved the name and functions of Fuchu to cover the reclaimed land, which had lain separated from the two old port towns until the end of the 16th century. As a result, Tokoroguchi, which had been both the castle town and a port town, was integrated with the other port town of Fuchu. This new inclusive town has since been referred to as Nanao. The residence-cum-political office of the lord moved from the top of the hill to the lowlands. Some feudatories also moved to the lowlands and built their residences around the lord's. The lord reset the borders of this expanded castle

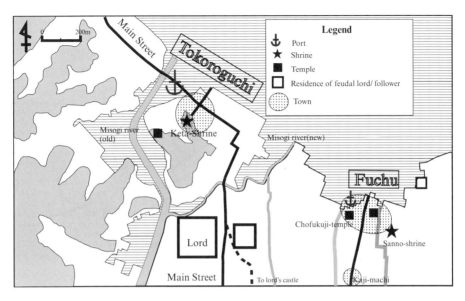

Figure 5.5: Medieval port towns in Nanao.
Source: Aki YAMAMURA.

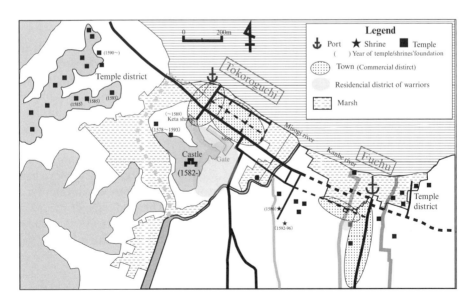

Figure 5.6: Nanao in the late of the 16th century.
Source: Aki YAMAMURA.

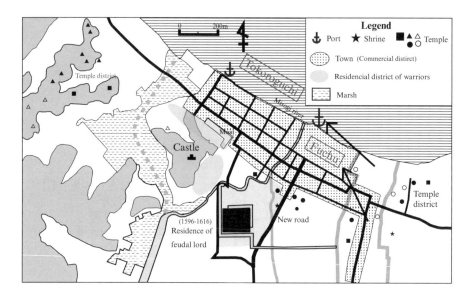

Figure 5.7: Nanao at the beginning of the 17th century.
Source: Aki YAMAMURA.

town, ordering the digging of a long line of moats. Inside this line, more streets and blocks were gradually developed, and at last the landscape turned into one that was typical of the early modern castle towns.

The example of Nanao illustrates how a castle town underwent changes in its landscape and landform during the medieval-modern transitional period as a result of occasional changes to its natural landscape, say, by the reclamation of its land. From the late 16th century onward, the lords had access to the means to change the routes of rivers and reclaim coves and marshes. He was thus in a position to reclaim most of the lowlands and obtain new stretches of flat land that were suitable for the construction or extension of castle towns. The development of the waterfront area was also used as a means to "take in" an old port town into the folds of a feudal lord's castle town. In the 17th century, the lord had reclaimed enough land to fulfill his urban layout, according to which each type of urban function was to be separately concentrated. The landscape of medieval castle towns was determined largely by their original landform. As the feudal lord's powers to utilize the lowlands increased, so did his powers to influence the landscape of his castle towns.

Early modern castle towns

After Hideyoshi's death around the end of the 16th century, Tokugawa Ieyasu, one of Hideyoshi's important feudatories but one that had been opposed to him, took over power and established the Tokugawa government in 1603. The Tokugawa government went on to function for about 260 years since then. Ieyasu constructed his headquarters in Edo, which was located on the eastern part of Honsyu Island and far from Kyoto and Osaka (Edo became Tokyo after the Tokugawa government collapsed). The period of the Tokugawa government's rule is referred to as the Edo era (1603–1867) and is regarded as the early modern times. While Edo developed rapidly as the new government capital, Kyoto retained its importance as headquarter of the emperors. Osaka, too, underwent a period of major development as it blossomed into the biggest commercial center in Western Japan during the Edo era.

The government established feudal domains (Han) all over Japan. The feudal lord who was allotted a particular domain by the government maintained a castle town as his headquarters. Many of the castle towns of that time were ones that had been constructed by the Hideyoshi regime, but some were newly constructed in fresh locations. On the way to (re)constructing these castle towns, the feudal lords ordered the abandonment of many medieval castle towns in order to unify their political and economic centers and base these inside their own castle towns. As a result, the early modern castle towns, with their uniform characteristics, superseded the old medieval towns, which were extremely diverse. Further, the populations of the abandoned castle towns flocked into the new or remodeled castle towns, and the population density of such towns increased. This relatively higher population density would go on to be another common feature of the early modern castle towns.

As described in the preceding section, the elements of the landscape in the early modern castle towns had first appeared in the castle towns set up by the Hideyoshi regime. However, the locations and spatial patterns of these elements differed in the early modern castle towns, according to their period of construction, topographical conditions, pre-existent town landscapes, and their political and social contexts. Thus, the landscapes of the early modern castle towns were not entirely uniform.

Yamori (1988) categorized the morphologies of these towns, focusing on the relationship between the outermost edge lines and the residential segregation that corresponded to the ranks of the inhabitants. The outermost edge lines were often made by artificial earthworks and moats. However, rivers and mountains also constituted the outermost edge line in some castle towns. Further, the concept of residential segregation divided the entire space into a certain number of quarters: these included the castle with its related facilities and quarters, the higher-class warriors' residential quarters, merchants' quarters, the temples' quarters, and the lower-class warriors' residential quarters. As Yamori (1988) explained, the morphology of the castle towns in the early modern times was classified into four types: (1) Sokaku-type, (2) Uchimachi-Sotomachi-type, (3) Machiya-Kakugai-type and (4) Kaiho-type (Figure 5.8).

In (1) Sokaku-type castle towns, the outermost walls with their moats enclosed the entire space of the towns. In such cases, the outermost walls functioned as

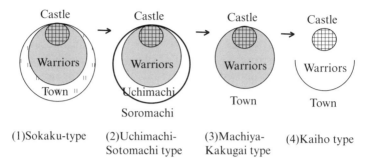

Figure 5.8: The morphology of the castle towns in the early modern times. Reference: Yamori (1988).

the town walls. (1) Sokaku-type castle towns were also divided into two types (Yamori 1970). One was a type wherein the agricultural fields and houses of farmers were distributed over a large area, and the residences of warriors and the houses of the merchants-cum-craftsmen were mixed within the town walls. The other was a type wherein these quarters were separated clearly; these towns had grid-patterned streets with rectangular-shaped blocks inside the town walls. The (1) Sokaku-type castle towns were promoted toward the end of the 16th century by Hideyoshi and his followers. However, castle towns in the 17th century were still being constructed in this mould, and the small domains (Han) that inherited pre-existent castle towns often accepted this type.

In (2) Uchimachi-Sotomachi-type castle towns, merchants' quarters was divided into two sections by the outermost walls. The castle's related facilities' quarters and the higher-class warriors' residential quarters were always within the enclosure, hemmed in by the outermost walls. However, only the major merchants' quarters (Uchimachi) were included into the enclosure. In some cases, the lower-class warriors' residential areas and temple quarters were also built outside the outermost walls. (2) Uchimachi-Sotomachi-type castle towns were established in the 17th century, at a time when the Tokugawa government was well established. Castle towns were being made, at that time, with the deliberate design to put some parts of the towns outside the outermost edge lines (Sotomachi). These castle towns, however, were not particularly popular. More commonly, when the merchants' quarters in some (1) Sokaku-type castle towns expanded to outside the town walls, these castle towns developed into (2) Uchimachi-Sotomachi-type castle towns. Such cases were also regarded as extension versions of the (1) Sokaku-type. Since the majority of the (2) Uchimachi-Sotomachi-type castle towns were originally built to have a (1) Sokaku-type form but ended up as (2) Uchimachi-sotomachi-type towns, Miyamoto (2005) classified the (2) Uchimachi-Sotomachi-type towns as a part of the (1) Sokaku-gata variety. Many of these are found in the areas surrounding Kyoto, Osaka and the western parts of Japan.

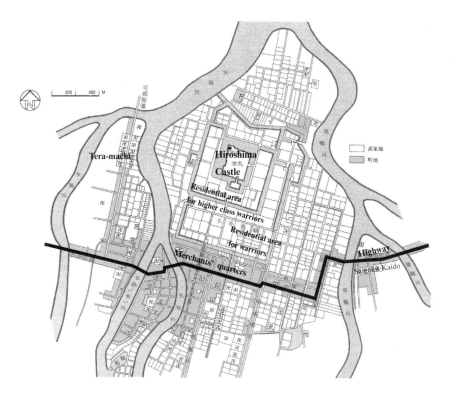

Figure 5.9: Hiroshima in the early modern times.
The original map was made by *Zushu Nihon Toshishi* (1993). The places painted gray mean the merchants' area.

Hiroshima, which was located on an unstable delta at the mouth of a river, was a example of a town being transformed from type (1) to type (2) (Figure 5.9). In 1591, the feudal lord who was subordinated to Hideyoshi had finished constructing the Hiroshima castle town. At that time, the whole town was surrounded by two tributaries that flowed near the castle. This meant that these tributaries were regarded as the outermost boundaries of Hiroshima. Hiroshima was, therefore, originally a (1) Sokaku-type town. The space around the castle was designed for the higher class warriors to live. The merchants' quarters was arranged along the highway. The route of this highway was shifted from its original course, so that it ran through the centre of the castle town. The temple district was set on the western fringes of the town. However, the feudal lord was sent down by the Tokugawa government in the early years of the 17th century. The Hiroshima castle town grew, and expanded across the two tributaries and became a (2) Uchimachi-Sotomachi-type castle town (Zusyu Nihon Toshishi 1993).

Among castle towns built in the 17th century or later, the outermost boundaries only enclosed the castle and its related facilities and the higher-class warriors' residential quarters. The other parts of the town, the merchants' quarter as well as the temples and the lower-class warriors' quarters, were built outside the outermost enclosures. These were the (3) Machiya-Kakugai-type castle towns. Many of the (3) Machiya-Kakugai-type castle towns were established in places that had been sites of medieval castle towns, and therefore incorporated several components of the landscape of the earlier towns. Further, this pattern was often accepted and endorsed by the powerful lords in the eastern part of Japan. In these castle towns, merchants' quarter was not enclosed by the outermost boundaries; this was an effort to promote commercial activities by facilitating the smoother movement of traffic along land and water, and enabling the expansion of commercial areas.

Yonezawa, located in the northeastern region of Japan, was a typical castle town of the (3) Machiya-Kakugai-type variety (Figure 5.10). The feudal lord of Yonezawa belonged to the Uesugi clan who were one of the most powerful feudatories in the Tokugawa government. Even before the Uesugi clan started the construction of the Yonezawa castle town in 1601, the place had a pre-existent landscape from the days of the medieval castle towns. The Uesugi clan went on

Figure 5.10: Yonezawa in the early modern times.
The original map was made by *Zushu Nihon Toshishi* (1993).

to move the old residential areas meant for the merchants and craftsmen of the medieval castle out of the outermost enclosures, outside the earthworks and moats. They set up the higher-class warriors' residential quarters in the place that had accommodated the merchants' and craftsmen's quarters in the medieval times. As a result, the space inside the outermost boundaries occupied only the castle and the warriors' residences (Zusyu Nihon Toshishi 1993).

After the last war between the feudal lords was over in 1615, the (4) Kaiho-type castle towns, which were less defensive in design, emerged. In those castles, even the warriors' residential quarters were not enclosed: the outermost walls and moats were omitted.

However, some of the biggest castle towns had more complex plans, having several urban cores in addition to the lord's castle. For example, Sendai encompassed some historical centers and its surrounding urbanized areas. At first, the warriors' quarters and merchants' areas were founded around the Sendai castle and the main street. In 1622, after the lord's retirement, another castle was built to the south of this castle town and the residences of the warriors were built in clusters around this new castle. In 1654, the Toshogu shrine, meant for the worship of Ieyasu, was established in the northern part of the town. The merchants' areas were then formed around the Toshogu shrine. Sendai had housed plural urban centers in its prime.

The other way of categorizing the castle towns focuses on the location of their main streets vis-a-vis their castle buildings (Yamori 1988). This basis yields two categories (Figure 5.11): Tatemachi-type and Yokomachi-type. In a Tatemachi-type castle town, the street that led up to the main gate of the castle was the town's main artery. Tatemachi-type castle towns were primarily constructed between the years 1570 and 1600, when the Nobunaga and Hideyoshi families controlled the central government of Japan. The Tatemachi-type castle towns were built to emphasize the castle as the center of the lord's territories. The segment of the

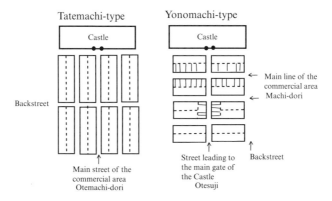

Figure 5.11: The types of the location of the main streets in early modern castle towns. Reference: Yamori (1988).

main line around the main gate was regarded as "the head," and the segment far from that gate was taken as "the tail." It was usually the case that the wealthier merchants lived in areas near "the head" while the poorer merchants lived in areas near "the tail."

In a Yokomachi-type castle town, an avenue orthogonal to the street leading up to the main gate was the primary axis or central line of the given town. In a Yokomachi-gata castle town, the main line went through the town and lead to other castle towns and to the three domestic central towns during the early modern times—Edo, Kyoto, and Osaka. This resulted in the flow of traffic being made easier. In contrast to the Tatemachi-type castle towns, the main line in a Yokomachi-type castle town did not have a "head" or a "tail," and the locations of the merchants' residences were not indicative of their relative wealth. Many of the Yokomachi-type castle towns were founded after Hideyoshi passed away and Ieyasu took control of Japan. Some castle towns were initially founded as Tatemachi-type castle towns but later modified to assume the character of Yokomachi-type towns.

The new capital, Edo

When Toyotomi Hideyoshi conquered the eastern region of Japan in 1590, he ordered Tokugawa Ieyasu to move from the original territory to there. Ieyasu decided to establish the ruling castle in Edo. Once Ieyasu came to power, Edo became the capital of the Tokugawa regime.

Edo was divided into two areas: uptown and downtown. The uptown area was on the highland. In contrast, the downtown area was on the lowland circumvented by several river mouths pouring into the sea. Lowlands were commonly reclaimed and made habitable. The Tokugawa regime turned the uptown area into residential quarters for the feudal lords and vassals owing allegiance to Tokugawa shogun. The downtown areas were used to build quarters for the merchants and craftsmen. The Edo castle was located at the edge of the highland, and the rulers of the castle could look down upon their downtown from the top of the castle. The temples were created in a cluster just outside the borders of the downtown area. This basic structure of Edo was completely formed by the late 1630s, when Ieyasu's grandson was the shogun.

In general, street blocks in the downtown area were not long and thin, but square (Figure 5.12). The center of the square blocks was the Kaisho-chi, a place jointly owned by the residents of a block. These square blocks and the Kaisho-chi were peculiar features of the original Edo castle town: only a few castle towns of the period have these characteristics. As the downtown of Edo expanded, new rectangular blocks without Kaisho-chis were added to the original structure of the town. The directions of the streets were not uniform: the administrators chose to accommodate old streets and pre-existent relief features.

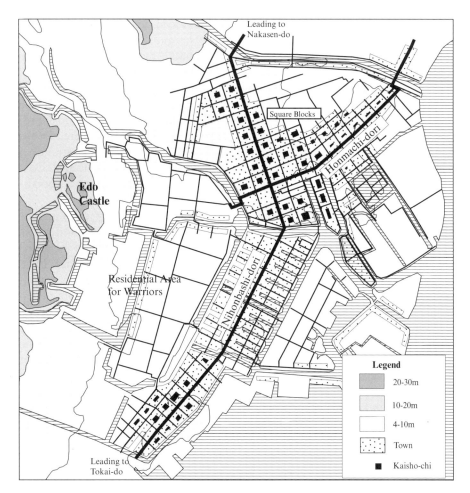

Figure 5.12: Downtown (*Shitamachi*) of Edo in the early 17th century.
Reference: *Zushu Nihon Toshishi* (1993).

Ieyasu founded Edo as a Tatemachi-type castle town, which had Honma-chi-dori as its main line; at that time, Ieyasu only controlled certain surrounding areas and Honmachi-dori led to these places. After Ieyasu took control of Japan, he made Nihonbashi-dori the main line, for it led to the two main traffic routes of Japan, the Tokai-do and the Nakasen-do. This changed the structure of Edo from that of a Tatemachi-type town to that of a Yokomachi-type town.

Ieyasu connected land transportation routes with sea and river transportation routes at Edo. Five highways were paved from Nihonbashi to the important towns corresponding to the directions of the main streets in the downtown area (outside Edo, inn towns were built along the highways). Ieyasu used a system of water moats and a river to make Edo a center of sea and river transportation networks. He also opened waterworks to provide water for merchants and craftsmen in the newly created downtown area. In early Edo, the transportation of goods largely depended on these water channels.

In 1635, the Tokugawa regime institutionalized a system under which feudal lords were required to spend every alternate year in residence in Edo. Feudal lords were also required to have their families stay in Edo. This policy increased the number of warriors' mansions. To serve the needs of these increased warrior class members in Edo, a larger number of merchants and craftsmen were needed. Consequently, the population in Edo increased, and Edo started to expand beyond its original borders.

In 1657, a fire destroyed not only Edo castle but also most of the warriors' mansions and merchants' and craftsmens' residential quarters. After this disaster, the erstwhile compact castle town of Edo underwent drastic expansion. Learning their lessons from the fire, the Tokugawa regime enforced three policies. First, the government moved the warriors' mansions and temples outside the outermost moats of Edo. Like many other castle towns of the time, Edo had been surrounded by moats along its outermost extremity before the fire. The Tokugawa government moved warriors' mansions and temples from inside to outside the moats in order to have buildings dispersed over a larger area and to expand the area of the town. Second, the government expanded the downtown area of the town. It reclaimed waterfronts, such as reservoirs, coastlines, and marshes in order to create new street blocks in the downtown area. Third, the Tokugawa government put firebreaks and enforced new policies concerning the streets and buildings of the town. It vacated several places inside and outside the castle and built banks with the view to ensuring breaks in the eventuality of another fire. The administration also widened existing streets, paved new streets, and enforced building regulations.

As a result of these policies, Edo town areas were radically expanded. Before the fire, the entire area could be covered by a circle with a 2 km radius. After the fire, the town area could only be covered by a circle with a radius of 5 km. Further, no clear border of the town was drawn, and the town gradually sprawled outward. Around 1719, when the number of wards in Edo downtown reached 933, the population of Edo went past one million. This number was significant in comparison to not only other Japanese towns but also with major towns all over the world (Zusyu Nihon Toshishi 1993).

Even though Edo expanded drastically, the basic structure was nevertheless largely retained. Warriors' mansions were on highlands; merchants' and workers' areas were on the lowlands; and temples were built outside the downtown. This basic structure was altered only after the Tokugawa regime collapsed in 1868 and Japan moved from the early modern times to the high modern times.

Port towns in early modern times

As seen in the last chapter, even in the 16th century, when enough technology was accessible for town planners to bury a lagoon, it was still technically impossible to construct buildings and streets along the coast. Medieval port towns developed along the highways that were orthogonal to the waterfront lines and led to a single wharf; the markets were set up around the edge of the highway near the wharf. In contrast, early modern port towns extended along the streets that ran parallel to the waterfront lines, to which many wharves were attached (Miyamoto 2006).

In the early modern port towns, each merchant's mansion, with its storehouses, was annexed to a wharf that was owned by the merchant. The mansion on its opposite side faced the main street that ran parallel to the line of the waterfront, and the goods unloaded from the wharf were sold on this side. The common wharves and marketplaces used by the merchants in the medieval times disappeared. Each mansion, with its storehouses, occupied one block; all blocks were identical in shape and size. The blocks were rectangular, and the sides that faced the waterfront and the main street were short, and the other sides were long. Each block had the same shape and size presumably to help every merchant secure equal access to the waterfront and the main street (Miyamoto 2006).

These ports were used only for intra-national trade. This was because in the early modern times, international trade was limited to special ports. The Tokugawa government issued a ban against Christianity in 1613 and by 1639 the Spanish and the Portuguese were ordered off Japan, while the British voluntarily abandoned their trading interests. After that, only Koreans, Chinese, and Dutch traders were allowed to visit Japan (by that time, the Japanese, too, were prohibited from leaving Japan and going abroad). After 1639, trade with the Dutch and the Chinese was confined to Nagasaki in Kyushu Island (to the west of Honshu Island). This period of isolation continued until 1853, when the US Admiral Perry demanded that the Tokugawa government open up the country.

Nagasaki was founded in 1571 as a port for trade with the Portuguese. The Society of Jesus had a church there, and it, along with the town surrounding it, was fortified with stone walls and moats (Zusyu Nihon Toshishi 1993). In 1580, Nagasaki was donated to the Society of Jesus. Governed by Christians, Nagasaki soon prospered as a port of international trade. Toyotomi Hideyoshi ordered the banishment of Christians in 1587, and in the following year, took Nagasaki out of the hands of the Society of Jesus. Hideyoshi broke the Society's buildings and removed the stone walls surrounding the town. Under his rule, Nagasaki expanded. Nagasaki continued to prosper even after the Tokugawa government assumed control of Japan.

However, the Tokugawa government took the "danger" of Christianity more seriously, and as a result, reclaimed the sea around one of the river mouths and created an artificial island to cage the Portuguese. The reclaimed land, which was referred to as "Dejima," was connected to the mainland only through an aisle that had a guarded gate. In 1639, the Portuguese were ousted from Japan and the Dutch were allowed to move in and live there. The Chinese lived in scattered communities across Nagasaki, but in 1689, they too were confined to an area that was surrounded by moats and bamboo fences. Trade goods arrived at these confined spaces and were then moved outside.

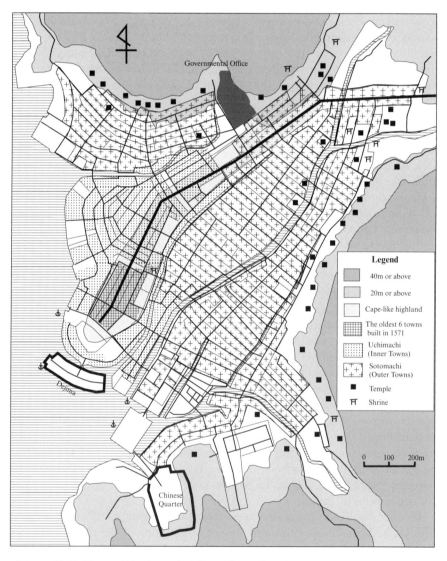

Figure 5.13: Nagasaki in the end of the early modern times.
Reference: *Zushu Nihon Toshishi* (1993).

The Tokugawa government ordered many feudal lords in the western part of Japan to guard Nagasaki. These lords placed their branch offices near the coast of Nagasaki. These offices included storehouses, and the lords sold rice and other products as well as borrowed money through these offices.

Nagasaki had been founded on a cape-like highland (Figure 5.13). This original town coupled with the additions made by 1605 was called "Uchimachi" (Inner Town). Highways ran through these quarters, orthogonal to the coastal line. Since these highways were the axes of these quarters, the rectangular street blocks were longer on the sides orthogonal to the coastal line. These quarters were surrounded by moats. The quarters added after 1605 were together termed as "Sotomachi" (Outer Town) because this part was constructed outside the Uchimachi. The street that ran orthogonal to the highways and rivers was the main axis of the town. As a result, many of the rectangular street blocks within these new quarters were longer on the sides that were horizontal to the coastal line. The street blocks were connected by arched bridges across rivers. In the 1620s, many temples were placed along the eastern border of Sotomachi. Later temples were built along the western border of Sotomachi. In this way, temples grew to surround the town. These quarters, in addition to Dejima and the Chinese quarter, constituted the whole town of Nagasaki.

In 1663, a fire destroyed the entire town of Nagasaki, with the exception of Dejima and a few other blocks. The town was rebuilt, with the streets being widened and the number of rooms in each house restricted. The structure of Nagasaki was fixed at this point; and it would remain so until Japan ended its self-imposed isolation around the end of the Tokugawa regime.

The transformation of early-modern towns into high modern towns

The Tokugawa regime was overthrown and a new regime called the "Restoration Government" was formed in 1868. This marked the end of the early modern times and the beginning of high modern times in Japan. In 1871, in order to increase the power and authority of the central government, the government deprived the feudal lords of their lands and ordered them and their subordinates to leave their castles and mansions. Most of the lords and their top-ranking subordinates went to Tokyo, the new capital of Japan. The castles and the surrounding warriors' mansions were placed under the ownership of the new government. This incident, as well as the construction of railroads and the advent of industrialization, transformed the landscape of historical towns in the high modern times (Yamori 1988).

The vacant lots where the castles used to be were converted in several ways. In the cases of middle- or small-sized ex-castle towns, many of the vacant lots were occupied by public offices or schools. In the cases of relatively large ex-castle towns, many of them became parks or military sites; after World War II, many of the military sites changed into non-military public spaces, particularly into public office sites. Low-profile ex-castle towns, however, were commonly made over into residential lots, forests or farmlands.

The castle moats were often filled and used for agricultural lands or residential lots. The vacant lots that housed the warrior mansions were utilized in various ways—as factory sites and schools, for instance. However, many of them eventually became residential lots or shopping districts.

After 1872, many railroads were gradually laid. Railroad stations had not been built in many of the inn towns and river port towns in the early modern times. These inn towns and river port towns declined in population and suffered economic losses. Railroad stations were placed at the circumference of many castle towns, and their development was made a priority. When a railroad station was built, a bustling shopping and entertainment district often emerged around the station. The new shopping and entertainment district frequently ran into competition with old merchants' quarters within the ex-castle towns. In some cases, this emergence of new shopping and entertainment districts was accompanied by the change in direction of adjacent main town. In this way, ex-castle towns as well as inn towns and river port towns were influenced by the development of the railway systems.

Industrialization was another crucial factor that transformed the landscape of historical towns into that of high modern towns (Yamori 1970). The Restoration Government tried to increase the powers and resources of the nation by introducing modern industry. Various plants were constructed in and around conveniently located towns. Many laborers came from outside these towns came and set up residences, which increased the population of these towns.

Even through these processes of modernization, the basic structure of the early modern towns was often preserved. Despite the fact that the residential and functional division of quarters in ex-castle towns had ceased to be enforced, and the towns often expanded far beyond their original area, the division of quarters still largely held, and the old streets and blocks of the original towns often retained their shapes.

Bibliography

Kido, Masayuki (2008), Azuchi-yama to Azuchi Sangecho (Azuchi Mountain and Azuchi Town), Niki, Hiroshi and Matsuo, Nobuhiro (eds.), *Nobunaga no Jokamachi* (Castle Towns Constructed by Nobunaga), Tokyo: Koshi Publishing, pp. 113–136.

Maekawa, Kaname (1991), *Toshi Kokogaku no Kenkyu* (Studies of Urban Archaeology), Tokyo: Kashiwashobo.

Matsuo, Nobuhiro (2008), Osaka Jokamachi (Osaka Castle Town), Niki, Hiroshi and Matsuo, Nobuhiro (eds.), *Nobunaga no Jokamachi* (Castle Towns Constructed by Nobunaga), Tokyo: Koshi Publishing, pp. 201–224.

Miyamoto, Masaaki (2005), Vista ni Motozuku Kukan Sekkei no Tenkai (The Development of Vista-Centered Spatial Planning), his *Toshi Kukan no Kinseishi Kenkyu*, (The Study of the Modernization of Urban Space), Tokyo: Chuo-Koron Bijutsu Publising, pp. 288–346.

────── (2006), Nihongata Minatomachi no Seiritsu to Ko'eki (The Emergence of Japanese Style Port Towns and Trade), Rekishigaku Kenkyukai (eds.), *Series Minatomachi no Sekaishi 2: Minatomachi no Topography* (Port Cities in World History Volume 2: The Topography of Port Cities), Aoki Shoten Publishing, pp. 79–110.

Nakai, Hitoshi (1990), Shokuhokei Jokaku no Kakki (The Epoch-making Techniques of Castle Engineering in the Nobunaga-Hideyoshi Era), Murata, Shuzo (eds.), *Chusei Jokaku Kenkyu Ronshu* (Essays on Medieval Castles), Tokyo: Shin Jinbutsuohrai Publishing, pp. 115–153.

Nakajima, Takashi (2008), Komaki Jokamachi (Komaki Castle Town), Niki, Hiroshi and Matsuo, Nobuhiro (eds.), *Nobunaga no Jokamachi* (Castle Towns Constructed by Nobunaga), Tokyo: Koshi Publishing, pp. 33–58.

Niki, Hiroshi (2001), "Odoi" he no Michi (Process to Odoi), The Japanese Society for Historical Studies (eds.), *Toyotomi Hideyoshi to Kyoto* (Toyotomi Hideyoshi and Kyoto), Kyoto: Bunrikaku, pp. 43–60.

────── (2008), 'Nobunaga no Jokamachi' no Rekisiteki Ichi (The Historical Significance of 'Castle Towns Constructed by Nobunaga'), Niki, Hiroshi and Matsuo, Nobuhiro (eds.), *Nobunaga no Jokamachi* (Castle Towns Constructed by Nobunaga), Tokyo: Koshi Publishing, pp. 275–304.

Senda Yoshihiro (1989), Komaki Jokamachi no Fukugenteki Kosatsu (The Reconstruction of Komaki Castle Town), *Historia*, 123, pp. 36–52.

────── (2000), *Shokuhokei Jokaku no Keisei* (The Innovation of Castles in the Nobunaga-Hideyoshi Era), Tokyo: Tokyo University Press.

Takahashi, Yasuo et al., (eds), *Zusyu Nihon Toshishi* (The Map Catalogue of the Urban History of Japan), Tokyo: Tokyo University Press.

Tamai, Tetsuo (1993), Toshi no Keikaku to Kensetsu (The Planning and Construction of Towns), Asao, Naohiro et al. (eds.), *Iwanami Koza Nihon Tsushi 11*, Tokyo: Iwanami Publishing, pp. 70–106.

Yokota, Fuyuhiko (2001), Toyotomi Seiken to Shuto (The Toyotomi Regime and the Capitals), The Japanese Society for Historical Studies (eds.), *Toyotomi Hideyoshi to Kyoto* (Toyotomi Hideyoshi and Kyoto), Kyoto: Bunrikaku, pp. 18–42.

Yamamura, Aki (2006), Chukinsei Noto-Nanao no Minatomachi to Jokamachi no Keikan (The Landscapes of Port Towns and Castle Towns in Noto-Nanao during the Medieval and the Early Modern Periods), Yada, Toshihumi and Senda, Yoshihiro (eds.), *Noto-Nanaojo, Kaga-Kanazawajo: Chusei no Shiro, Machi, Mura* (Noto-Nanao Castle and Kaga-Kanazawa Castle: Medieval Castle, Towns, and Villages), Tokyo: Shin-Jinbutsuohrai Publishing.

Yamori, Kazuhiko (1970), *Toshi Plan no Kenkyu* (The Study of Urban Morphology), Tokyo: Taimeido.

——— (1988), *Jokamachi no Katachi* (The Forms of Castle Towns), Tokyo: Chikuma Shobo.

PART 3

Rural landscapes

CHAPTER 6

Ancient and medieval rural settlement

Akihiro KINDA

The ancient land system

The ancient land system of Japan was introduced during the Great Reform of 645, and amended over the next few decades. Conversion to this land system, which was based on the *ritsu-ryo* (the basic penal and administrative laws), was completed by the enactment of the administrative codes of 701 (the *taiho-ryo*); the system was periodically reinforced by subsequent administrative codes with some minor changes. These various laws regulated the condition of arable land as well as other types of land. All land was initially classified into one of three types[1]:

Type 1. Arable land
Arable land was the most important economic base for the people, and the administrative base for the ancient state. Such land was administered directly by the state through the provincial government.

Type 2. Garden and housing land
It was held that this type of land was to be planted with mulberry trees, lacquer trees, hemp and so on, in order to generate and pay produce taxes, and with millet and vegetables for domestic consumption. This type of land was privately owned and could be inherited.

Type 3. Mountains, rivers, bushes and swamps
This type of land could be used by members of all communities that lived within range for food gathering, hunting, wood collecting and, presumably, slash-and-burn agriculture. Some areas with this type of land where trees were planted or managed could be privately owned.

Arable land consisted basically of rice fields, which were usually irrigated paddies, but sometimes included dry fields, especially where and when a shortage of paddies occurred in some provinces[2]. Arable land had begun to be allocated to individuals in some provinces near the imperial capital and the practice was adopted by almost all provinces during the seventh century. Allocations of arable land were made once every six years, and on the basis of the most recently available census register; under the official decree, allocations were made two years after the last census. Every individual above the age of six received arable land based on the unit of the household according to the following formula: two *tan* (approximately 2,400 square meters) to a male commoner; two-thirds of this area to a female commoner; one-third of a male commoner's allocation to a male subordinate; and one-third of a female commoner's allocation to a female subordinate. When the holder of an allocation of arable land died, the land was subsumed by the state at the next allocation. This system meant that the state was both allocating and assuming arable lands.

There were some arable lands that were kept outside of this allocation system: these included, for example, imperial domains, lands for particular persons with high court rank or special merit, lands bestowed imperially, temple or shrine lands, central- and local-governments' office lands, and station office lands[3]. All of these lands were cultivated primarily by hired labor and sometimes by subordinates. Otherwise, they were rented, with the exception of imperial domains, which were cultivated by corve'e labor, and some temple and shrine lands. Surplus land left after each allocation was rented annually to commoners under the jurisdiction of provincial governors.

The *ritsu-ryo* tax system consisted fundamentally of three types of taxes:

a. land taxes,
b. production taxes, and
c. labor levies or produce paid in lieu of them.

It had also become a duty to pay interest on state loans of rice seeds[4].

All arable lands were subject initially, according to their size and quality, to land taxes that amounted to approximately three percent of the yield from a first class paddy crop. Surplus lands left after allocation were to pay rent at a similar rate. Both tax and rent were paid to the provincial governments. However, imperial domains and temple/shrine lands that had been established before the codes of 701 had come into effect were exempt from any taxes. The basic unit that received land allocations and paid taxes was the household; every household was a registered unit. A household under the ancient land system was much larger than the average size of a present-day family: it could contain 24 persons, which was the average number of household members in a local administrative district[5]. Under this system, the rate of land taxes was relatively low; further, lands were strictly administered by the state government through provincial governments, although some of the older temples were allowed to retain the mountainous lands or forests they had enclosed in a period prior to the enactment of the *ritsu-ryo* tax system. Furthermore, some powerful aristocrats and temples, even in the early eighth century, had tended to illegally occupy mountainous areas and wastelands that had been intended for public use (the land type 3 mentioned above).

Change of the land laws

Arable land was basically administered by the state, and private ownership was prohibited under the original *ritsu-ryo* codes. However, the combination of certain factors—the shortage of arable land for allocation, a movement in favor of the private occupation of lands, and the intentions of the policy-makers of the time—led to an innovation: a tenure system for privately owned arable lands was introduced. The first change in the *ritsu-ryo* ruled that newly reclaimed paddies could be privately owned only by the developer himself and not his descendants if these paddies used an irrigation system that was already in existence. However, in cases where an irrigation system had been newly established by the developer, these lands could be passed on to his descendants for three generations. Then, a further change in the law came to rule that any of the newly reclaimed paddies could be owned privately, although upper limits to the size were set out according to the official status or court rank of the individual. The sizes ranged between 10 *cho* (12 hectares) and 500 *cho* (600 hectares), and permission of the provincial governor was mandatory in all cases. Bigger temples were given special grants and donations, and the largest temple, the Todai-ji Temple, was allowed to possess paddies of up to 4,000 *cho* (4,800 hectares).

After the enactment of the first change, the number of newly reclaimed paddies increased quickly as a result of acquisitions by, both, powerful families of aristocrats and bureaucrats as well as ordinary families of commoners. The units allocated to the aristocrats and bureaucrats were usually large, whereas those of the commoners were smaller. When these developers died a few decades later, their reclaimed paddies had either to be returned to the state or passed on to their descendants. This was quite likely a difficult decision to make, because the irrigation systems, which held the key to such decisions, had to be repaired or revamped at least annually, and sometimes it was impossible to separate the new systems that had been constructed for private reclamation from the old ones. This was one of the reasons why the second edict was enacted, which stipulated that any paddies newly reclaimed by an individual were to become privately owned by him. It was therefore no longer necessary to make difficult decisions about the categorization of irrigation systems.

Both new laws cited above are considered by many historians to have triggered the process of the collapse of the Japanese *ritsu-ryo* land system[6]. Although the Japanese *ritsu-ryo* system was based on the Chinese system, it had initially, unlike the original, not regulated the private ownership of arable land. Recent scholars, including this author, have argued that this had nothing to do with the disintegration of the land system, and that the collapse had resulted from problems associated with the administration of the *ritsu-ryo* land laws. This series of changes in the laws had nevertheless made it possible to fit land policies to the actual ground conditions of that time[7].

Even if the assessment of the process divides scholars, it is generally agreed that the procedure of land administration had become more complicated after the introduction of the revised laws. Under the original *ritsu-ryo* land system, the re-registration and allocation of arable lands would begin on the first day of October and would be completed within three months. These procedures, which took seven months starting from November, were to be carried out two years after the beginning of the six-yearly census, as stated already. The procedure of re-registering and allocating the lands was estimated to take a shorter period than the census did. Such a period would have to have been long enough for the procedures of arable land allocation to be carried out, since all arable land, with a few exceptions, was directly administered by the state, and the procedure would not have been very complicated[8].

However, under the new policies, every newly reclaimed paddy had to be inquired into and registered by the bureaucracy if it was to be exempted from being counted as arable land for allocation. This new procedure would have been extremely complicated for that era, and each re-registration and allocation could well have taken an entire season to complete. In fact, from the middle of the eighth century, it was an observed practice for any allocation to be carried out three years after its census, and every registration check, two years after its census[9].

The allocation system of arable land survived with some minor changes made to the number of paddies available for allocation and the interval between allocations until the end of the ninth century in certain regions and the beginning of the tenth century in others[10].

Minor place-name in the original procedure of land registration

The *ritsu-ryo* allocation system of arable land was thought by earlier scholars to have been carried out in tandem with the *jori* plan[11], which was also considered to have been introduced for the enforcement of policy at the time of the Great Reform of 645[12]. However it has become clear that the *jori* plan—a cadastral system that indicated the location of lands by a systematic numbering method based on a grid pattern—had been introduced approximately one century after the Great Reform and several decades after the establishment of the allocation system[13]. We should consider the fact that the *jori* plan was not used under the original *ritsu-ryo* land system in the first half of the eighth century. The formulation of the *jori* plan was completed at around the same time that the already mentioned changes in land policy were being implemented, that is, around the middle of the eighth century[14].

We can find many documents from the eighth century describing lands according to the administrative codes; further, we can also find some examples of descriptions of lands with accompanying minor place-names. A minor place-name at that time was a kind of field name that was used to indicate a certain place within the lowest unit of local administration, and it seems to have had an important role in the procedure of land registration. This understanding is gained from documents of that period that list the size of each paddy using only a minor place-name to identify its location[15].

Such minor place-names covered certain areas which varied in size. Some of them seem to have been original or actual place-names indicating certain areas spanning several hectares or more. Others corresponded to a small group of paddies representing subdivided patterns of the name. An example was the case of the subdivision into an upper, middle and lower part of an original place-name. In the case of such a pattern, a subdivided unit often corresponded with the *cho* (1.2 hectares) unit of paddies, which was usually one section of a grid pattern. Many of them were still used after the completion of the *jori* plan, as per the official records of the second half of the eighth century[16]. It is also notable that minor place-names that underwent such patterns of subdivision seem to have been attached only to groups of paddies that were either directly administered for allocation by the state or had a land tax or rent imposed on them by the state. Minor place-names were not attached to land used for gardens, housing or community use. Such evidences of usage encourage two assumptions: first, the subdivided patterns of minor place-names were only to facilitate the bureaucratic procedures of land registration; second, lands such as gardens and so on, not under the direct administration of the state, did not need such subdivision of place-names to correspond to a unit in order to receive the treatment accorded to official land[17].

Thus, allocated lands were identified under the original *ritsu-ryo* land system by both minor place-name subdivisions and the amounts of land and their boundaries as indicated by cardinal points. Such a system might have caused difficulty, confusion or ambiguity with regard to the location of the lands. This may have been a result of the possibility of similarities among place-names and the relative newness or uncommon nature of a given place-name that had been derived from minor place-name subdivisions[18]. Even if any difficulties had occurred, the problems or confusion would not have been very serious, because all arable lands were basically state lands and re-allocation would be done before long.

However, under the new policies permitting privately owned land, such difficulties and confusion must have become so serious that another system that sidestepped these problems was required. This system was the *jori* plan, which though available had never been intended for implementation under the original *ritsu-ryo* allocation system; however, the new situation that emerged after the regulation of privately owned arable lands necessitated its adoption[19].

Outline of the *jori* plan

The *jori* plan was a uniform system of indicating location by a numbering method which was based on the unit of *cho* (approximately 1.2 hectares, 109 meters on a side), with the lands arranged in a grid pattern; it was, first and foremost, a cadastral system. Consequently, it was not necessary to construct the permanent grid patterns on the ground since the pattern was represented and characterized by an interlacing network of paths and ditches, at least in the latter periods. The *jori* plan, in other words, originally contained two components: one was the *jori* place indication system as a cadastral method; the other was the *jori* grid pattern on the ground as a factor of the landscape[20].

The *jori* indication system had some local varieties of terminology, and measures with regard to the extent and direction of the grid lines. The basic land unit had generally been called *bo* in the eighth century. This name was changed to *tsubo* (this word will be used as a general term hereafter in this paper; the same applies to *bo*, the eighth century term) during and after the ninth century, although both represented sections containing an area of one *cho*. A square consisting of 36 basic sections was called a *ri*, forming a square of 654 meters on a side. A linear arrangement of *ri* was usually called a *jo*, combining together to form the term *jori*. This *jori* indication system was generally arranged in a uniform manner in each unit of the county in every province. The typical numbering method was as follows: each *tsubo* was numbered from 1 to 36 within each *ri*, and each *ri* was also numbered within each *jo*. An example of the way this system worked is cited here:

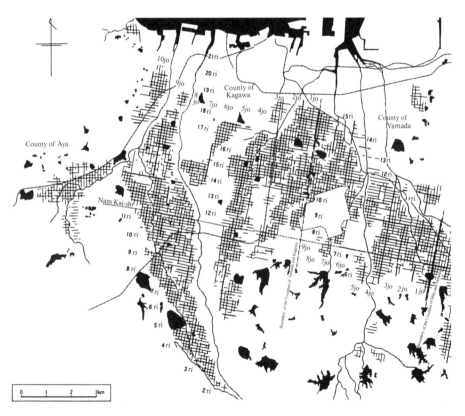

Figure 6.1a: *Jori* plans in Takamatsu plain in Sanuki Province.
Source: Akihiro KINDA.

"24 *tsubo*, 3 *jo* 8 *ri*, Yamada-county, Sanuki-province" [in Japanese the arrangement is read in reverse]. In contrast to this example of *jo* and *ri*, which consists of only ordinal numbers, there were other cases in some provinces in which each *ri* had an individual name. There were also certain cases that had involved sub-units within the *jori* plan of a county.

It was not only the *jori* indication system but also the *jori* grid pattern that had a uniformity or planned standard in each county within a province, although such uniformity or standard varied across the various provinces in accordance with their physical features, depending on whether they had large alluvial plains or a scattered distribution of many small valleys, for instance[21].

In a principal plain in the province of Sanuki (present Kagawa Prefecture), a standard of planning seems to have been very clear[22].

Figure 6.1b: Outline of *jori* plans, Nankai-*do* (an imperial highway) and county boundaries in Sanuki Province.
Source: Akihiro KINDA.

In ancient times, a main national highway, the Nankai-do, ran from the foot of a hill on the east corner of the plains through a pass crossing over the mountains on the west corner. County boundaries had also been set out as straight lines from conspicuous peaks at right angles with the highway. The straight lines of the highway had been established by the end of the seventh century, and the straight county boundaries are thought to have been set out by the codes of 701 at the latest. The north-south principal line of the *jori* plan is considered to have coincided with the east boundary line of each county, and the east-west base line coincided with the highway. The *jori* plans of this plain have been reconstructed as shown in Figure 6.1. The numbering of the *jo* began from the east and counted westward and the numbering of the *ri* began from the foot of the southern mountains moving onward to the northern coast. The numbers of *ri* were not always the same as that of the *ri* in the neighboring *jo*, and depended largely on the width of the plain at particular points. As a result, such a standard reveals the fact that the *jo* at the west end of each county was often incomplete or of narrow width, and that the road bed of the highway was excluded from the survey units of *ri* along the highway. Both of these patterns show that the *jori* plan was completed at the same time or just after the establishment of the highway and county boundary lines.

Evidence of the usages of *jori* plans and the construction of *jori* grid patterns in ancient times has been found widely in Japan. Source materials and remains of the *jori* grid patterns have been found in places such as the northern Honshu Island and its southern end as well[23]. Source materials that used *jori* plans as well as the remains of *jori* grid patterns are found typically on the alluvial plains in western Japan, especially in and around the former capital district, and on the plains along the Setonai-Kai Inland Sea, including the area shown in Figure 6.1, and in northern Kyusyu, all of which have been densely populated since ancient times.

Land division within a *tsubo* section

The typical morphology of land division within a *tsubo* section was a rectangle containing a *tan*. Two types of rectangles for a paddy have been dominant: the long type, 10.9×109 meters, and the short type, 21.8×55 meters, both containing 0.12 hectares (*tan*) or a tenth of a section, as shown on Figure 6.2. Such land divisions within a *tsubo* were also considered by early scholars to have been established for the allocation of arable lands in the seventh century, but this is again an incorrect interpretation. Such land divisions were the result of the implementation of the *jori* plans, as already mentioned.

The unit of allocation was formally two *tan* for a male commoner as already explained, but acreages for other people were different from each other and could not be depicted using integral numbers of tan. We can refer to an extensive example to illustrate this point. The provincial government order issued in the year 766 records 447 pieces of land that were owned by the Todai-ji Temple,

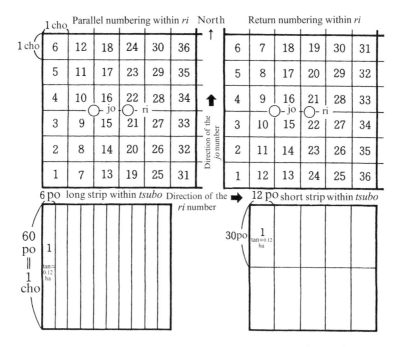

Figure 6.2: *Jori* numbering system and land division within *tsubo* section.

originally on account of allocation, rent, confiscation, reclamation, re-registration and exchange. 304 pieces of land among these had odd areas or were smaller than a *tan,* while the rest of the 143 pieces were in integral numbers of *tan.* This evidence suggests that the regular sizes of land units that contained a *tan* could not always be represented in terms of practical units; such diversity in the sizes of land holdings was common in the eighth century, a period that represented stage I of the historical *Jori* plan.

However, since the tenth century, coinciding with stages II and IIIa of the *jori* plan, many title deeds recorded lands that could be marked in integral numbers of *tan.* Furthermore, management within a manor was also often based on *tan* units, which functioned as the standard size in the construction of housing lots, in the course of cultivation and in discharging responsibilities to pay rent. These title deeds and standard units within a manor were especially dominant in the provinces near the capital, although there are examples to the contrary in other manors and provinces. Thus, the units of the *tsubo* and those of the *tan* began to predominate in the construction of regular shapes in the course of the land division along, both, the *jori* grid pattern and within a given grid section.

Evidence of such a process has been found in archaeological data, and it has been reported that regular rectangles that served as land divisions within a *tsubo* became common both during and after the tenth century.

Process of the establishment of the *jori* plan in the provinces

The first instance of the usage of the *jori* indication system, as already mentioned, has been found to have been in 743; the edict regulating privately owned paddies was also enforced in the same year. There is also evidence to suggest that the allocation of arable lands had been carried out during the term that began in October 742. This seems to suggest that the edict of 743 was introduced to solve the problems revealed during the allocations of 742: the *jori* indication system was thus originally intended to facilitate new bureaucratic procedures related to land re-registration immediately after land allocation as well as to inquire into lands before upcoming allocations[24].

Using established *jori* plans, cadastral plans were prepared each time to undertake the allocation or re-registration of lands[25]. In the case of one of the provinces, there is a document still in existence, which lists up to 86 roll plans for every year, pertaining either to the allocation/re-registration of arable lands or to inquiries into lands in and after the eighth century. These roll plans were maintained by the provincial government. It is considered that these plans, each of which was a very long roll with sections corresponding to each *jo* of the *jori* plan, covered whole areas of the provinces where paddies existed. When the roll plans were prepared for the allocation/re-registration of lands, they were also appropriated to the inquiries related to the next occasion. When the roll plans were prepared to inquire, they were used again for allocation/re-registration at the next time[26]. The first roll plans were prepared for the allocation/ re-registration which began in October 742 and were, at least in a few provinces, completed by the following year[27]. The existence of such cadastral plans provides additional evidence of the introduction of *jori* plans in the years 742 and 743.

In some provinces, however, the *jori* plans were established several years after 742[28]. Based on available evidence, we may suppose that these plans were established after 756 in certain provinces, and by 755, 762, and 767 in others. These precise dates coincide with the presumed dates resulting from the morphological analysis of the *jori* grid patterns as demonstrated in Figure 6.1. These examples show, at the same time, that the *jori* plans were a practical system rather than an idealistic or political one, because they was established in response to the needs of each province, without any political or legal statements by the state government or the emperor.

Prior to the establishment of the *jori* plan, the imperial capital of those days, Heijo-kyo, had used a systematic place indication system that relied on a numbering method consisting of *jo* and *bo* which, in turn, were based on a grid pattern. Although the Chinese capitals were also based on grid street patterns and square units for facilities and residences, the locations were indicated, by the proper name *fang* that referred to every square unit; locations within a *fang* were shown by directions from corners, gate openings at cardinal points and street crossing at the center[29]. However, the methods used in China and Japan were different from each other despite the fact that both the units *bo* and *fang* used the same character, and despite Japanese capitals being under a strong Chinese influence at that time.

In the case of rural areas in China, the fields belonged to the people and the locations of fields were generally indicated only by the local administrative units. If details were required, the direction and distance from a prefectural town or some another major place were also described[30]. Thus it has not been possible to find any numbering methods in China, which could have been a model for the *jori* plans of Japan to emulate. The Japanese capital was the only possible model for producing a numbering method according to a grid pattern in the middle of the eighth century. Therefore, the systematic methods adopted in Heijo-*kyo* could have been a model for the *jori* indication system[31].

Changing functions of the *jori* plan

Stage I: During the eighth and ninth centuries

After the establishment of the *jori* plan, registries of lands had relied on their cadastral plans that had been prepared for each *jo*, and registers that had been amalgamated into the households. In either case, the locations of lands were described according to the *jori* plans. Provincial governors made annual reports to the state government on the condition of cultivation and the actual cultivators, who were also incorporated into each household. Their locations were indicated in the *jori* plan. These reports were transferred to the state government. Incidentally, in 845, the annual report was changed to an occasional one by a government order. For these procedures, the *tsubo* section of the *jori* plan was the basic unit of land administration[32].

The *jori* plan was so systematic that it was effective in overcoming the troublesome bureaucratic procedures. However, some problems, which are known to us from documents that have survived from the eighth century, still remain. One of them was the tendency to misjudge non taxable land (Type 2: for example, dry fields, which were in the same category as gardens) and treat it as taxable arable land (Type 1) within a *tsubo* section[33]. A further problem developed as a result of the ambiguity of the actual location or boundary of the section itself, although it might have been evident on the cadastral plan[34]. This situation was presumably caused by the lack of a clearly constructed grid pattern on the ground in places such as marshy alluvial plains and narrow valleys. Under such physical conditions, the construction of land divisions according to a grid pattern was often difficult and impractical. Differences in direction between the standard grid patterns and natural slopes or water courses may have tended to create irregular and unaccounted for patterns of land. Even if the basic physical condition was suitable for constructing grid land divisions, confusion or ambiguity of boundaries happened often, especially after the temporary abandonment of cultivation following a disastrous flood and other similar situations. This will be discussed further in the latter part of this chapter.

In spite of such difficulties of identifying particular lands, they were addressed to re-registry of misjudged lands by provincial governments in the following year or at the next allocation. Many surviving documents, in fact, have recorded changes of tenure or registration, as well as information related to the dealings and inheritance of lands. The main function of the *jori* plan, in the second half of the eighth and ninth centuries, was to create a grid cadastral scheme for a regularly ordered and numbered land identification system. This period can be categorized as stage I of the *jori* plan[35]. Stage I was effective in inquiring, allocating and registering lands under a national land system, which was expressed as a cadastral system with a grid pattern that represented typically actual land divisions on the ground.

Stage II: During the tenth and twelfth centuries

The land administration system established in the middle of the eighth century as a national system continued as the basis of provincial administration despite the break-down of the allocation/re-registration system of arable land at the beginning of the tenth century. From the tenth to the twelfth centuries, manors became dominant units of land holding and management, although their land tenure varied according to the origin and manner of grants. On the other hand, the provincial governor's power was, in general, strengthened within state guidelines, with the result that almost all manors were still under the authority of provincial governments and held limited rights that consisted of occasionally fragmented interests. The majority of the revenue of the lords of manors was generated by the interest on their lands; this in turn enabled them to pay only a part of their tax amounts to the provincial government.

Even in the case of manors established by the authority of state ministries, the lords of manors had to submit applications that listed lands they expected to be exempt from tax. These applications were submitted to the provincial governor every time a new governor was appointed at the province[36]. The manors established by the authority of the provincial governor himself also had to submit applications, but these tended more often to be strongly swayed by the governor's policy. Both types of applications usually listed lands according to the *jori* plan. Under each new governor, the provincial government checked the applications, consulting both the cadastral plans maintained by the provincial government and newly surveyed lists of lands ordered by the governor. Permission to gain exemption from tax could be granted after the completion of these procedures, but if the application or evidence on a prior grant was deficient, the manor could even be confiscated by the provincial government. In the case of manors established by the authority of the governor, the location of lands could be changed by the governor's policy, even if the application was appropriate in all respects.

It may be pertinent here to discuss one case in particular[37]. A manor of a temple consisted of scattered lands spread over two counties during and after the year 1018, but the manorial lands were consolidated around the temple during the administration of two governors in the period after 1138. However, in 1156, the manorial lands were dispersed again by the governor following a petition by the temple itself, because the temple could not manage any new manorial areas at that time.

For these procedures, all land was generally indicated as per the *jori* plan and the *tsubo* section was the basic unit for all permissions and grants. The *jori* plan managed to enforce more stringently the boundaries of land ownership as well as the rights and responsibilities to pay taxes as compared to the original *ritsu-ryo* system of the eighth and ninth centuries for both provincial governors and land owners of various sizes[38].

In the eleventh century, a new custom was established, which enabled a land owner to expand his rights within a *tsubo* section if he was the sole land owner and if he had reclaimed or cultivated more than the acreage of his original ownership within the section[39]. There was another change which held that the land owners or operators in a section were jointly responsible for paying taxes or rent even if they had originally been levied separately on their respective parts of the section[40]. In other words, the grid lines of the *jori* plan gained an additional function as boundaries of rights, interests and duties, for parties who intended to expand them as well as those who intended to control them.

Thus, the *tsubo* section came to be the basic unit in the functioning of Japan's agricultural economy and society. In this period, new cadastral plans were no longer prepared, as the old plans were persisted with. Such plans, which had been maintained since the eighth and ninth centuries by the provincial government, were used as a kind of ledger. In these cadastral plans, all changes with regard to land rights were written down, and only such descriptions on the basic cadastral plans could secure an owner formal rights to a piece of land. This type of usage of the *jori* plan can be categorized as stage II[41].

This period witnessed the emergence of an intense rivalry between the provincial government and the lords of the manors. Both were, over time, connected with and variously supported by political allies of the state government, such as powerful aristocrats and the bigger temples. At the end of this period, during and following the twelfth century, many manors established complete rights within their boundaries and excluded the administration of the provincial government. In many such cases, the provincial government wielded only a nominal or honorary power, retaining control over a limited set of bureaucratic functions[42].

Stages III and IV: In and after the twelfth century

After the establishment of complete rights by the lords of manors within their manorial boundaries, the *jori* plan as a uniform system throughout a county should ordinarily have become redundant, but in many cases it was still used as before or with a few modifications.

For many of the manors in the provinces near the capital, the *jori* plan was still useful for identifying or re-confirming boundaries with neighboring manors because the sizes of the manors were relatively small and many of them were adjacent to each other. In these cases, the *jori* plans survived and continued to be used until the sixteenth century, typically in the provinces near the capitals. For larger manors, their boundaries were often fixed by physical features like rivers and hills, or other clear landmarks and it was not necessary to use the *jori* plans standardized throughout the county. However, within a manor, a system for identifying and managing manorial lands was still necessary. The methods which were used in this situation are generally categorized as stages III or IV of the *jori* plan, with four popular manifestations, as follows:

(i) A special *jori* style indication system, which was framed and completed within a manor but followed and coincided with grid patterns on the ground, was produced only for the area of the manor[43].

(ii) A special jori style indication system that was also completed within a manor and followed the style of stage I but without both any grid indication systems and grid land divisions on the ground. Such a system was produced only for the area of the manor[44].

(iii) Minor place-names within a manor that were used for identifying the location of lands; these minor place-names corresponded to grid patterns that continued as actual land divisions on the ground[45].

(iv) Minor place-names, used when there were no grid patterns that coincided with the former *jori* plan[46].

Both types (i) and (ii) more or less followed an element of the *jori* plan, and can be categorized as stage III of the *jori* plan. This can be sub-divided into stages IIIa [corresponding to (i)] and IIIb [(ii)][47]. Type (iii) can be categorized as stage IV, having no *jori* style indication systems but having *jori* grid patterns on the ground. There were some variations too, such as a combination of types (i) and (ii), and a complex of type (i) along the central part and type (iii) along the margin of a manor. Type (iv) had been common in areas where *jori* grid patterns were not dominant, such as mountainous areas or fringe zones of the ancient state.

However, by the end of the sixteenth century, lands patterned along type (i) had adopted type (iii), and type (ii) lands had also changed overwhelmingly into type (iv); in addition, lands that had followed stage II had directly made the transition to stage IV[48]. Stage IV corresponding to type (iii) was the final stage of the *jori* plan and this had continued, in many cases, well into the modern times until the practice of land consolidation intervened[49].

The *jori* grid patterns on the ground

Jori grid patterns were found widely on the ground until drastic changes were effected by land consolidation, which was initiated to bring about the modernization of agriculture. Yet some *jori* grid patterns have remained to this day. Such grid patterns have, in many cases, been fitted to a standardized *jori* plan within the county as a whole, making it possible to reconstruct the original *jori* plan on the basis of these centuries-old grid patterns as shown in the example in Figure 6.1.

However, the distribution of *jori* grid patterns on a plain often consists rigidly of many smaller patterns and presents a mosaic or groups of grids that can be observed in detail on large scale maps such as those with a 1: 2,500 scale or in aerial photographs. Groups of grid patterns are generally discrepant from each other. They can be distinguished by an interval or a difference of direction or discrepancy of grid lines as shown in the example in Figure 6.3. The average size of each group of grid patterns is approximately a hundred *cho* or slightly smaller. In other words, each group of grid patterns contains less than or around a hundred grids.

This size is similar to the average area of a group of paddies belonging to any of the major temples in the second half of the eighth century. Such a coincidence is presumably because of the similarity between micro-geomorphologic units such as a flood plain with a back marsh surrounding natural levees on a deltaic plain and a group of relatively thick soil deposits between channels on a larger

Figure 6.3: *Jori* grid pattern on the ground with nucleated villages in Nara basin (1961) (Geographical Survey Institute No. KK-61-8, C4-9).

alluvial fan. A group of paddies necessarily corresponds to such a physical unit not only for reasons related to cultivation but also for its irrigation. Consequently, the units of land under reclamation and irrigation in ancient and medieval times are thought to have been limited by such physical conditions.

The reasons that made up groups of grids within a *jori* plan have been categorized as follows :

(i)   In cases where some grid patterns were constructed in a plain before the completion of the *jori* plan, these were established either by organizing the various groups of grids according to the units of the paddies, or by including the paddies reclaimed or rearranged in the various periods.

(ii) In general, the construction of the *jori* grid patterns did not admit discrepancies consciously. However, even in cases where grid patterns were constructed under the *jori* plan, there would be errors, which would occur during surveying and constructing, and irregularities, which were the result of limitations in technology. Moreover, adaptation to physical conditions tended to make groups of grids within a unit of the *jori* plan.

(iii) Even in cases where a standardized grid pattern had once been constructed, groups of grids within a *jori* plan were often created by post-flood rehabilitation or land-improvement efforts or a period of abandonment caused by social or natural factors.

The case described in category (i) is a rather theoretical one. Remains of such grids are rarely ever found on the ground, given their antiquity—created as they were in the first half of the eighth century. Despite, processes in many cases involved in category (iii). The main reasons for the existence of groups of grids within a *jori* plan are the cases described in categories (ii) and (iii). In many cases where sub-surface remains of *jori* grid patterns have been found, grid lines below the surface and on the ground have been found to have shifted a little from each other. Such examples vividly show the processes involved in the case of category (iii) *jori* plans.

Thus, the *jori* grid patterns have demonstrated in the past as they continue to do today various units of groups of grids, despite of their very standardized and regularized pattern as a whole.

A great number of subsurface remains of paths and ditches, coinciding with *jori* grid patterns on the ground, have been found as a result of the progress of archaeological excavations. Although the earliest example of a subsurface *jori* grid pattern has been dated back to the second half of the eighth century, most of these have been dated as significantly later constructions by archaeological methods[50]. Many such paths and ditches were constructed in and around the twelfth century[51], and had existed until very recently—until land consolidations related to modern land divisions on the ground [that is to say, stage IV] took over.

Thus the period when many of the *jori* grid patterns were found as subsurface remains corresponds to the end of stage II or the beginning of stage IIIa of the *jori* plan. At this stage, the significance of grid lines in the *jori* plan as boundaries was generally strengthened. This has already been explained. This process could explain the fact that grid lines on the cadastral plans had come to be fixed as physically constructed lines on the ground like paths and ditches[52]. Once the grids were constructed, it is apparent that they were persisted with as the basic units of agriculture, even in a period by when the *jori* indication system had become redundant [stage IV]. In many regions, rural communities continued with the patterns despite floods and other disasters. Such evidence collated on the strength of archaeological data supports the theory that the function of the *jori* plan has evolved from stage I through to stage IV.

The rectangular section *tsubo* was a basic unit of land in the rural areas of Japan in ancient times—in stages I and II of the *jori* plan—which was associated with certain implicit rights and duties relating to agriculture. On the other hand, the larger unit *ri* as well as *jo* was originally not a very practical unit[53] but rather a cadastral one, despite the fact that the *ri* was once thought, by early scholars, to have been a unit of the rural community or village under the *ritsu-ryo* land system. This is because these early scholars found some villages in a few provinces that fitted the dimensions of a *ri*, and took them to be wholly representative of the remains of the ancient landscape[54]. However, such villages were formed no earlier than the twelfth century and some villages, much later. It is important to note here that this period when villages which fitted the *ri* of the *jori* plan were formed was toward the end of stage II of the *jori* plan.

Rural land use and settlement pattern

In the early stages of the establishment of the *jori* plan, the distribution of arable lands was generally limited to selective areas that were suitable for cultivation even within a plain.

Some documents reported that only 17-77% of the formal agricultural fields were actually cultivated, or that 12-44% of the fields were not used at all during the eighth century. Some other documents listed that around one third of a manor was paddy, one third was dry field, and the other third was wild; this was in the twelfth century.

Since the twelfth century through the medieval times, the use of agricultural land intensified and progress was made not only on account of agricultural resources but also owing to novel engineering methods and social control. The agricultural resources involved in driving such development include fertilizers such as ashes of plants, which were introduced in the twelfth century, and the introduction of profitable crops such as cotton at some time during the thirteenth or fourteenth century. The engineering innovations included the construction of irrigation channels or irrigation ponds including rectangular and shallow ponds with a supplementary function as rice paddies in Nara Basin in the late twelfth century, and the leveling down of paddies for effective irrigation. Social control, in this context, implies the improvement in the social management of irrigation water witnessed among many medieval manors.

The gradual intensification of agricultural land use was above all witnessed in and around the capital district, and its neighboring regions, depending upon their economic situations or morphological conditions. These innovations generally percolated from the capital region that acted as the political and economic center to the outer regions. Intensive land use of rice paddies usually brought about typical *jori* grid patterns on the ground as per the strict land rights and ownerships.

The distribution of rural houses between the eighth and twelfth centuries was generally sparse; the houses were primarily of the hamlet type during this period.

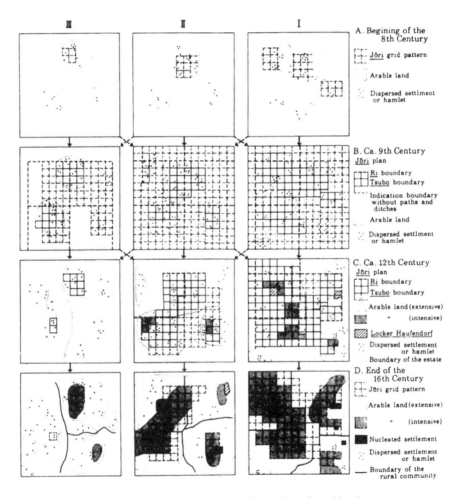

Figure 6.4: Process of the formation and transformation of rural landscapes.
Source: Akihiro KINDA.

Some settlements began to form nucleated types of villages around manor houses or manor offices in the capital district during the twelfth century, presumably owing to the ease of management. Thereafter, such a tendency became popular in many developed regions, although some regions remained with sparsely distributed farm houses or hamlet-type settlement patterns. In some areas like Tonami Plain in the middle of Honshuh Island, the distribution of rural settlements became sparser and more dispersed. Even in the rural areas, some of the larger villages or small towns were developed or planned as nodal points from the point of view of transportation and markets. These were very important as service centers in rural regions.

Notes

1. T. Iyanaga, Land ownership under the *"ritsuryo"* system, in *Iwanami Lectures in Japanese History*, Vol. 3 (Tokyo, 1962). T.Miyamoto, Land system under the *"ritsuryo"* system, in R. Takeuchi (ed.) *History of Land System,* Vol. 1 (Tokyo, 1963).
2. It was popular in the provinces of Yamashiro and Awa.
3. Iyanaga, *op.cit.* Miyamoto, *op.cit.*
4. T. Yoshida, *The Ritsuryo State and the Ancient Society* (Tokyo, 1983) 420–421.
5. K. Hirata, *Discussion on the Register System in Ancient Japan* (Tokyo, 1986) 314–320.
6. Problems in the previous studies are pointed out by T. Torao [*Discussion on the History of Land Laws in Ancient Japan* (Tokyo, 1981) 242–272.
7. Yoshida, *op.cit.* 263–266. A. Kinda, *An Historical-geographical Study of the Jori Plan and the Rural Landscape* (Tokyo, 1985) 126–136.
8. Kinda (1993a), *Landscape of Ancient Japan* (Tokyo, 1993a), 3–14.
9. T. Torao, *A Study on the System of Allocating and Returning Arable Lands in Ancient Japan* (Tokyo, 1961) 307–316. Kinda, *ibid.*
10. Torao, *ibid.*, 317–336.
11. The edict of 646, regulating the allocation system of arable lands, is contained in the first official chronicle *Nihonshoki*, but it was arranged by the editors of *Nihonshoki* in the 720s according to the administration codes of 701.
12. S. Hotta, The system of *"jori"*, *Shigaku-zatshi* 12 (1901) No. 11, 12. J. Yonekura, The *jori* system as a rural planning policy, *Chiri-ronsou* 1 (1932).
13. Kinda (1993a), *op.cit.* 3–14.
14. Kinda (1985), *op.cit.* 77–125.
15. T. Kishi, A document concerning with the system of renting arable lands in the Nara period of Japan, *Historia* 12 (1955). Kinda (1985), *op.cit.* 43–59.
16. Kinda (1985), *op.cit.* 39–64.
17. A. Kinda, Land administration and minor place-names in the Nara period of Japan, *Shirin* 78 (1995) No. 4.
18. Kinda, *ibid.*

19. The average size of the *"jori"* grid was varied regionally; for example: 109.2 meters in Nara Basin and Fukui Plain, 109.2 meters in Sanuki Plain, 107 meters in Shizuoka Plain, approximately 120 meters in the Kawage-gun, Ise Plain, and 110.3–111.4 meters in Ibo River Plain of Hyogo Prefecture. [A. Kinda, Morphology and complexity of the *"jori"* grid pattern, *Jorisei-kenkyu* 11 (1995)].

20. Kinda (1985), *op.cit.* 54.

21. There are many works that have reported on the distribution of the *"jori"* grid patterns and reconstructed the *"jori"* plan. Two of them are very detailed reconstructions on a very large scale; they cover the entire area of one or two provinces with more than one hundred sheets of 1: 5,000 maps [Kashihara Archaeological Research Institute (ed.) *Reconstruction of the Jori Plan in Yamato Province* (Nara, 1980): A. Kinda (ed.) *Reconstruction of the Jori Plan: History of Fukui Prefecture, Material Series* Vol. 16B (Fukui, 1992).]

22. A.Kinda, *"Jori"* plan and rural life, in Kagawa Prefecture (ed.) *History of Kagawa Prefecture*, Vol. 1 (Takamatsu, 1988). Kinda (1993a), *op.cit.* 16–41.

23. The northern-most example is reported by Torao [(1981), *op.cit.* 273–284] and the southern-most is cited by J. Yonekura [the southern limit of the distribution of the *"jori"* grid patterns, *Shigaku-kenkyu* 66 (1957)]. Among many works, the following books contain many figures for reconstructing *"jori"* plans: T. Tanioka, *A Geography of Plain* (Tokyo, 1963); T. Tanioka, *Development of Plain* (Tokyo, 1964); H. Watanabe, *A Study of the Jori System* (Osaka, 1968); T. Mizuno, *An Historical-geographical Study of the Jori System* (Tokyo, 1971); M. Hattori, *An Historical-geographical Study of the Ritsuryo State* (Tokyo, 1983). Many prefectural histories and municipal histories also contain more detailed reconstructions as shown in the note (21).

24. Kinda (1985), *op.cit.* 127–130. Kinda (1993a), *op.cit.* 3–11.

25. Torao (1961), *op.cit.* 331–335. A. Kinda, Manorial maps and the *"jori"* plan in the eighth and ninth centuries, in A. Kinda *et al.* (eds.) *Maps of Ancient Manors in Japan* (Tokyo, 1996).

26. Torao (1961), *op.cit.* 331–335. Kinda (1995), *op. cit.*

27. T. Kishi, *A Study of the Registers in Ancient Japan* (Tokyo, 1973) 391–414.

28. Kinda (1995), *op.cit.*

29. Kinda (1985), *op.cit.* 77–96.

30. Kinda, *ibid.*

31. Kinda (1985), *op.cit.* 96–112.

32. Kinda (1993a), *op.cit.* 250–264.

33. Y. Murai, Development and structure of the manor system, in *Iwanami Lectures: Japanese History*, Vol. 4 (Tokyo, 1962).

34. Kinda (1993a), *op.cit.* 250–264.

35. Kinda, *ibid.*

36. S. Sakamoto, Discussion on the National Organization of Dynastic Japan (Tokyo, 1972) 19–52.

37. A. Kinda, *Micro-geomorphology and Medieval Settlement* (Tokyo, 1993b) 109–131.
38. Kinda (1993a), *op.cit.* 264–275.
39. Sakamoto, *op.cit.*
40. Murai, *op.cit.*
41. Kinda (1993a), *op.cit.* 264–275.
42. Y. Amino, Formation and structure of the manor based administration system, in R. Takeuchi (ed.) *History of Land System,* Vol. 1 (Tokyo, 1973). S. Ishii, *A Study of History of the Japanese Medieval State* (Tokyo, 1970) 118–174.
43. Kinda (1993b), *op.cit.* 176–202.
44. T. Ueshima, On the *jori* plan of the manor of Yano in Harima Province, in *Memoirs for the Retirement of Professor J. Kobata* (Kyoto, 1970).
45. This case has been most popular in the regions where the *jori* grid patterns are dominant.
46. This case has been most popular in the region where the *jori* grid patterns have never existed, although this case is also found in some regions where the *jori* grid patterns have partially existed.
47. Kinda (1993a), *op.cit.* 275–286.
48. Kinda (1985), *op.cit.* 64–70. Kinda (1993b), *op.cit.* 182–192.
49. Minor place-names themselves often changed, individually according to local events, and systematically according to the local administration.
50. For example: S. Nagamune, Underground remains of *jori* grid patterns in Hazukashi, Otokuni County, *Jorisei Kenkyu* 4 (1988).
51. For example: K. Nakai, A regional study, in Nara National Research Institute of Heritage (ed.) *Problems of the Jori System* (Nara, 1981); K. Hirose, *Jori* grid patterns in the provinces around ancient capitals, *Koukogaku Journal* 310 (1989).
52. Kinda (1993a), *op.cit.* 297–305.
53. Kinda (1985), *op.cit.* 136–175.
54. J.Yonekura, *Jori* system as a rural planning policy, *Chiri Ronso* 1 (1932). Meaning and influence of this paper was critically reviewed by Kinda (1985), *op.cit.* 4–21.

CHAPTER 7

The early modern rural landscape

Taisaku KOMEIE

An enormous amount of new arable land emerged in early modern Japan from 1603 to 1867, under the reign of the Tokugawa government, or 'Pax Tokugawana.' Thousands of wet swamps, marshes, crescent lakes, lagoons, tidal flats, dry table-lands, and river terraces were transformed into well controlled and domesticated spaces. In many instances this work involved creating geometric patterns in the landscapes of fields and new settlements. *Kaihotsu*[1], or land reclamation, was a primary feature of rural Japan from the seventeenth to nineteenth centuries. This reclamation was accompanied by a steep rise in population, which had a severe impact on the natural vegetation that surrounded settlements. Almost all land, including uncultivated space, was officially divided and allocated to neighboring villages as commons, meaning that each village controlled, and occasionally destroyed, the natural landscape surrounding it. In early modern Japan, both arable land and the natural environment were altered greatly as a result of aggressive human activity. This section begins with an overview of the great land reclamation that occurred in the Pax Tokugawana period and introduces several cases related to landscapes surrounding the new villages that arose from the reclamation. Focus then shifts to the changes that took place in the natural landscape and the manner in which people used, controlled, and destroyed the environment.

The era of great land reclamation

It is quite safe to say that approximately twenty thousand square kilometers of newly exploited land was acquired in early modern Japan. Many of the settlements formed during this period incorporated the word *shinden*[2] in their names, a term used officially by the Tokugawa and local governments to identify both newly exploited fields and new settlements. According to a place name database (Kadokawa Shoten 2002), the names of at least 4,297 villages, for example Nakatomi-shinden or Kōnoike-shinden, had *shinden* as a suffix, many of which have survived as place names to this day. *Shinden* was clearly one of the most important features of Japan's early modern historical geography and has been a constant source of inspiration to historical geographers (Kikuchi 1958, 1963,

137

1986; Kitamura 1981; Fukuda 1986) and local historians (Kimura and Itō 1960; Kimura 1964).

During early modern times the growth of reclaimed acreage was not always steady; rather, it was characterized by two distinct peaks. The first major increase in the number of villages and the second, more gradual, rise are shown in Table 7.1. The first of these, which took place between 1645 and 1697, saw 6,186 or more new

Table 7.1: The number of villages in early modern Japan.

Province	1645	1697	1829	1873
Tōhoku Region				
Mutsu				
– Mutsu	499	501	1,012	1,088
– Rikuchū	530	530	537	728
– Rikuzen	–	702	702	703
– Iwashiro	1,005	1,306	1,305	1,328
– Iwaki	963	1,326	963	1,069
Dewa				
– Ugo	872	1,232	1,239	1,295
– Uzen	816	1,195	1,204	1,249
Kantō Region				
Hitachi	1,546	1,677	1,723	1,848
Shimotsuke	1,133	1,359	1,365	1,304
Kōzuke	1,058	1,213	1,217	1,265
Shimousa	928	1,186	1,623	2,074
Kazusa	–	1,149	1,194	1,205
Awa	–	272	280	247
Musashi	2,425	2,987	3,042	3,028
Sagami	605	679	671	678
Chūbu Region				
Izu	–	285	284	283
Suruga	725	795	780	860
Tōtōmi	–	1,093	1,094	1,239
Mikawa	–	1,267	1,292	1,494
Kai	730	849	769	772
Shinano	–	1,697	1,615	1,774
Hida	–	414	414	416
Mino	1,245	1,631	1,602	1,507
Sado	251	260	261	262
Echigo	2,779	3,964	4,051	4,409
Ecchū	1,372	1,441	1,376	1,591

(*Continued*)

Table 7.1: (*Continued*)

Province	1645	1697	1829	1873
Noto	644	681	666	871
Kaga	745	770	768	1,021
Echizen	–	1,541	1,533	1,537
Wakasa	–	255	255	253
Kinki Region				
Ōmi	1,357	1,516	1,516	1,579
Ise	1,166	1,400	1,325	1,324
Shima	56	56	56	56
Iga	182	182	182	182
Kii	–	1,413	1,337	1,369
Settsu	–	870	955	1,285
Izumi	–	317	320	341
Kawachi	–	511	545	551
Yamato	–	1,405	1,354	1,441
Yamashiro	–	450	477	484
Tamba	786	902	880	1,040
Harima	–	1,800	1,796	1,847
Awaji	234	238	251	258
Chūgoku Region				
Tango	293	392	388	412
Tajima	–	627	623	683
Mimasaka	592	592	628	771
Bizen	620	648	673	680
Bicchū	–	464	484	542
Bingo	460	530	530	563
Aki	433	436	436	522
Suo	152	178	252	296
Nagato	149	173	150	295
Inaba	515	535	553	561
Hōki	703	710	754	778
Izumo	500	504	504	561
Iwami	–	489	451	547
Oki	61	61	61	61
Shikoku Region				
Awa	417	455	455	585
Sanuki	–	385	377	394
Iyo	–	959	955	971
Tosa	463	1,076	1,076	426

(*Continued*)

Table 7.1: (Continued)

Province	1645	1697	1829	1873
Kyūshū Region				
Chikuzen	–	901	901	847
Chikugo	–	709	710	789
Bungo	–	1,516	1,473	1,812
Buzen	–	668	677	771
Hizen	–	1,418	1,400	849
Higo	–	1,124	1,116	1,910
Hyūga	–	398	483	376
Ōsumi	223	230	230	242
Satsuma	–	258	258	309
Iki	27	50	50	22
Sum				
41 Provinces with 1645 data	30,260	36,446	37,124	39,461
(increase)		(+6,186)	(+678)	(+2,337)
30 Provinces lacking 1645 data	–	25,357	25,355	27,269
(increase)		(?)	(−2)	(+1,914)
sum	–	61,803	62,479	66,730
(increase)		(?)	(+676)	(+4,251)

Source: Kikuchi (1963: 223–225). Numbers in the table are based on the national survey by the Tokugawa government, whilest some provinces lacking the data in 1645.

villages. In the second case, from 1829 to 1873, the number of villages rose from 62,479 to 66,730. It should also be noted, however, that villages were occasionally divided or integrated for purely political reasons. The figures mentioned above possibly reflect the two great waves of settlement and reclamation, which involved significant economic and political changes: firstly, the shift from a medieval society to the Tokugawa regime, and secondly, to the Meiji Restoration and the Japanese industrial revolution. The amount of reclaimed land is also believed to have had two peaks, reaching one million *cho* (or 9,917 square kilometers) in both the seventeenth and nineteenth centuries (Table 7.2), although early numbers regarding acreage are imprecise. This observation is reinforced by rough estimates of the number of irrigation projects implemented for the reclamation (Table 7.3). In short, the seventeenth and nineteenth centuries were eras of great land reclamation, whilest the eighteenth century was characterized by stagflation.

The distinct pattern of land reclamation—a rise followed by a plateau, and then another rise—reflects demographic changes and the exploitation politics of the time. Firstly, recent historical demographic findings suggest that an increase

Table 7.2: Acreage from the seventeenth through nineteenth centuries.

$$(1 \ cho = 0.00992 \ km^2)$$

Year	Area (*cho*)	Source
c. 1600 (a)	1,635,000	Ōishi (1975: 28)
	2,000,000	Kimura (1964: 4)
	2,065,000	Hayami and Miyamoto (1988: 44)
	2,060,000	Kikuchi (1963: 3)
c. 1720 (b)	2,970,780	*Chōbu shimogumi chō* (Ōkurashō 1926: 216–265)
Early 19th century (c)	3,233,408	Meiji Zaiseishi Hensan Iinkai (1904: 361–378)
1873–1881 (d)	4,129,771	Meiji Zaiseishi Hensan Iinkai (1904: 361–378)

(a) The amount in the beginning of early modern times lacks any record. It has been sur-mised by scholars based on *kokudaka* or the estimated productivity of land at the Toyo-tomi Land Survey, c.1600.

(b) Presumably an official calculation by the Tokugawa government. Not including Tsushima Province lacking original data.

(c) *Kyū tanbetsu* or the 'former acrage' calculated after *Chiso Kaisei* or the Rivision of Land Tax, 1873–1881. The 'former acrage' is supposed to inherit largely the figures on the land surveys during the late Tokugawa regume (Fukushima 1975: 231–232).

(d) The Grand Land Survey at the Rivision of Land Tax, 1873–1881 (Meiji Zaiseishi Hensan Iinkai 1904: 380–387).

Table 7.3: Number of new irrigation projects and *shinden*.

	Reservoir	Ditch	Shinden
1551–1600	3	11	14
1601–1650	66	55	122
1651–1700	93	121	220
1701–1750	27	52	103
1751–1800	23	31	88
1801–1867	99	139	450
Sum	311	409	997

Source: Kimura (1964: 5) and Hayami and Miyamoto (1988: 45). The number caluculated here is based on the cases pre-sented in Doboku Gakkai (1936).

in population was both the cause and consequence of the great land reclamation. Table 7.4 presents two distinctive rises in population. The first was a 'popula-tion explosion' in which the existing twelve million people were joined by nearly twenty million more in the seventeenth century, and secondly, an increase of approximately ten million people in the late nineteenth century. Due to the lack

Table 7.4: Estimated change in regional population.

(1,000 persons)

Region (1)	Hokkaidō	Tōhoku	Kantō	Chūbu	Kinki	Chūgoku	Shikoku	Kyūshū	Sum (2)
1600	7.1	1,072.9	2,018.9	2,373.6	3,682.1	1,227.3	625.0	1,266.1	12,273.0
1721	18.7	3,408.6	6,148.4	6,491.6	6,080.0	3,602.9	1,838.6	3,689.8	31,278.5
1750	26.2	3,218.9	6,056.8	6,586.9	5,767.5	3,681.4	1,874.7	3,798.4	31,010.8
1756	27.2	3,173.5	5,972.3	6,666.4	5,899.0	3,758.6	1,929.0	3,856.3	31,282.5
1786	31.6	2,842.4	5,250.8	6,577.5	5,663.5	3,872.7	1,993.8	3,871.5	30,103.8
1792	32.9	2,862.0	5,161.5	6,503.9	5,568.6	3,862.7	1,989.4	3,888.9	29,869.7
1798	34.5	2,930.5	5,220.6	6,836.1	5,582.9	4,033.2	2,043.1	3,884.6	30,565.2
1804	54.5	2,967.7	5,154.9	6,898.0	5,539.9	4,059.2	2,112.6	3,959.6	30,746.4
1822	74.3	3,071.9	5,091.4	7,378.1	5,725.3	4,297.2	2,235.9	4,039.6	31,913.5
1828	78.0	3,151.2	5,212.7	7,604.0	5,784.1	4,412.9	2,276.3	4,106.4	32,625.8
1834	81.4	3,157.7	5,004.5	7,574.3	5,709.9	4,489.7	2,319.4	4,139.7	32,476.7
1840	77.2	2,806.6	5,157.3	7,092.7	5,443.9	4,186.6	2,260.2	4,077.6	31,102.1
1846	85.1	3,024.4	5,326.1	7,391.9	5,605.1	4,371.3	2,331.8	4,161.7	32,297.4
1873	123.7	3,503.9	5,220.4	7,518.4	5,061.7	4,249.6	2,459.2	4,997.0	33,133.9
1880	163.5	3,781.6	5,820.3	8,011.0	5,445.3	4,496.4	2,620.2	5,265.1	35,603.3
1890	421.7	4,406.5	7,296.0	9,015.3	6,201.9	4,816.2	2,868.8	5,872.3	40,898.5

(1) Hokkaidō: Yezo Province. Tōhoku: Mutsu and Dewa Provinces. Kantō: Hitachi, Kōzuke, Shimotsuke, Awa, Kazusa, Shimousa, Musashi, and Sagami Provinces. Chūbu: Sado, Echigo, Ecchū, Noto, Kaga, Echizen, Wakasa, Kai, Shinano, Hida, Izu, Suruga, Tōtōmi, Mikawa, Owari, and Mino Provinces. Kinki: Yamato, Yamashiro, Settsu, Kawachi, Izumi, Ōmi, Iga, Ise, Shima, Kii, Awaji, and Harima Provinces. Chūgoku: Tango, Tajima, Inaba, Hōki, Oki, Izumo, Iwami, Mimasaka, Bizen, Bicchū, Bingo, Aki, Suō, and Nagato Provinces. Shikoku: Awa, Sanuki, Iyo, and Tosa Provinces. Kyūshū: Chikuzen, Chikugo, Hizen, Iki, Tsushima, Buzen, Bungo, Higo, Hyūga, Ōsumi, and Satsuma Provinces.

(2) not including Ryūkyū Province.

Source: Kitō (2000: 16–17).

of reliable records prior to the national demographic survey of 1721, figures pertaining to the seventeenth century are calculated demographically. A clear parallel pattern of increases can be found in the number of villages (Table 7.1), the number of irrigation projects (Table 7.3) and the arable land area (Table 7.2). As Hiroshi Kitō (2000) argues, the first steep rise in population, which would have begun at some point in the fourteenth or fifteenth centuries, involved small-scale independent family farming, labor-intensive agriculture and the development of a market economy, and saw the population trebling in many regions between 1600 and 1721. On the other hand, a population plateau was reached in the eighteenth century, for a variety of reasons: the impact of a cooler climate in northeastern Japan (particularly in the Tōhoku and Kantō regions); the relocation of unmarried immigrants to Edo (now Tokyo) and Osaka; and the practicing of population control measures and infanticide in order to sustain economic growth. The increase that took place in the nineteenth century was the result of a recovery from the stagflation of the eighteenth century and reflected the beginning of modern industrialization, which continued for two centuries. Both periods of population growth were accompanied by increases in new arable lands and reclaimed lands.

Secondly, changes in exploitation politics with respect to *shinden* were crucial for land reclamation because those who planned exploitation were typically required to obtain permission from the Tokugawa government or that of their local feudal lord. Despite the desire of rulers to acquire more arable land, and thus increase their tax incomes, these governments found it necessary to shift their reclamation policies from encouragement to restriction in the late seventeenth and early eighteenth centuries. Faced with decreasing supplies of green manure and forage gathered from marshlands, swamps and woodlands, which were rapidly becoming arable lands, the existing villages and farmers began to demand the prohibition of new land reclamation. Accordingly, Morimitsu Tsuji, auditor of the Tokugawa government in the early eighteenth century, issued the following statement (Kikuchi 1963: 16):

> Although it is admirable to reclaim new land, there are no spaces for exploitation today because all lands that could be *shinden* were already reclaimed sixty or seventy years ago. In recent years we have received many requests to exploit grasslands where peasants gather fertilizer and forage for their horses. To transform these lands into arable lands is disagreeable because it reduces the fertility of existing fields and hinders the breeding of horses.

It is evident from Tsuji's discourse that the deceleration of *shinden* in the eighteenth century was not due to a lack of uncultivated space but rather to the need to maintain a certain area for subsistent agriculture, which was greatly dependent on green fertilizer. Governments were therefore able to allow new reclamation only if neighboring villages did not object. The second rise in the nineteenth century was, as suggested by Motoi Kimura (1964: 6), achieved thanks to the general introduction of fish fertilizer and increased farmers' income from cash crops, which made it possible to purchase the fertilizer. Thus, the change from green manure to a purchasable one led to another rise.

Expansion into drier and wetter conditions

The geological conditions targeted by early modern reclamation and, alternatively, the types of land that were restricted until the seventeenth century and then permitted in order to allow the population explosion, are certainly open to question. The case of the Kantō region, where the population tripled in the period from 1600 to 1721 (see Table 7.4), indicates the typical geology of new villages at the time. As shown in Figure 7.1, the new *shinden* villages were predominantly located on river terraces and alluvial plains, with a few settlements in the mountainous areas (Fukuda 1986). For centuries, river terraces had been maintained as woodland or grassland and not used for human habitation due to their lack of drinking water. It should be noted that since the Japanese population had not developed pasturage for religious reasons, the dry terraces that were inappropriate for habitation had held no interest except for the purposes hunting for game such as wild boar, deer and hares and the gathering of green manure, mushrooms, fiddleheads, etc. A Portuguese missionary named João Rodrigues, who lived in Japan from 1577 to 1610, recorded the following (Cooper 2001: 88):

> There is a large desert or plain called Musashi-no, that is, Musashi Field, in this Kingdom [Musashi Province], and it is covered with hay and grass without a single grove of trees... There are many mountain pigs or boars in this desert as well as much hunting of innumerable animals, wild ducks that come from Tartary in the winter, many cranes, swans, etc.

The conversion of river terraces into arable lands essentially required new aqueducts or irrigation systems. Finally, it was the Tamagawa Canal, constructed in the 1650s, with its many branch streams, that transformed Musashino Terrace into an open landscape with new settlements and arable fields.

The back marshes, swamps and flood plains that lay along the lower rivers had also been excluded from human occupation until the Japanese learned how to artificially control the strong flow and flooding of the rivers. The case of the central area of the Kantō region exemplifies the struggle between rivers and humans. A series of enterprises that involved the construction of new canals and dikes (the most important canals are presented in Figure 7.1), approved by local lords and the Tokugawa government for the purpose of defending the new capital city Edo, and water carriages and drainage systems for land reclamation, were carried out between 1594 and 1654. These constructions integrated a network of many small

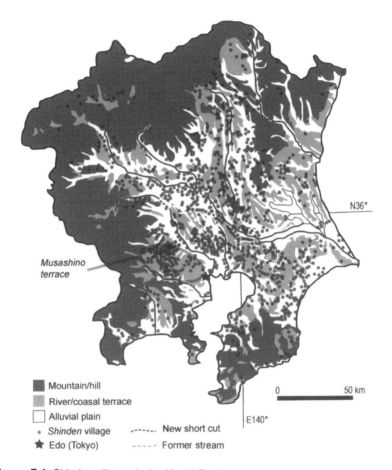

Figure 7.1: Shinden villages in the Kantō Region.
Source: Fukuda (1986: 108), Geographical Survey Institute (1990: plate 2.1), Harada (1999: 15).

streams that led them to rivers which, in turn, carried the water directly to the sea. Once several streams had been dammed to construct irrigated reservoirs, the marshes and swamps in the northern plain of Edo were converted into rice paddy fields or controlled 'artificial swamps' with numerous new settlements. In 1878 an English traveler named Isabella Bird observed the landscape on her travels from Edo (Tokyo) to Nikkō (Bird 1973: 36–37) as follows:

> The country is a dead level, and mainly an artificial mud flat or swamp, in whose fertile ooze various aquatic birds were wading, and in which hundreds of men and women were wading too, above their knees in slush; for this plain of Yedo [Edo] is mainly a great rice-field, and this is the busy season of rice-planting...On the plain of Yedo, besides

the nearly continuous villages along the causewayed road, there are islands, as they may be called, of villages surrounded by trees, and hundreds of pleasant oases on which wheat ready for the sickle, onions, millets, beans, and peas, were flourishing.

Dry river terraces and wet marshes in plains were both important expansion targets for habitation purposes in early modern Japan, whereas the medieval population had not completely conquered the over-dry or over-wet areas. As shown by Harada (1999), the medieval villages in the Kantō region generally had three types of landscapes within which inhabitants were safe from flood flows and enjoyed easy access to water: (i) at the foot of mountains with adequate spring water, (ii) within a small valley near the brink of terraces or tableland, or (iii) on a natural levee surrounded by swamps. Compared with western Japan, with its relatively developed irrigation systems that allowed the exploitation of terraces, the case of the Kantō Region illustrates the typical distinction between the medieval and early modern landscapes used for settlements. The Kantō region had an enormous amount of space potentially available for reclamation, while demand for food suppliers increased rapidly in the areas surrounding the capital city, Edo. Numerous cases of *shinden* can be observed in all of Japan's regions, however, with the exceptions of colonial Okinawa and Hokkaidō. The next section looks at various cases regarding the effects of settlements and the new landscapes they created.

Landscapes of *shinden*

The planning and construction of new settlements left visible features in the landscape. In settlements located on terraces or plains, geometrically ordered landscapes were particularly essential, not only for planning irrigation or drainage systems but also due to the apportionment of land among the participants or subscribers of reclamation projects. One case concerning a dry terrace and two cases involving wet plains are introduced below, while one characteristic case involving rice paddy stairs in a mountainous area is discussed toward the end of the section.

On river terraces

The first case, which concerns Ogawa Village in Musashi Province, on the Musashino terrace (Figure 7.2; now Ogawa-chō, Kodaira City, Tokyo), highlights the typical landscapes of a 'road-village' (Kikuchi 1963: 160–162). Ogawa Village dates back to 1656 when a farmer named Krobē Ogawa submitted a request to the local government of Tokugawa for a new reclamation of woodland. Ogawa was a wealthy farmer who owned 3.6 *cho* (0.036 km²) of arable lands and had several servants, and a resident of the village of Kishi, an old settlement located at the

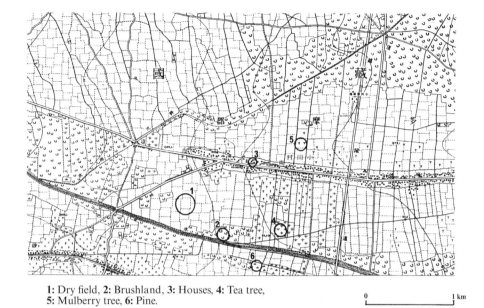

1: Dry field, 2: Brushland, 3: Houses, 4: Tea tree,
5: Mulberry tree, 6: Pine.

0   1 km

Figure 7.2: Ogawa village.
Source: Topographical map "Ogawa Mura" (1: 20,000), 1896.

foot of a small hill on the terrace. His project depended on two factors. The first of these was the aqueduct system of Tamagawa Canal, originally constructed in 1654 to supply water to Edo, and the second was Ōme Highway, which conveyed fuel and lime to Edo from the western mountains. Expecting a subordinate income from transportation labor on the highway, Ogawa excavated a small stream from the canal along the highway in 1657 to create a supply of drinking water. At least 114 families had applied for settlement by 1680 and were obligated to pay rent to Ogawa's family. The total exploited area reached 92 *cho* (0.91 km²) by 1664, 183 *cho* (1.81 km²) by 1669, 330 *cho* (3.27 km²) by 1674 and 394 *cho* (3.91 km²) by 1689, although it did not include any rice paddy due to the limited supply of water, a feature that remains to this day. A map from 1791 (Figure 7.3) illustrates the new landscape of a road-village, which resembled a German Waldhufendorf in shape. One hundred and six farmers' houses were located along the highway, behind which were strip-shaped lands that were 250 *ken* (453 meters) in length and 10 *ken* (18.2 meters) or more in width. This strip-shaped village was typical of *shinden* located on terraces.

Drainage of marshland

The second case concerns the drainage of a lagoon known as Shiunji-gata (Figure 7.4) in the Echigo Province (now Shiunji Town, Niigata Prefecture) and highlights a typical reclamation project that involves marshland lying beside lower

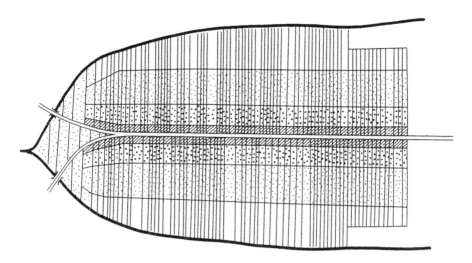

Figure 7.3: Map of Ogawa village (1719).
Source: Kikuchi (1963: 161).

rivers (Kikuchi 1963: 89–93). Following several failed drainage projects by the local Domain of Shibata, a mine proprietor named Gonbē Takemae presented a reclamation plan in 1726 that had three objectives: new ditches for a drainage system that would cut across the Niigata dune and flow around and within the lagoon, a new dike closing River Sakai or the existing outlet of the lagoon, and a new irrigation canal. With the Tokugawa government's authorization and the support of an experienced engineer named Yasobē Izawa, dispatched by the government, the project was completed successfully in 1734. Furthermore, 740 peasant families, 42 villages, and 1,996 *cho* (19.79 km²) of arable land were registered in 1736. Covering the unexpected expenses ended up bankrupting the planner, Takemae, but the government was able to sell the lands to local merchants, who became landowners, with many peasants under their dominion. Figure 7.4 demonstrates the technical achievements of the time in terms of water control and new landscapes. There were new settlements along the banks of the former lagoon, and the newly exploited rice paddy fields were divided into strip-shaped areas of land that ran parallel to the drainage ditch. Lineal houses or villages controlling a bundle of oblong-shaped lands were typical in Japan's early modern *shinden* landscapes, although a rectangular pattern was also used, as illustrated in the next case.

Drainage of tidal flats

The third case concerns approximately 50 estates of Settsu-Kawaguchi Shinden (Figure 7.5) located on and beside the estuary of the Yodo River in Settsu

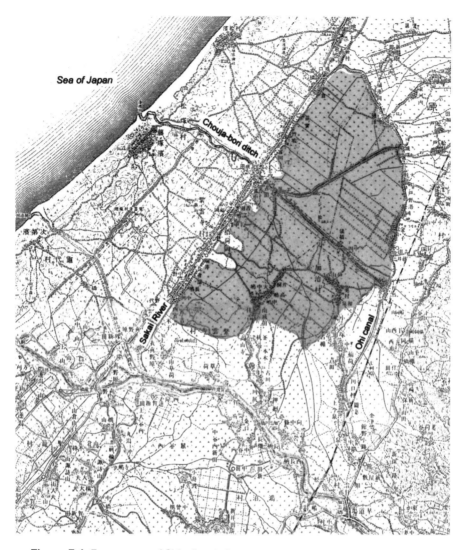

Figure 7.4: Former area of Shiunji-gata Lagoon.
Gray area: Former Shiunji-gata.
Source: Topographical map "Nakajo" and "Shibata" (1: 50,000), 1913.

Province (now Osaka City, Osaka Prefecture), and involves one of the largest capitalistic projects of the time for creating a drainage system (T. Fujita 1989: 411–422; Kimura 1964: 151–157). The tidal flat that grew continually westward of Osaka's Uemachi terrace was an excellent target for investment by Osaka merchants. In 1698 the Tokugawa government appointed three officers as directors of the reclamation of the estuary area and called for merchants to invest their own funds towards the draining of the flat. Many merchants in Osaka and other cities

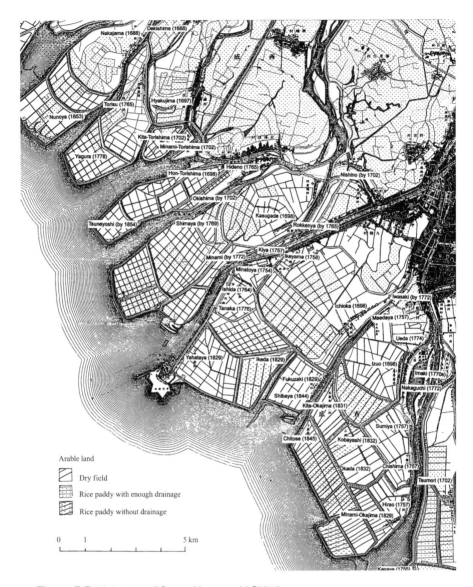

Figure 7.5: Main area of Settsu Kawaguchi Shinden.
Source: Topographical map (1: 20,000), "Amagasaki", 1898 and "Temupozan", 1877.

answered the call and, as a result, became owners of the embanked estates. By 1702, 14 *shinden* estates of approximately 450 *cho* (4.46 km²) had been added to the nine antecedents reclaimed between 1596 and 1647. Twenty-one more farms emerged by 1780 and 13 followed by 1854. In total, at least 2,000 *cho* (19.8 km²) of mud flats was transformed into arable fields.

Development of new lands was not only supported by capital provided by merchants but also by technical advancements related to dikes and lockage. In the early eighteenth century, stonewalling dikes were used to replace mounds, while a system of lockage with gates—which were designed to be vertically mobile by using pulleys—was installed to drain water at low tide. Figure 7.5 presents the names of various *shinden*, with their year of construction in parentheses. The patchwork landscape of parallelograms of these *shinden* was marked by ditches, with lineal settlements on the dikes. The prevalence of salty soil, however, along with the lack of pure drinking water and the frequent bursts of water through the dikes, combined to restrict the development of rice paddy fields and settlements. As recently as 1877, many farms included dry fields (the white areas in Figure 7.5) that provided the urban population with vegetables and cotton. These *shinden* villages based on landlordism were not official 'villages' but rather private 'estates' that belonged to merchants, in which peasants did not have the opportunity to improve their 'own' lands or form social organizations.

More expansion: Aggregation of micro-reclamation

The three abovementioned cases represent the macro-reclamation of a vast area of new lands and communities, but many micro-reclamation projects were taking place throughout the country at the same time as a result of individual efforts, although these did not result in the official addition of any new villages. This type of micro-*shinden* was called '*kiri-zoe*' or '*mochi-zoe*,' which means additions to private property. The contribution of micro-reclamation to the aggressive increase in arable acreage was just as significant as that of macro-reclamation. The case of a mountain village named Shimo-hiramaru (Figure 7.6) in the Echigo Province (now Myōko City, Niigata Prefecture) illustrates the aggregation of small-scale hillside exploitation efforts. Shimo-hiramaru occupied a slope of Kubiki Hill and continued to transform the hillside, which was prone to landslides, into arable fields, including many shreds of *tanada* or rice paddy stairs. Based on the land registers of 1683, 1724 and 1780, Tsutomu Igarashi (1983) presented a case study of progressive land reclamation through a handwritten map from 1869 (Figure 7.7). The map covers the area from the main settlement, at an altitude of 320–400 meters, to the surrounding slopes and the northern base of a new community called Subundo, located at an altitude of 500–550 meters. By relocating or commuting to Subundo, lower-class peasants had, by 1724, added 19.2 *cho* (0.19 km²) of arable lands surrounding Subundo to the existing 6.9 *cho* (0.07 km²) of lands. Most of the new lands were shifting cultivation or swidden fields, which offered peasants a new means of livelihood without requiring a great deal of expensive investment. By 1778, another increase of 26.5 *cho* (0.26 km²) in arable lands and the conversion of 2.6 *cho* (0.026 km²) of existing land into paddy terraces had been achieved. Hillside rice paddy stairs did not require large-scale irrigation mechanisms and entailed less personal effort during construction than

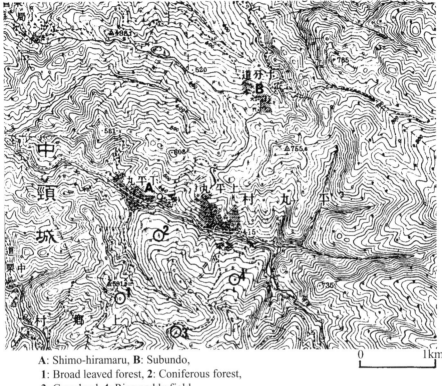

A: Shimo-hiramaru, **B**: Subundo,
  1: Broad leaved forest, **2**: Coniferous forest,
  3: Grassland, **4**: Rice paddy field.
Blank area without any symbol represents arble field

Figure 7.6: Shimo-hiramaru village.
Source: Topographical map "Iiyama" (1: 50,000), 1930.

did paddy fields on alluvial plains. They also provided peasants with an important means for remaining independent. However, the reclamation of hillsides was restricted by the lack of green manure, which prevented the village from expanding swidden or other fields after 1780.

Changing natural land cover

The growth in population and acreage of arable lands had a severe impact on the natural woodland and forests. Huge demand for timber, woody fuel, and green manure led to drastic changes in the natural land cover of early modern Japan. The extreme use of biomass, which did not allow the natural recovery of vegetation, caused thinner second growth and sometimes led to bald landscapes in both suburban and mountainous areas. As demonstrated by Yoshihisa Fujita (1995a: iii, 1995b), it is possible to reconstruct mid-nineteenth century

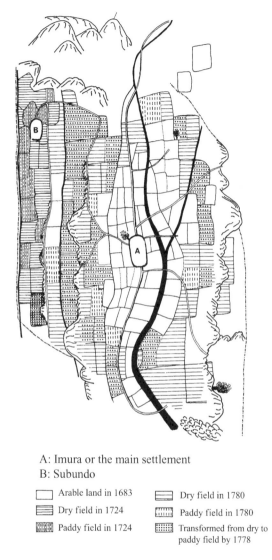

A: Imura or the main settlement
B: Subundo

☐ Arable land in 1683   ▤ Dry field in 1780

▤ Dry field in 1724   ▦ Paddy field in 1780

▦ Paddy field in 1724   ▦ Transformed from dry to paddy field by 1778

Figure 7.7: Progressive land reclamation in Shimo-hiramaru.
Source: Igarashi (1983: 449).

land cover through topographic maps based on the modern Ordnance Surveys of the early twentieth century. Figure 7.8 demonstrates that, by the end of the nineteenth century, most areas that had been covered by original vegetation were converted into second-growth pine forests, grassland for green manure or bald land, particularly in western Japan. As demonstrated by environmental archaeologists (Yasuda 1985; Tsuji 1997), palynological records suggest the

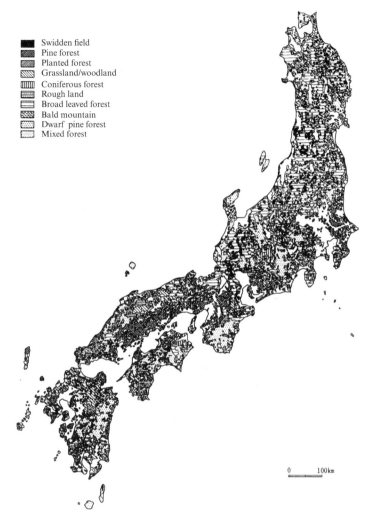

Swidden field
Pine forest
Planted forest
Grassland/woodland
Coniferous forest
Rough land
Broad leaved forest
Bald mountain
Dwarf pine forest
Mixed forest

0   100km

Figure 7.8: Forest, wooland and grassland in the mid-nineteenth century.
Source: Fujita (1995a: iii).

occurrence of drastic changes in land cover. These records indicate an accelerated expansion of pine trees from the last century of the medieval period through to early modern times, although pines had been spreading since rice cultivation began in ancient times. The pine or grass landscapes on the hillsides surrounding Kyoto were also represented in many nineteenth century paintings (Ogura 1992). As shown in Chiba (1973, 1991), red pine (*Pinus densiflora*) serves as a typical index of human impact on Japanese natural vegetation because of its tendency to rapidly occupy open spaces, such as after logging of natural forests. It also continues to remain dominant when young trees are artificially cut for fuel or manure.

The emergence of vast areas of pinelands due to early modern human activities remains one of the most violent examples of destruction of original vegetation in Japan's history.

Control of *iriai* or 'tragedy of the commons'?

Changes in vegetation did not occur due to disordered usage of natural resources or the lack of any kind of control system. Instead, they took place under traditional spatial management, namely *iriai*[3], the system of commons. *Iriai* is the traditional relationship between Japanese people and nature wherein a village or a group of neighboring villages share and use certain areas under common rule, and it served to institutionalize membership, method and the spatial and temporal range of gathering, hunting and fishing. Some medieval historians claim that the need for control over natural resources encouraged the social formation of local village communities in medieval times (Tamura 1994; Mizuno 2000; Takagi 2008). Guarding natural spaces from other communities and strangers helped determine the destiny of every local society during both medieval and early modern times. The question of what happened within these controlled spaces is discussed below.

In the mid-seventeenth century, the Tokugawa and local feudal governments observed that trees were being uprooted so frequently that huge amounts of sand and stones were being carried down into streams. For example, Tokugawa dignitaries proclaimed the following in 1660 (Tsukamoto 1993: 192–193): 'Because of the extraction of trees from hillsides in Yamashiro, Yamato and Iga Provinces, dirt is overwhelming the River Yodo and Yamato with flood flow. Henceforward, disrooting must be prohibited; afforestation must be promoted.' This announcement reflects the fact that vegetation in the Kinki Region had become so thin that people were resorting to digging out roots for fuel. In 1709 a Confucian named Banzan Kumazawa also forewarned that 'a disrooted mountain remains bald for thirty or fifty years even if under conservation' (Chiba 1991: 141–142). According to Kumazawa's observation, an excessive number of poor people were forced to cut or dig up trees in order to obtain their daily food and fuel, and therefore the implementation of a conservative policy was never realistic. In 1722 a Tokugawa officer discussed the problem of overuse in *iriai* forests in an administrative essay (Takimoto 1923: 256–257), describing it as a 'tragedy of the commons' (Hardin 1968).

> In a local commons, the members dig out roots of trees so competitively that no young trees are able to grow, because all members may use *iriai* forest. This creates a lack of timber for public or personal use. If one peasant takes a rest due to illness, no one leaves green manure or fuel for him. In this case, forest commons could be divided into private property according to one's status. Every peasant can afforest and manage the gathering of manure or fuels under their hands whenever

they need to do so. Trees grow up to be available for construction of houses. Division of ownership is good and should be promoted unless it presents a problem.

In the officer's opinion, the overuse of commons had an irreversible impact on vegetation. In the Kansai region, at least, bald mountains overlapped with *iriai* space (see Figure 7.9). However, the appropriation of *iriai* as private property

Figure 7.9: Bald mountains and commons around Osaka in the 1890s.
Source: Chiba (1973: 165).

would lead to the trade of tenancy, which would mean that an even higher number of poor people would lack the right to use natural resources.

Bald mountains, those without any trees, were not necessarily unsuitable or 'destructive' for some peasants, although governments at the time were seeking a solution to the problem of floods. Minami and Hisatake (2001) traced an interesting case from the early twentieth century in which the local people in the Okayama Prefecture had opposed the promotion of afforestation for river control. The local peasants believed that afforestation on the mountain would obstruct the flow of water into streams and reduce the amount of irrigation water available for arable lands. Faced with such a strong claim, the foresters were required to conduct a series of experiments, which eventually supported the peasants' assertions. Mountains or hillsides with thin vegetation functioned as rainwater catchments, which provided downstream areas with water for irrigation. The bald landscapes of the early modern period, therefore, were not necessarily an undesirable by-product. On the contrary such landscapes were sometimes even the result of the intentional conversion of natural woody landscapes. In other words, increases in the number of villages, population, and agricultural economy in the lower areas brought about drastic changes, both accidental and intentional, to the natural vegetation.

From lord's forestry to agro-forestry

Population increase and economic development of urban areas in the seventeenth century also encouraged the timber industry, which rapidly changed the landscape of deep mountains. Enormous amounts of timber were systematically cut and transported through rivers (Totman 1995), and the timber industry became such an important part of the economy, in fact, that many feudal lords advocated enclosing deep mountains and transforming rivers into logging streams for timber rafts in order to monopolize the timber industry as 'lord's forestry'. One typical case was the upper region of the River Kiso in the Owari (Nagoya) Domain, (now the southwestern part of Nagano Prefecture), which served as a good timber repository, particularly for *hinoki* or Japanese cypress (*Chamaecyparis obtuse*). A Confucian named Ekiken Kaibara observed during his journey of 1709 that 'thousands of loggers' (Y. Fujita 1995a: 90) congregated in the Kiso mountains, and myriad timber rafts could be seen traveling down the Kiso River. However, as Yoshihisa Fujita (1995a: 86–120) argues, the systematic lord's forestry served only to exhaust the timberland within a century. Owari Domain was forced to reduce the size of its timber industry in the early part of the eighteenth century and shift to a more conservative policy due to the depletion of its forests. Almost all of the upper areas of the Kiso River were reserved for natural regeneration, where logging was prohibited along with gathering and hunting by local people. In the late seventeenth and early eighteenth centuries, many feudal domains that contained rivers for transportation exhausted the enclosed timberlands within their territories and therefore began to conserve those mountains that lacked mature trees. Because the lords were forced to wait for cypress or cedar trees to re-grow, the lord's forestry never regained economic viability. The decrease in timber supply did, however, encourage another timber industry, that of systematic plantation forestry.

One of the first established afforestation systems was achieved through shifting cultivation or swidden agriculture in the mountainous regions in which the monopolistic lord's forestry had not developed. The case of the upper part of the Kino (Yoshino) River, Yoshino County in Yamato Province (Nara Prefecture), illustrates how mountain dwellers managed to succeed in plantation forestry and change the original vegetation into artificial forests (Izumi 1992; Fujita 1998; Komeie 2005). The conditions in Yoshino County, with its warm and wet climate and excellent logging stream, the Kino River, which connected the area to Osaka, are favorable for forestry. With an increase in the demand for timber in the late seventeenth century, plantations for *sugi* or Japanese cedar (*Cryptomeria japonica*) derived from swidden plantation of tea, Japanese lacquer, and paper mulberry, became widespread. Swidden agriculturists in the region cultivated not only millets and vegetables but also trees that were able to grow on fallow land. Shifting cultivators referred to both swidden fields and cedar forests as *yama-bata* or 'mountain fields.' A patchwork landscape made up of many small compartments of cedar plots (Figure 7.10) was generated from the small-scale shifting cultivation or agro-forestry carried out by peasants.

Two devices supported the evolution from swidden to afforestation, the first of which was the commons system of villages, which made it possible for peasants to use the mountain space surrounding their settlements as swidden, and consequently develop cedar plantations. Cultivators were required to pay soy beans or money as a fee to their villages in order to maintain the system. The second device was the high-density planting of trees in a small area. Because the cedar plants grew to maturity over the course of twenty-five or thirty years, mountains dwellers could not use the space for agriculture, but they could earn their livelihood by slowly but steadily cutting off parts of the young trees, thus gradually reducing the density of the trees. In early modern Japan, however, this kind of plantation forestry succeeded only in those mountainous regions that were not monopolized by major lords and that were connected through rivers with the urban areas of Osaka, Kyoto, Nagoya, and Edo. On the other hand, the Yoshino style of forestry became a model for modern foresters in the late nineteenth and twentieth centuries (Fujita 1995a).

As shown above, early modern Japan witnessed not only an enormous increase in the amount of new arable land and the number of settlements but also severe impacts on the natural landscapes surrounding its settlements. It is often believed that the most drastic changes in Japan's landscape took place during the twentieth century, but in fact the changes in early modern Japan, particularly in the seventeenth century, are among the country's greatest landscape changes. The previous landscape should therefore be treated as if it were a different country altogether. In that era, numerous natural spaces were converted into domesticated

Figure 7.10: An aerial photo of Ido, Kawakami village, Nara prefecture.
Aerial photo CKK 76-4, 1976.
With permission of the Geographical Survey Institute, Japan.

cultural landscapes or second-growth land. This was the time when the Japanese people discovered that human activities could irreversibly and unexpectedly alter the natural landscape.

Notes

1. Nowadays, the word *kaihotsu* is pronounced as *kaihatsu* in Japanese.
2. The Japanese word *shinden* literally means new (shin-) arable land (-den).
3. The word *iriai* originally meant several villages or communities using an area of forest or sea.

Bibliography

Akaha, Takishi (ed.) (1984), *Meiji nōsho zenshū* (*Agricultural literatures in Meiji Period*), Vol. 13, Tokyo: Nōsangyoson Bunka Kyōkai.

Bird, Isabella L. (1973), *Unbeaten Tracks in Japan: An Account of Travels in the Interior including Visits to the Aborigines of Yezo and the Shrines of Nikko*, Tokyo: Charles E. Tuttle Co.

Chiba, Tokuji (1973), *Hageyama no bunka* (A culture of bald mountain), Tokyo: Gakuseisha.

——— (1991), *Hageyama no kenkyū* (A study on bald mountain), revised version, Tokyo: Soshiete.

Cooper, Michael (ed.) (2001), *João Rodrigues's Account of Sixteenth-century Japan*, London: The Hakluyt Society.

Doboku-Gakkai (ed.) (1936), *Meiji-izen Nippon doboku-shi* (An history of Japanese civil engineering before Meiji Era), Tokyo: Iwanami Shoten.

Fujita, Teiichirō (1989), 'Shinden kaihatsu (Land reclamation)', in Shinshū Osaka-shishi Hensan Iinkai (ed.), *Shinshū Osaka-shishi* (New edition of Osaka City history), Vol. 3, Osaka: Osaka City, pp. 411–422.

Fujita, Yoshihisa (1995a), *Nippon ikusei ringyō chiiki keisei ron* (The making of plantation forestry regions), Tokyo: Kokon Shoin.

——— (1995b), 'Kinsei-matsu (1850 nen goro) no rin'ya riyō (Forest use circa 1850)', in Yukio Himiyama et al. (eds.), *Atlas: Nippon rettō no kankyō henka* (Atlas: Environmental change in modern Japan), Tokyo: Asakura Shoten, pp. 78–79.

——— (1998), *Yoshino ringyō chitai* (Timber region of Yoshino), Tokyo: Kokon Shoin.

Fukuda, Tōru (1986), *Kinshei shinden to sono genryū* (Early modern land reclamation and its origin), Tokyo: Kokon Shoin.

Fukushima, Masao (1975), 'Kin-gendai (Modern times)', in Masamoto Kitajima (ed.), *Tochi seidoshi* (A history of the institution of land), Vol. II, Tokyo: Yamakawa Shuppansha, pp. 195–394.

Geographical Survey Institute (1990), *The National Atlas of Japan*, revised edition, Tokyo: Japan Map Centre.

Harada, Nobuo (1999), *Chūsei sonraku no keikan to seikatsu* (Landscape and life of medieval settlements), Kyoto: Shibunkaku Shuppan.

Hardin, Garrett (1968), The tragedy of the commons, *Science*, 162, pp. 1243–1248.

Hayami, Akira and Miyamoto, Matao (1988), 'Gaisetsu: 17–18 seiki (An overview: Seventeenth and eighteenth centuries)', in Akira Hayami and Matao Miyamoto (eds.), *Keizaishakai no seiritsu* (Establishment of economic society), Tokyo: Iwanami Shoten, pp. 1–84.

Igarashi, Tsutomu (1983), Kinsei sanson ni okeru kōchi kaihatsu to sonraku kōzō (Land reclamation and social structure in early modern mountain village), *Jimbun chiri* (Japanese journal of human geography), 35 (5), pp. 51–69.

Izumi, Eiji (1992), Yoshino ringyō no tenkai katei (Development process of Yoshino foresty), *Ehime daigaku nōgakubu kiyō* (Bulletin of Faculty of Agriculture, Ehime University), 36 (2), pp. 305–463.

Kadokawa Shoten (ed.) (2002), *Kadokawa Nippon chimei daijiten CD-ROM* (Kadokawa gazetteer of Japan CD-ROM), Tokyo: Kadokawa Shoten.

Kikuchi, Toshio (1958), *Shinden kaihatsu* (Land reclamation), Tokyo: Kokon Shoin.

——— (1963), *Shinden kaihatsu* (Land reclamation), Tokyo: Shibundo.

——— (1986), *Zoku shinden kaihatsu: Jirei-hen* (Land reclamation volume two: Case studies), Tokyo: Kokon Shoin.

Kimura, Motoi (1964), *Kinsei no shinden mura* (New settlements in early modern times), Tokyo: Yoshikawa Kōbunkan.

Kimura, Motoi and Itō, Kōichi (1960), *Shinden sonraku: Musashino to sono shūhen* (New settlements: Musashino and its surroundings), Tokyo: Bungadō Shoten.

Kitamura, Toshio (1981), *Shinden sonraku no shiteki tenkai to tochi mondai* (Historical development and land issue in new settlements), Tokyo: Iwanami Shoten.

Kitō, Hiroshi (2000), *Jinkō kara yomu Nippon no rekishi* (Japanese history from the viewpoint of demography), Tokyo: Kōdansha.

Komeie, Taisaku (2005), *Chū-kinsei sanson no keikan to kōzō* (Landscape and structure of medieval and early modern mountain villages), Tokyo: Azekura Shobō.

Meiji Zaiseishi Hensan Iinkai (ed.) (1904), *Meiji zaiseishi* (A history of public finance in the Meiji Era), Vol.5, Tokyo: Maruzen.

Minami, Kazuhiko and Hisatake, Tetsuya (2001), 'Kanbatsu to hoanrin: Yamamoto Tokusaburō ron nōto (Drought and protection forest: A note on Tokusaburō Yamamoto)', *Kōnan daigaku kiyō: Bungaku-hen* (Memoir of Kōnan Univeristy: Letters Series), 117, pp. 84–138.

Mizurno, Shōji (2000), *Nippon chūsei no sonraku to shōen-sei* (Village and manor system in medieval Japan), Tokyo: Azekura Shobō.

Ogura, Jun'ichi (1992), *Ezu kara yomitoku hito to keikan no rekishi* (A history of human beings and landscapes shown in paintings), Kyoto: Yūzankaku Shuppan.

Ōishi, Shinzaburō (1975), 'Kinsei (Early modern times)', in Masamoto Kitajima (ed.), *Tochi seidoshi* (A history of the institution of land), Vol. II, Tokyo: Yamakawa Shuppansha, pp. 21–194.

Ōkurashō (ed.) (1926), *Dai Nippon sozeishi* (A history of Japanese tax), Vol. 1, Tokyo: Chōyōkai, pp. 216–265.

Takagi, T (2008), *Nippon chūsei chiiki kankyōshi no kenkyū* (A study on regional environmental history in medieval Japan), Tokyo: Azekyra Shobō.

Takimoto, Seiichi (ed.) (1923), *Zoku Nippon keizai sōsho* (The sequel to the corpus in Japanese economy), Vol. 2, Tokyo: Daitōkaku.

Tamura, Noriyoshi (1994), *Nippon chūsei sonraku keisei-shi no kenkyū* (A study on the making of Japanese medieval village), Tokyo: Azekyra Shobō.

Totman, Conrad (1995), *The Lumber Industry in Early Modern Japan*, Honolulu: University of Hawai'i Press.

Tsukamoto, Manabu (1993), *Chiisana rekishi to ōkina rekishi* (Micro-history and macro-history), Tokyo: Yoshikawa Kōbunkan.

Tsuji, Sei-ichirō (1997), 'Kantō-heiya ni okeru Yayoi-jidai ikō no shokusei-shi to ningen katsudō (Vegitational history in relation to human activities since the Yayoi Period in the Kanto Plain, Central Japan)', *Kokuritsu rekishi minzoku hakubutsukan kenkyū kiyō* (Bulletin of the National Museum of Japanese History), 72, pp. 103–138.

Yasuda, Yoshinori (1985), 'Mori no tami to shite no Nippon-jin no kūkan ninchi (Spatial cognition of Japanese as forest people), *Rekishi chirigaku kiyō* (Annals of the Association of Historical Geographers in Japan), 27, pp. 15–38.

CHAPTER 8

Modernization of the countryside

Taisaku KOMEIE

The Meiji Restoration of 1868, during which a political transition took place from the feudal Tokugawa government to a centralist government under the rule of Emperor Meiji, was a starting point for the modernization of Japan's landscape. Japan's incorporation into the world economy brought with it a steep rise in international trade, an industrial revolution in manufacturing and the pursuit of imperial expansion. Along with these developments was a major increase in the country's population from 33.3 million in 1873 to 83.9 million in 1950 (Kitō 2000: 16). Such political and economic changes had an impact on rural land use and land cover in the late nineteenth and early twentieth centuries (Table 8.1). Approximately, the area of paddy/dry fields rose from 41,000 square kilometers in 1870s to 59,000 square konometers in 1940s (compare Table 7.2 and Table 8.1). In particular, the colonization of Hokkaidō Island, the construction of new estates on uplands and growing international demand for silk led to a sharp increase in the amount of dry fields, pastureland and tree crops. Japan's final, and largest, land reclamation took place in the eras of Emperor Meiji (1868–1912) and Taishō (1912–1926).

Two major features of modern rural Japan are large migration and the development of commercial agriculture. One of the most important slogans of the Meiji government was *shokusan kōgyō*, the promotion of founding industries. This encouraged colonial expansion and also corporate reclamation and the operation of new farms and estates, in which aristocrats, politicians and the bourgeoisie attempted to introduce western methods of stockbreeding and pasturing. The Japanese people's eating habits changed too, in terms of publicly consuming pork, beef or cow's milk, which they had not done previously due to their Buddhist beliefs. In addition, the development of the silk filature industry and trade resulted in mulberry, tea, citrus and apple being planted in large quantities on uplands or hillsides, compared to the small number of these trees that had been cultivated in early modern times.

Agriculture was introduced to landscapes that had not previously been cultivated and, in addition, two 'improvements' were made to the existing cultivated lands that completely changed the landscape. The first improvement was the regulation, or geometrization, of small disorderly fields into larger rectangular ones. This project helped encourage the repartition of properties and intensive agriculture, but it also abolished the traditional use of lines to demarcate farmland

Table 8.1: Major agricultural land use in modern Japan.

(1,000 *cho***)**

Year	Paddy fields	Dry fields	Sum of paddy and dry fields	Grassland/ pastureland	Mulberry trees	Tee trees
1885	2,641	1,886	4,527	988	94*	–
1895	2,748	2,289	5,037	1,074	266	58
1905	2,827	2,389	5,216	1,158	340	50
1915	2,863	2,379	5,242	1,337	454	48
1925	2,954	2,754	5,708	1,633	549	44
1935	2,988	2,876	5,864	1,971	582	39
1945	2,994**	2,946**	5,940**	2,053**	242	32

Source: Nōrin Tōkei Kenkyūkai (1983: 4–16). 1,000 *cho* equals 9.92 km². * 1884, ** 1944.

boundaries, which had been useful resources for historico-geographical study. The second improvement was the afforestation of bald mountains, or 'rough land.' Enormous demand for timber encouraged the government to protect bald mountains in order to allow the regeneration of vegetation and the conservation of deep mountains as national forests.

This chapter presents an overview of the major cases involving newly created 'modern' landscapes, then shifts the focus to improvements effected in existing landscapes. This examination is significant because landscape changes brought about in this period can hinder this reconstruction of the pre-modern landscape.

The colonization of Hokkaidō

The colonization of Hokkaidō Island was one of the most important projects implemented by the Meiji government. The first reason for this is that the northern frontier of Japan was disputed land, claimed also by Russia. The second reason is that the island had the potential for the development of agriculture and mining, so it was sometimes used to accommodate redundant population groups, particularly former *samurai* soldiers who had lost their feudal privileges. This was the first case of colonization by the Japanese government with the intention of fully controlling a vast area of land in a modern manner. Most parts of Hokkaidō were uninhabited and were covered with wild forests or grasslands that could be cultivated by new Japanese immigrants. The southern peninsula, however, had been occupied by Japanese people since late medieval times. The native people of Hokkaidō, known as the Ainu, were mainly hunters and gatherers but planted millet as a secondary means of income, and had not developed the concept of land ownership and territoriality. Under the modern system of colonization, it therefore became possible for the Japanese to openly prevent the native people from owning land.

In 1872, *Hokkaidō Kaitaku-shi,* or the Hokaido Colonization Bureau, began
distributing uncultivated land, allowing each immigrant to own a maximum of
100,000 *tsubo* (approximately 0.33 km²) (Hokkaidō 1971: 287–292). Encouraged
by the bureau's support, many peasants, former *samurai* groups and several reclamation corporations moved to the island to settle and reclaim the land through
trial and error methods. Under the rule of the bureau, 73,231 immigrants were
registered between 1869 and 1881 (Hokkaidō 1971: 346). The majority of these
early colonists established their settlements along rivers or roads and constructed
road villages that were arranged as linear series of houses. For example, 203

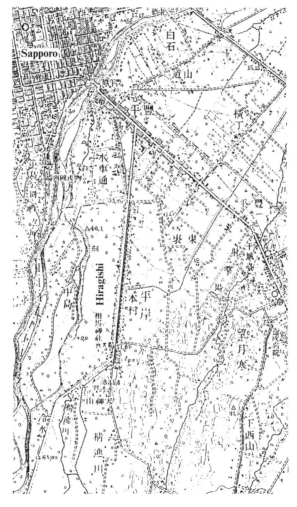

Figure 8.1: A road village of Hiragishi.
Source: Topographic map "Sapporo" (1: 50,000), 1916.

former *samurai* immigrants and peasants from the Sendai domain established a settlement in Hiragishi (Toyohira Ward, Sapporo City, Hokkaidō Province) along a straightened stream and road in southern Sapporo (Figure 8.1).

Early soldier villages

Early colonial settlements were also formed as compact complexes of road villages for *tonden-hei,* or farmer-soldiers, deployed for frontier development and to defend the country against Russia (Tsutsu'ura 1968; Hokkaidō 1971: 367–397). Between 1875 and 1898, most of the 26 soldier-villages were located on the Ishikari plain, where the early colonization had taken place. Most of these villages were occupied by the equivalent of one army company (a maximum of 240 soldiers), while 10 villages were occupied by the equivalent of two, three, or half an army company. The Colonization Bureau supplied applicants with funds to pay for travel, agricultural equipment, grain seeds, houses, and at least 15,000 *tsubo* (approximately 0.05 km²) of uncultivated land for reclamation. Nopporo village (Ebetsu City, Hokkaidō Province), established in 1886, typifies a plan in which one company occupied barracks located along either side of several parallel roads (Figure 8.2). The village also comprised an army office, a drill ground, and an elementary school in the center (Tsutsu'ura 1968: 71–73; Yamada 1971). Each household was allotted 4,000 *tsubo* of land (a space approximately 72.7 meters wide and 181.8 meters deep) along with a house inside the settlement and 11,000 *tsubo* of land outside the settlement. The

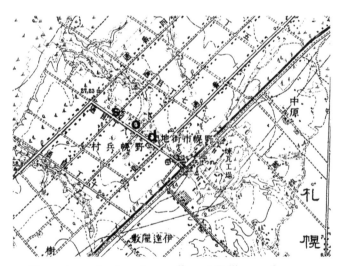

s: Elementary school,   o: Army office,   d: Drill ground.

Figure 8.2: Nopporo Soldier-Village.
Source: Topographic map "Ebetsu" (1: 50,000), 1916.

farmer-soldier system played a pioneering role in reclaiming Hokkaidō's wild frontier until it was dissolved in 1904 with the establishment of a conscript system.

Dispersed settlements on the colonial grid pattern

In contrast to the early road-village patterns, the most common settlement pattern in Hokkaidō was that of dispersed settlements based on *Shokuminchi Kukaku,* the colonial grid pattern that consisted of squares 300 *ken* in length on each side (approximately 545.5 meters) (Tateishi 2002). As the example of the area around the mouth of River Ishikari shows (Figure 8.3), the colonial grid pattern was not adopted uniformly throughout Hokkaidō. Many settlements consisted of a number of local mesh units of various orientations along the major rivers or highways in the region. This system of spatial partition was Hokkaidō Province's method of providing immigrants with uncultivated land for reclamation following the establishment of the provincial government in 1886. As Kinda (2002) argues, the township system found on the western frontier of the United States in the late

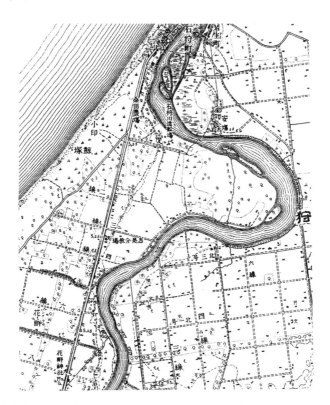

Figure 8.3: Colonial grid patterns around the mouth of River Ishikari.
Source: Topographic map "Ishikari" (1: 50,000), 1910.

eighteenth century was used as a reference while adopting the system, albeit only in terms of spatial partition and apportionment.

Surveying, measuring and mapping of the areas were critically important for the development of modern Hokkaidō's rural landscape (Satō 1986: 355–400). By 1889, the government had completed a full survey of the distribution of the entire island's potential arable land. It was the same year, 1889, that the government first adopted the colonial grid pattern for the village of Shin-totsukawa (Shin-totsikawa Town, Hokkidō Province). Each unit of squares was divided into six small rectangles, each measuring 150 by 100 *ken* (272.7 by 181.8 meters), so that one immigrant household could purchase one small rectangle of 15,000 *tsubo* (approximately 0.05 km²). Consequently, colonists tended to disperse and settle in their own properties, although some congregated into nucleated settlements. Progress in the development of topographical maps that covered the entire island led to the publication of *Shokuminchi kukaku zu,* or Colonial Grid Plans, on a scale of one to 25,000, starting in 1893 (Endō 1992). The published plans covering the major plains and uplands in northern and eastern Hokkaidō (Figure 8.4) show areas with the modern landscapes of reclaimed land and dispersed settlements as they existed after 1886, which cannot be seen in any other region of Japan.

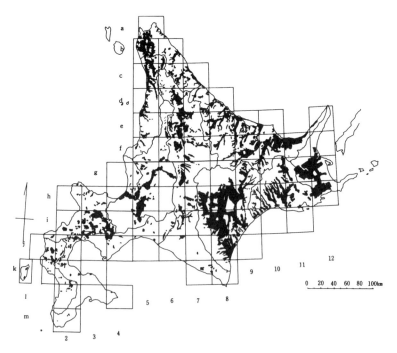

Figure 8.4: Coverage of publication of Colonial Grid Plans.
Source: Endō (1992: Figure 2.2).

Landscape of *shokusan kōgyō*

Shokusan kōgyo, the national promotion of modern industry, impacted the rural landscape in two major ways. Firstly, it led to large farms being reclaimed from uncultivated lands in which aristocrats, former *samurai*, and members of the bourgeoisie tried to introduce capitalist agriculture, including commercial stockbreeding. Expansive pastureland for cows, oxen, horses, and sheep was foreign to many contemporary Japanese despite their use of cattle and horses for plowing and drafting. The second major impact was the monoculture of commercial crop trees such as mulberry. These new forms of land usage came about not only in Hokkaidō but also in mainland Japan, where replaced previous usage.

Introduction of breeding farms

As Tsubaki (1996a) demonstrated, by 1921 the reclamation of at least 213 new estates had been completed in the mainland, and further reclamation continued until 1927 (Table 8.2), with approximately three-quarters of these new farms being situated in northeast and central Japan. The reason for this is that in national or common lands, large wild woodlands or grasslands remained on the uplands, at the foot of the mountains and in the marshlands of northeast and central Japan, rather than in western Japan (Figure 8.5). To promote land exploitation and stockbreeding, the government sold approximately 7,200 *cho* (71 km²) and lent 13,600 *cho* (135 km²) of national land to applicants between 1871 and 1884, as well as continuing to dispose of national land (Tsubaki 1996b). Many former feudal lords and *samurai* attempted, unsuccessfully, to construct their own farms, but by 1924, at least 82 landowners each owned more than 500 *cho* (approximate 4.96 km²) in the form of estates (Hatade 1963: 4). They preferred to refer to their

Table 8.2: Number of major reclaimed estates.

Year	Number of estates
1868–1877	28
1878–1887	45
1888–1897	38
1898–1907	23
1908–1917	41
1918–1927	10
no data	28
Sum	213

Source: Tsubaki (1996a: 883).
Numbers do not include estates in the colonies
or cases that failed by 1927.

Figure 8.5: Distribution of major reclaimed land (1927).
Source: Tsubaki (1996a: 882).

properties with the modern word, *nōjō* (farm), which means an estate or manor. Early modern landlords, in contrast, ruled over their lands rather than owning and operating them. The main national policies for building the economy and creating new landscapes in rural Japan were not only the rehabilitation of former *samurai* but also and the establishment of modern capitalist landownership.

Many estates adopted stock breeding, partly because they could neither reclaim nor depend on alluvial plains or fans to grow paddy, and partly because the national promotion encouraged the introduction of western methods of breeding or mixed farming. In particular, early Meiji government aristocrats aimed to lead the modernization of Japanese agriculture by introducing breeding and pasturing. As shown in Table 8.3, the stock of cattle and hogs increased slowly in modern times, although cow's milk, beef, and pork did not become staple components of the daily food of ordinary people. An example of a typical national promotion scheme for farming that the early Meiji government introduced is one of the early breeding efforts in Nasuno-ga-hara (Nasushiobara City, Tochigi Prefecture) (Tsubaki 1993). Approximately 100 square kilometers of Nasuno-ga-hara, or the wild woodlands of Nasuno, located on the acidic soil of the southern foot of the

Table 8.3: Major breeding in modern Japan.

(**1,000** heads)

Year	Cattle for drafting, plowing, and beef	Dairy cows	Horses	Hogs
1885	989	4	1,548	42*
1895	–	16	1,531	–
1905	979	33	1,368	228
1915	1,078	54	1,580	333
1925	1,133	65	1,553	673
1935	1,307	100	1,448	1,063
1945	2,079	93**	1,121	206

Source: Nōrin Tōkei Kenkyūkai (1983: 14–15). * 1887, ** 1946.

volcanic Mount Nasu, had been a vast commons for neighboring villages until the 1870s, when the Home Ministry surveyed the wild woodlands for potential reclamation. D. W. Jones, an adviser invited from the United States, visited the uncultivated land surrounding Kanto Plain, and recommended sheep breeding in Nasuno-ga-hara and other places. In 1878, understanding that western methods of breeding would succeed on the vast wild land of Nasuno, the government lent money to Tochigi Prefecture to establish and manage the Nasu Farm, built with 1,719 *cho* (17.0 km²) of fields. By 1905 the government had lent funds for the same purpose to at least 31 major private farms belonging to aristocrats, politicians, and political merchants.

The landscapes of these baronage estates embodied modernity (Tsubaki 1999), such as the west side of Nasuno, illustrated in Figure 8.6. Dry fields or pasture land expanded along the grid compartment in the woodland that belonged to two estates established by political figures. The first of these was Mishima Farm (1,037 km²), established in 1881 by Viscount Michitsune Mishima (later Governor of Tochigi Prefecture), and the other was Sembonmatsu Farm (1,640 km²), established in 1889 by Viscount Masayoshi Matsukata, the Home Minister and later the fourth Prime Minister of Japan. Both farms enjoyed access to national or public infrastructure: Riku'u Highway (1884), planned by Viscount Mishima himself, the Tōhoku railway line (1886), Nasu Canal (1886), and later Shiobara Tracks (1912), which linked the farms with the railway station. Mishima Farm, which contained a local government office, postal office, telegraphic office, elementary school, and shops, was planned more as a new town than merely as a new farm. Viscount Mishima commissioned Yuich Takahashi, the artist who was patronized by Mishima and became one of the founders of modern Japanese oil painting, to create landscape paintings of the farm (Figure 8.7). Mishima viewed the landscape painting of the estate and the office building in western style as being a consequence as well as a representation of modernity, since noble

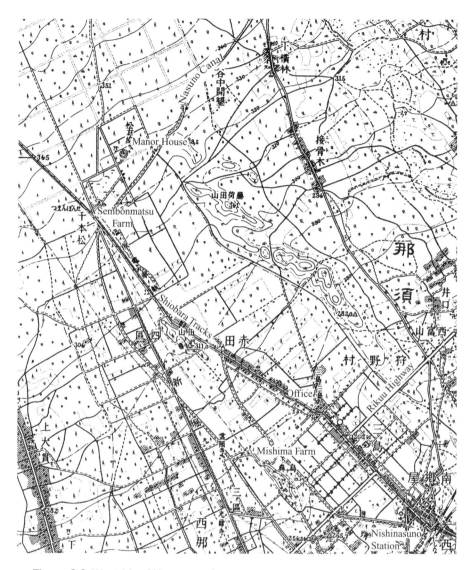

Figure 8.6: Westside of Nasuno-ga-hara.
White area: dry field or pastureland.
Source: Topographic map "Shiobara" (1: 50,000), 1929.

European landowners had commissioned artists to create paintings of their properties (Seymour 2000).

Most estates in Nasuno introduced breeding (of cattle, sheep and/or horses) or mixed farming. Faced with technical difficulties and the slow development of the market, many farms, including the Nasu Farm, had collapsed by the early

Figure 8.7: Mishima farm painted by Yuichi Takahashi (1884).
Collection of Nasunogahra Museum.

twentieth century, only to be purchased by other capitalists or divided into small holdings. Only Sembonmatsu Farm, which was also involved in forestry, managed to survive as a breeding farm, although it was transferred to Hōrai Corporation in 1928. Despite the difficulties that many modern farms faced, some of them could be taken as models for the modernization in agriculture and the creation of a new modern landscape.

Plantation of commercial trees

Another new modern landscape witnessed in the Japanese countryside was plantations containing commercial tree crops, which resulted from the industrial revolution and developments in international trade. In particular, the transformation of ordinary fields into commercial plantations of the Japanese mulberry tree known as *kuwa* (*Morus bombycis*) spread to mainland Japan. Tea and silk were the only two major exports that the early Meiji government had expected to experience an increase in international trade. To promote the silk industry, the government established the first silk filature factory in 1872 in Tomioka, in Gumma Prefecture, for which modern equipment was imported from France, leading to the factory becoming a model for the silk industry. The silk filature industry succeeded, largely due to the cheap labor provided by female workers, thereby causing a huge amount of demand for the cocoons of silkworms, which fed on mulberry leaves. Sericulture and mulberry plantations therefore became important means for peasants to earn their livelihood. The acreage of mulberry trees rose to 714,176 *cho* (7,082 km²) in 1929 thanks to the enthusiasm for a sericulture economy (Nōrin Tōkei Kenkyūkai 1983: 16). Records show that up to 80 percent of the dry lands of several counties were covered by mulberry plantations (Figure 8.8). Furthermore, an analysis of the Ordinance Survey topographical maps (Figure 8.9) reveals that the flat suburban terraces around Tokyo, as well as Japan's central mountainous areas, were covered with mulberry trees. As Arizono (1995a, 1995b) pointed out, the large monoculture of crop trees resulted in quite a modern landscape. Although mulberry, tea, and citrus had been cultivated before

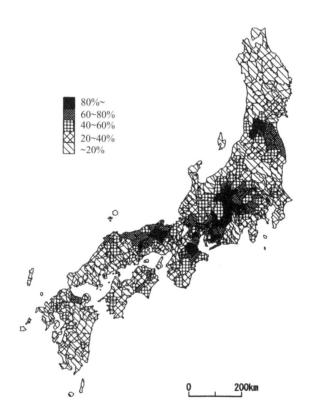

Figure 8.8: The ratio of mulberry plantations in dry field (1929). Source: Nakanishi (2003: 31).

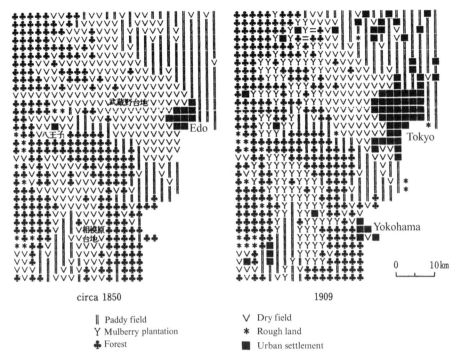

Figure 8.9: Changing land use around Tokyo.
Source: Arizono (1995b: 51).
The symbols represent the largest amount of land use in each two kilometer mesh.

early modern times, they had been planted as supplementary crops on the edge of paddy/dry fields and were thus only a small part of the landscape.

Modernist control of rural landscapes

The creation of modern landscapes resulted not only from the exploitation of new lands but also from improvements achieved in previous land usage and cover. In addition, more intensive agriculture was required to meet the demands of an increasing population, and more specialized timber was sought from the mountains in order to meet the demands of growing industries and urban areas. There was consequently a transition from a rural life vulnerable to natural forces into one characterized by artificial improvements in one's natural surroundings. The modernist belief that human beings could and should control nature was realized typically in two cases: land readjustments in existing fields and the conservation of mountains. Both cases have sparked heated academic debate in modern Japan and influenced many inhabitants of rural areas.

Geometrizing fields

The modernist wave of *kōchi seiri*—the land readjustment of existing disorderly unsystematic paddy fields into orderly rectangular fields, was one of the most important movements of modern rural Japan. *Kōchi seiri* involved many peasants and landowners, who shaped the rural landscape according to geometrical patterns. The origins of the movement are based partly on voluntary indigenous efforts but mostly on the recommendations of agronomists emulating the western methods of large-scale agriculture, particularly those of Germany or the United States (Tomita 1989). These agronomists attempted to alter the traditional rural landscape, which was characterized by small patchwork fields, into a vast series of large oblong fields. Spatial regulation generated many patterns in the landscape within the mainland as in colonial Hokkaidō, described above.

Following local voluntary efforts undertaken in the 1870s and 1880s came the enactment of *Kōchi Seiri Hō,* or the Land Readjustment Act, which enabled rural people to perform land readjustment as long as they had the agreement of at least two-thirds of the landowners. In his book, one advocate of agronomy, Eizaburō Ueno from Tokyo Imperial University, highlighted four benefits of such land readjustments (Ueno [1905] 1989: 5–18). The first of these was that larger fields, created through the exchange of land ownership, were more suitable for plowing with larger implements and with horses/cattle. According to Ueno, the average size of a Japanese paddy field unit was a mere 200 *bu* (approximately 661 m²), which had prevented the widespread use of plowing. Secondly, the integration of small field units involved the removal of banks or hedges and increased the acreage of arable lands. Thirdly, the installation of drainage ditches in such a way that they were detached from the irrigation system meant that they could be used as dry fields during the winter season, particularly in western Japan, thereby increasing their productivity. Finally, the construction of roads facing all field units helped in transportation.

Thanks to a series of revisions of the act that encouraged the installation of drainage ditches, approximately 12,100 km² of land in 34,000 districts was improved between 1900 and 1939, particularly in eastern Japan, where the ancient and medieval system of land plotting through *jori* (see Chapter 6) had never prevailed. After several local efforts in spatial planning, a system adopted in 1902 in the town of Kōnosu (Kōnosu City, Saitama Prefecture) came to be regarded as the most suitable model, as mentioned in Ueno's textbook (Figure 8.10). The Kōnosu system consisted of basic rectangular units of 300 *bu* (991.7 m²) measuring 10 *ken* (18.2 m) by 30 *ken* (54.5 m). Each unit faced a road, irrigation stream and drainage ditch. Figure 8.11 presents the case of Kibe Village (Sakai City, Fukui Prefecture) before and after the start of the readjustment in 1903. Facing the mouth of the Kuzuryū River and other small streams, Kibe's former settlements and dry fields were located on natural levees, whereas the paddy fields were spread across the flood plain. This variety of land usage demonstrates how the local people had adapted historically to the geological

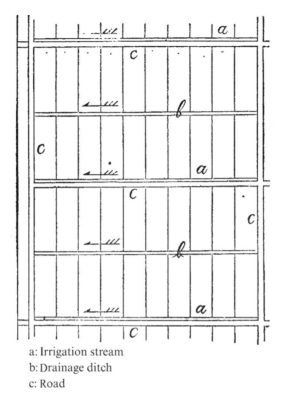

a: Irrigation stream
b: Drainage ditch
c: Road

Figure 8.10: Kōnosu system of land adjustment.
Source: Ueno ([1905] 1989: 279).

conditions of lagoons, marshlands and small, slender uplands. After the replotting, almost all areas, with the exception of land that contained houses, were converted into rectangular paddy fields along roads and ditches. As a result, the village of Kibe not only enjoyed increased arable land—from 552 *cho* (5.47 km²) to 617 *cho* (6.12 km²)—but also a greater number of paddy fields available as dry fields in the winter (Fukui Prefecture 1994: 502–504). This extraordinary growth of new and more productive acreage was brought about partly by the local inhabitants but mostly through the encouragement of the local government and squirearchy. For example, in Fukui Prefecture, the local government and agricultural association actively encouraged the readjustment projects. By 1921, at least 176 districts, mostly in downstream marshy areas like the village of Kibe, witnessed an increase of 699 *cho* (6.93 km²) in terms of acreage and increased rice production (Fukui Prefecture 1994: 502–504).

The end of the nineteenth century marked the start of modern land readjustment. Maintaining large and precise rectangular paddy fields required considerable

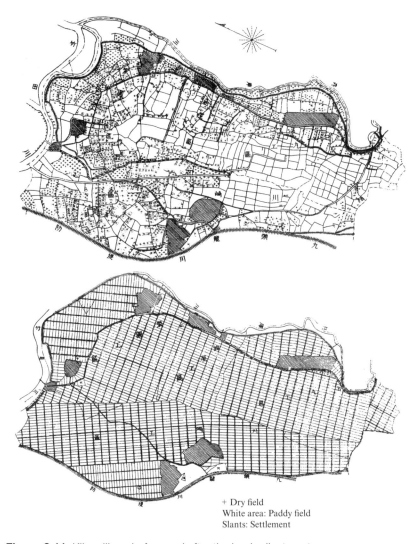

+ Dry field
White area: Paddy field
Slants: Settlement

Figure 8.11: Kibe village before and after the land adjustment.
Source: Fukui Prefecture (1922: plate 6). Scale of 1: 20,000.

amounts of effort and funds. Despite this, however, the unquestioned and uniform adoption of 300 *bu* as the standard size of paddy units led Ueno (1989:
262–284) to draw attention to the need for flexibility in unit sizes in accordance
with geological conditions. In the 1920s, agronomist Tokiyoshi Yokoi criticized
the mandatory readjustment as '*gobanme-shugi*' (gridism) and urged the provi-
sion of support for agronomical productivity and intensive agriculture rather
than land reformation (Hatade 1989). However, in 1949 the Land Improvement
Act was revised as the Land Readjustment Act, resulting in the replotting of at

least 1,769 districts by 1956 (Nishikawa 1995). The geometrization of landscapes has now succeeded in most parts of rural Japan, but pre-modern land usage cannot be found at all in the landscape of many regions.

Conservation of mountains

Another important target of landscape improvement was the 'bald' or 'rough' mountains. As seen in the previous chapter (see Figure 7.8), early modern Japan had numerous *iriai,* or commons, consisting of grassland or woodland areas, produced by humans using natural resources provided by them such as fuel, green manure and forage. Based on cases in the northeastern areas of Aichi Prefecture, Arizono (2007: 55–89) presents a typical landscape of *sato-yama* or grasslands/woodlands surrounding a settlement that fell under human control (Figure 8.12). However, a mountain without any trees gives visitors the impression of desolation. In 1868, a German geographer named Ferdinand von Richthofen observed 'ein rötliches ödes Aussehen' (a red desolate scene) in the bald hillsides of Shizuoka Prefecture (Tiessen 1907: 6). Foresters in the Meiji government who had similar impressions strove to declare numerous local commons and former lords' forests as national forests, citing the need for urgent national modernization. To this day, a Japanese version of 'combination of planting and patriotism' (Daniels 1988: 47) or a kind of nationalistic environmentalism can be seen in the politics involving modern forestry.

Three main factors supported the modern political movement for the afforestation of mountains, one of which was plantation for flood prevention. In 1873, Johannis De Rijke, an advisory engineer invited to Japan from the Netherlands, reported the existence of bald mountains in the catchment basins of the Yodo and

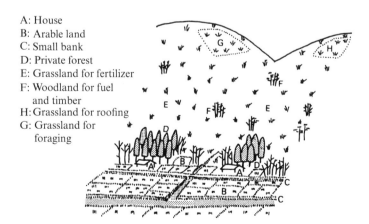

A: House
B: Arable land
C: Small bank
D: Private forest
E: Grassland for fertilizer
F: Woodland for fuel
   and timber
H: Grassland for roofing
G: Grassland for
   foraging

Figure 8.12: A typical landscape of modern countryside.
Source: Arizono (2007: 74).

Kiso rivers, the result of tree-felling in the local commons by the indigenous people (Chiba 1973: 30–31). In terms of modern civil engineering, one of the aspects that De Rijke stressed was the conservation of mountains. The second factor was that, by 1888, the Meiji government had come to own a huge area of mountain terrain through the Land Tax Revision –approximately 770 million *cho* (7.64 million km^2) (Fujita 1981: 220). Moreover, it forcefully nationalized vast mountain areas, including any local commons that could not provide sufficient evidence of being a part of private property or belonging to a taxpayer. In addition, once municipalities were granted permission to own forests, they incorporated at least 229 million *cho* (2.27 million km^2) of local commons by 1930 (Fujita 1981: 221–2). The academic forester, Zentarō Kawase, and others belonging to the German school of jurisprudence supported the national policy, regarding commons as public spaces, not for the exclusive used of individuals or the government (Fujita 1977). Thus, national and local governments intended to develop the timber economy and undertake afforestation in the grasslands or woodlands that they came to own, thereby restricting the access of indigenous people to resources. The third factor was the odd but influential idea that red pines would convert Japan into desert, proposed toward the end of the nineteenth century by Seiroku Honda, a professor of forestry at the Tokyo Imperial University (Chiba 1973: 18–28). Honda argued that a red pine forest is representative of the scenario wherein local people gather fallen leaves from the ground, causing it to dry up and turn into desert. This theory prejudiced both foresters in the government administration and academics who were against the growth of grassland or woodland, which had been used by locals for fuel, green manure and forage and now were a target of 'improvement.'

Along with nationalism, an environmentalist idea that condemned thin vegetation but lacked an understanding of the traditional use of grassland or woodland, flourished in the 1930s. As Nakashima (2000a, 2000b) argued, the afforestation movement dates back to the introduction of Arbor Day in elementary schools in 1895, followed by the series of policies implemented by the Bureau of Forestry in the Department of Agriculture and Commerce, between 1907 and 1929. These policies were intended to encourage the development of plantations on both private and municipal mountains. Meanwhile, local and colonial associations of private foresters instituted regional Arbor Days with the slogan 'love for forest.' Most of these forest days took place on April 3, day on which Japan's mythical first emperor, Jimmu, died. Flourishing trees symbolized prosperity, both for the country and for the emperor of Japan, as advocated by Professor S. Honda in 1928 (Nakashima 2000a: 10–11):

> Originally, the plantation and cultivation of trees, or even of just one tree, is done to admire and commemorate the flourishing family of the Emperor. Afforestation leads not only to large properties but also to developments in industry, ground water recharging and conservation in the country. Those who look up to trees should imagine and commemorate imperial benevolence forever.

'Love for forest' was therefore associated with 'love for the nation.' Through this ideological combination of love for both forest landscapes and nationalism, planting came to be regarded as not just an activity of the timber industry but also a symbol of the national landscape. The expansion of the Japanese empire also led to the spread of the planting movement to the colonies. Thus, the movement expanded from being a national one to an imperial one and, particularly in Korea, was used to justify colonial control of forests in the name of 'improvement' (Komeie 2005).

Despite the 'love for forest' propaganda, the movement did not manage to cover all of Japan's rough mountains with trees. In 1953, the Forestry Agency, which had replaced the Bureau of Forestry, surveyed the distribution and degree of devastation and found 27,388 km^2 of bald mountains in need of conservation (Chiba 1991: 52), a large part of which was located in the western part of Japan (Figure 8.13). In reality, there still remained adequate grassland and woodland areas for agricultural resources and swidden agriculture until the 1950s (Fujita 1995). Ironically, the development of these lands into mature forests has taken place in the latter half of the twentieth century, due partly to conservation

One point means 100 ha.

Figure 8.13: Distribution of bald mountains (1953).
Source: Chiba (1991: 52).

and afforestation but mostly to a decrease in the exploitation of vegetation. Increased use of fossil fuels, artificial manure, and agricultural machines has diminished the agricultural importance of grassland and woodland. The green landscape of Japan's mountains today is not a consequence of human control but rather a lack of it.

As noted above, colonial expansion, the promotion of modern industry and modernist control of land had a drastic impact on the rural landscape. Not all of these changes were successful; breeding and afforestation in particular did not spread as widely as hoped. In addition, mulberry plantations that had been developed in most parts of Japan vanished rapidly in the late twentieth century. The expansive landscape of dispersed settlements on regular geometrical lands in rural Hokkaidō was and remains so 'exotic' that today's Japanese tourists still find novelty in the scenery. It is difficult, even for Japanese people, to imagine the presence of grass or bald mountains close to all human habitation. The modern landscape has changed so rapidly that some rural landscapes created during modern times are regarded as landscapes of the past. However, the modernist belief that human beings could change the environment and control the landscape has prevailed in modern Japan. Both the geometrical division of land and a raging debate on landscapes were distinctive features that marked the late nineteenth and early twentieth centuries in Japan.

Bibliography

Arizono, Shōichirō (1995a), 'Meiji-Taishō-ki (1900 nen goro) no nōchi riyō (Agricultural land use circa 1900)', in Yukio Himiyama *et al* (eds.) (1995), *Atlas: Nippon rettō no kankyō henka* (Atlas: Environmental change in modern Japan), Tokyo: Asakura Shoten, pp. 48–49.

—————— (1995b), 'Meiji-Taishō-ki (1900 nen goro) no nōchi kaihatsu (Development of agricultural land use circa 1900)', in Yukio Himiyama *et al* (eds.) (1995), *Atlas: Nippon rettō no kankyō henka* (Atlas: Environmental change in modern Japan), Tokyo: Asakura Shoten, pp. 50–51.

—————— (2007), *Nōkō-gijutsu no rekishi-chiri* (An historical geography of agricultural skills), Tokyo: Kokon Shoin.

Chiba, Tokuji (1973), *Hageyama no bunka* (Culture of bald mountains), Tokyo: Gakuseisha.

—————— (1991), *Hageyama no kenkyū* (A study of bald mountains), revised version, Tokyo: Soshiete.

Daniels, Stephen (1988), 'The political iconography of woodland', in Denis Cosgrove and Stephen Daniels (eds.), *The Iconography of Landscape: Essays on the Symbolic Representation, design and use of past environments*, Cambridge: Cambridge University Press, pp. 43–82.

Endō, Tatsuhiko (1992), 'Shokuminchi kukaku-zu no database-ka ni tsuite' (The making of database on Colonial Grid Plans), *Hokkaidōritsu bunshokan kenkyū-kiyō* (Bulletin of Hokkaidō Archives), 7, pp. 33–126.

Fujita, Yoshihisa (1977), 'Iriai-rin'ya to rin'ya shoyū o megutte (Commons and landownership of forest)', *Jimbun chiri* (Japanese Journal of Human Geography), 29 (1), pp. 54–95.

—————— (1981), *Nippon no sanson* (Mountain villages in Japan), Kyoto: Chijin Shobō.

—————— (1995), 'Dainiji sekai taisenin izen no rin'ya no kōhai to sohōteki riyō (Rough land uses in mountain areas before World War II), in Yukio Himiyama *et al* (eds.) (1995), *Atlas: Nippon rettō no kankyō henka* (Atlas: Environmental change in modern Japan), Tokyo: Asakura Shoten, pp. 82–83.

Fukui Prefecture (ed.) (1922), *Fukuiken-shi* (An history of Fukui Prefecture), part 3, Vol. 3, Fukui: Fukui Prefecture.

—————— (ed.) (1994), *Fukuiken-shi: Tsūshi-hen* (An history of Fukui Prefecture: Historiography), Vol. 5, Fukui: Fukui Prefecture.

Hatade, Isao (1963), *Nippon ni okeru dainōjō no seisei to tenkai* (The making and development of large estates in Japan), Tokyo: Ochanomizu Shobō.

—————— (1989), 'Kaidai: "Keizai-gawa no kōchi seiri" (Commentary on "Economical phase of land readjustment")', in Nōgyō Doboku Gakkai Koten Fukkoku I'inkai (ed.), *Nōgyō doboku koten senshū* (Classics in civil engineering in agriculture), Vol. 3, Tokyo: Nippon Keizai Hyōron-sha, pp. ix–xviii.

Himiyama, Yukio *et al* (eds.) (1995), *Atlas: Nippon rettō no kankyō henka* (Atlas: Environmental change in modern Japan), Tokyo: Asakura Shoten.

Hokkaidō (ed.) (1971), *Shin Hokkaidō-shi* (A new history of Hokkaidō), Vol. 3, Sapporo: Hokkaidō Province.

Hokkaidō-shi Hensan-gakari (ed.) (1945), *Shinsen Hokkaidō-shi* (A newly compiled history of Hokkaidō), Vol. 4, Sapporo: Hokkaidō Province.

Kinda, Akihiro (2002), 'Hokkaidō shokuminchi-kukaku no tokusei to keifu (An approach to the origin and characteristics of the emigrating regions in the modern era of Japan)', *Rekishi chirigaku* (The Historical Geography), 44 (1), pp. 11–19.

Kitō, Hiroshi (2000), *Jinkō kara yomu Nippon no rekishi* (Japanese history from the viewpoint of demography), Tokyo: Kodansha.

Komeie, Taisaku (2005), Colonial environmentalism and shifting cultivation in Korea: Japanese mapping, research, and representation, *Geographical Review of Japan*, 79 (12), pp. 664–679.

Motoki, Yasushi (1997), *Gendai Nippon no suiden kaihatsu* (Paddy field reclamation in modern Japan), Tokyo: Kokon Shoin.

Nakanishi, Ryōtarō (2003), *Kindai Nippon ni okeru nōson seikatsu no kōzō* (Structure of rural life in modern Japan), Tokyo: Kokon Shoin.

Nakashima, Kōji (2000a), 'Jūgo-nen sensō-ki no ryokuka-undō: sōdōin taisei-ka no shizen no hyōshō (Afforestation campaigns in Japan during the Fifteen Year War: representation of nature under the national mobilization regime)', *Hokuriku shigaku*, 49, 1–22.

————— (2000b), 'Nationalism, colonialism and the representation of nature: forest and country in the afforestation campaign in modern Japan', in Korean Association of Spatial Environment Research (ed.), *Second International Critical Geography Conference*, Dargu: Korean Association of Spatial Environment Research.

Nishikawa, Osamu (1995), 'Nōchi no kiban-seibi (Agricultural land improvement)', in Yukio Himiyama *et al* (eds.) (1995), *Atlas: Nippon rettō no kankyō henka* (Atlas: Environmental change in modern Japan), Tokyo: Asakura Shoten, pp. 64–67.

Nōrin Tōkei Kenkyūkai (ed.) (1983), *Todōfuken nōgyō kiso tōkei* (Basic agricultural statistics in Prefectures), Tokyo: Nōrin Tōkei Kyōkai.

Satō, Jinjirō (1986), *Meiji-ki sakusei no chiseki-zu* (Cadastral map in Meiji Japan), Tokyo: Kokon Shoin.

Seymour, Susanne (2000), Historical geographies of landscape, in Brian Graham and Catherine Nash (eds.), *Modern Historical Geographies*, Harlow: Pearson Education Limited, pp. 193–217.

Tateishi, Tomo'o (2002), 'Okhotsk engan no shokuminchi-kukaku (The colonial plan on the coast along Sea of Okhotsk, Hokkaidō)', *Rekishi chirigaku* (The Historical Geography), 44 (1), pp. 1–10.

Tiessen, E. (ed.) (1907), *Ferdinand von Richthofen's Tagebücher aus China*, Vol. I, Berlin: Dietrich Reimer.

Tomita, Masahiko (1989), 'Kaidai: "Kōchi seiri kōgi" (Commentary on "Lecture on land readjustment")', in Nōgyō Doboku Gakkai Koten Fukkoku I'inkai (ed.), *Nōgyō doboku koten senshū* (Classics in civil engineering in agriculture), Vol. 3, Tokyo: Nippon Keizai Hyōron-sha, pp. i–viii.

Tsubaki, Machiko (1993), 'Nasuno-ga-hara ni okeru kindai kaitaku jigyō no tenkai kōzō (The changing structure of modern reclamation work in Nasunogahara, Tochigi Prefecture), Tokyo gakugei daigaku kiyō: III (Bulletin of Tokyo Gakugei University: Ser. 3), 44, pp. 121–137.

————— (1996a), 'Kindai Nippon ni okeru kaitakuchi no chiiki-teki tenkai: Nōrinsuisan-shō hen "Kaikonchi ijū keiei jirei" no bunseki (The development of reclaimed land in modern Japan: an examination of the *Kaikonchi ijyu keiei jirei*)', *Chirigaku Hyōron* (Geographical Review of Japan), 69A (11), pp. 879–891.

————— (1996b), 'Nippon ni okeru "kindai kaitaku son" kenkyū no seika to kadai (Studies of reclamation settlements in modern Japan: outcomes and problems)', *Jimbun chiri* (Japanese Journal of Human Geography), 48 (6), pp. 24–42.

————— (1999), 'Bunka-keikan to shite no kindai kaitaku nōjō: frontier ni okeru modernity no hyōshō ni kansuru ichi-shiron (Modern reclaimed farm as a cultural landscape: An essay on representation of modernity on frontier)', *Gakugei-chiri*, 54, pp. 43–56.

Tsutsu'ura, Akira (1968), 'Tondenhei-son no haichi to genjō ni tsuite (Collocation and condition of farmer-soldier village)', in Hokkaidō Kyōiku Iinkai (ed.), *Tondenhei-son* (Farmer-soldier village), Sapporo: Hokkaidō Kyōiku Iinkai, pp. 67–94.

Ueno Eizaburō (1989), 'Kōchi seiri kōgi (Lecture on land readjustment)', reprinted in Nōgyō Doboku Gakkai Koten Fukkoku I'inkai (ed.), *Nōgyō doboku koten senshū* (Classics in civil engineering in agriculture), Vol. 3, Tokyo: Nippon Keizai Hyōron-sha, pp. 1–461.

Yamada, Makoto (1971), 'Tondenhei-son no bangai-chi ni kansuru ichi-kōsatsu (On extra space in soldier-villages)', in Oda Takeo sensei taikan kinen-jigyō-kai (ed.), *Jimbun chiri-gaku ronsō* (Essays in human geography), Kyoto: Yanagihara Shoten, pp. 155–166.

PART 4

Landscape, materials and representation

CHAPTER 9

Landscapes and maps

Akihiro KINDA and Kazuhiro UESUGI

Maps in the ancient times

The ancient national government is known to have directed the provincial governments to create maps of the provinces and counties, and to transfer them to the national government in 738. These maps were stored and used by governments in that era. In 796, a similar directive was issued mainly because most of the maps had suffered damage from their long use. Besides such relatively small scale maps, there were various large scale maps that were commissioned and used by the governments in the ancient times.[1]

The ancient constitution, *ritsu-ryo*, had a ground rule that all lands basically belonged to the state or the emperor. All people who were older than six years were entitled to the allocation of a certain area of paddies that entailed the payment of certain taxes. Two *tan* of land was allocated to a male freeman, and two thirds of this area was allotted to an adult female. Besides land taxes, people were obliged to pay poll taxes, including labor levies, that were regulated primarily according to the age and sex of the tax payer.

As an administrative procedure, the state commissioned family registers once every six years and informal registrations were carried out right through this six-year period. Land registers and maps were also made once in six years as a part of this procedure. The land registration and allocation procedures were carried out in accordance with the *jori* plan since the middle of the eighth century, as already mentioned. The processes of the completion, change, and disintegration of the *jori* plan, and its functions in ancient and medieval Japan have been comprehensively analyzed and explained in a previous chapter.

The *jori* plan was completed by the application of the *jori* indication system to the *jori* grid pattern in the middle of the eighth century. Although the *jori* plan was effective in enforcing the *handen-shuju* (inquiry and allocation of farmlands), the process was closely connected with new land laws proclaimed in 723 and 743 which permitted private land ownerships. The main reason was presumably to find a solution to the sharply increasing complexities of the administrative procedures related to lands.

The *jori* plan was used formally for procedures related to the administration of lands, especially with regard to entries in the land register and in the formulation of large rural plans. The *jori* plan was depicted clearly as part of the rural plans known as *handen-zu* (large scale maps on a 1: 4000–5000 scale that showed the results of the *handen-shuju* procedures) and *kohden-zu* (usually used for inquiring into paddy lands before allocations; these were very similar to the *handen-zu* maps, and the two could be used as alternatives to each other with some revises by the procedure of *handen-shuju*). There were two types of rural plans; one kind was drawn as a linear arrangement of *ri* (654 square meters within 36 sections), and the other depicted each *ri* separately. Nevertheless, both types basically involved the drawing of grid patterns based on the *jori* plan.[(2)]

We can also witness the process of the completion of the *jori* plans on such rural plans or manorial maps of the eighth century. For example, the oldest known manorial map was drawn for an estate of the Gufukuji temple in Yamada County, Sanuki province; this corresponds to the center of Figure 6.1a,b. This map was originally drawn in 735 AD and was duplicated by the new owner of the estate in the second half of the eleventh century as shown in the northern part of the estate on Figure 9.1.

This map was drawn on paper and represents rectangular sections of one *cho* (1.2 ha; the same size and acreage as defined by a *tsubo* section within the *jori* plan). On each section was generally written a kind of minor place name, the acreage of the temple's property and the yield of the land. The manor was separated into two parts—to the north and the south—each of which consisted of several sections in the four directions. Although no numbers derived from the *jori* indication system were written within each section, the minor place names were indicated for the paddies. This type of minor place name was not generally used after the establishment of the *jori* indication system, so we may refer to this type as the pre-*jori* minor place names. A document written in 757 also shows similar conditions. Properties of other temples in the neighboring county documented in the same manuscript were also indicated by similar style place names. Thus, it is evident that the farmland was laid out as units of one *cho* square sections in the rural plans or cadastral methods, but it offers no indication that the *jori* grid pattern had yet been translated onto the rural landscape. The *jori* grid pattern for land planning and land registration was, in other words, used in this region during the first half of the eighth century. The pre-*jori* minor place name was also used side by side along with it.

A few decades later, the property of the same temple that was the owner of the estate shown in Figure 9.1 was described in terms of the *jori* numbering system using certain minor place names that were similar to the pre-*jori* place names witnessed on documents that were issued in 763. This was several years after the other example that has been mentioned in this context. These show that place indication functions were carried out both by the *jori* numbering indication system and the minor place names, which were akin to the pre-*jori* place names

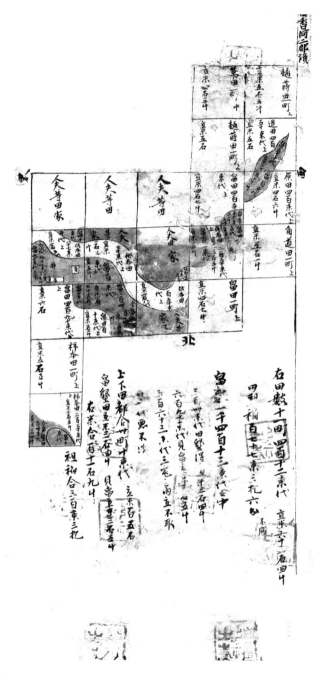

Figure 9.1: Manorial map of the Gufukuji temple in Sanuki province (northern part, original in 735, duplicated in the 11th century).
Private collection.

(hereinafter, in this chapter, "pre-*jori* place names" will be written as "ancient minor place names"). As a result, it is clear that the *jori* plan was completed in Sanuki Province by the introduction of the *jori* indication system between 757 and 763.[3]

In the other provinces, the earliest documents on which the *jori* indication system has been found include manuscripts found in Yamashiro Province dating back to 743 and in Iga Province dating back to 748; both these finds have unearthed documents that were created before the ones excavated in Sanuki Province.

Famous collections of manuscripts include seventeen ancient maps known as the Todaiji *Kaiden-chizu* that were drawn on hempen cloth. Many of them are original maps drawn between 751 and 767 that had been stored at Shosoin, a repository that served the Todaiji Temple in Nara (formerly Heijo-*kyo*). These maps depict a one *cho* grid pattern and the *jori* indication system, ancient minor place names and acreages of the temple's properties in each grid as shown in Figure 9.2. The map on Figure 9.2 has representations of coastal hills (sand dunes) with rich vegetation, a pond within a fish and an irrigation canal from a well as well as descriptions of the temple's properties in the *jori* grid pattern. One particular map, which represents a specific part of the Settsu Province, is slightly different from the other Todaiji *Kaiden-chizu* in the collection. In the case of this map, drawn in 756, there is no numbering *jori* indication system, although there is a grid pattern. The overall pattern, however, is very similar to the other maps as shown in Figure 9.1.

The *jori* plan had been widely implemented by the time these manorial maps were drawn for each manor in every province, case by case, in the eighth century. Although these remaining ancient maps were not original rural plans such as the *handen-zu*, they must have been edited as manorial maps and incorporated additional information; these presumably included pictorial subjects such as hills, vegetation and so on, to go with the formal rural plans drawn up in the eighth century.[4]

Besides this type of maps that were both manorial maps based on the formal rural plans and rural plans in themselves, there were other types of maps that served the occasional needs of the manor lords or governors of provinces. Although such maps that catered to occasional needs were often a little simplified or drawn in a slightly different style, large scale ancient maps were, on the whole, very effective in the analysis of land use at the time and in the reconstruction of landscapes in the ancient times.

They should, of course, be used carefully, since they are not modern scientific maps. The most characteristic nature of such rural plans was that they comprised notations with regard to the various phenomena on lands in each section according to the land policies of that time. For example, if there were a huge villa that ranged across a few sections in a rural region, the villa could reasonably be expected to be independently registered in each section of the *jori* plan, just lake a few premises in each of those sections of the *jori* grid pattern. However,

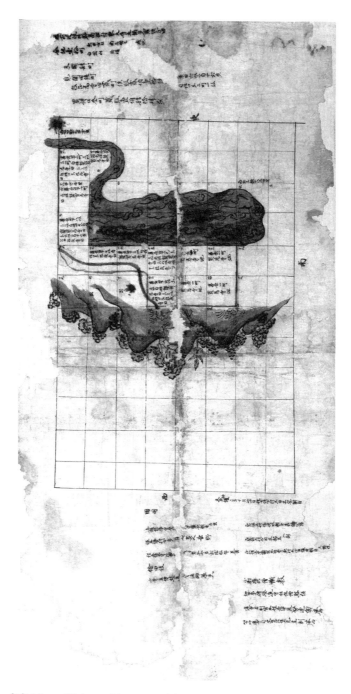

Figure 9.2: Map of Takagushi, a manorial map of Todaiji temple (766). Collection of Nara National Museum.

if there were a series of geographical features like, for example, a river and a mountain—these were viewed as public property—they would be drawn or visually depicted by some other means. There were several cases in which formal notations within a section indicated curiously different land use from the visually drawn parts of the same section on the same manorial map. Such cases might have happened owing to different writers and painters being appointed independently to work on a manorial map, or as a result of painters having drawn independently series of geographical phenomena and then copied faithfully the notations from the original rural plans.

Apart from the rural plan, city plans of the capitals must have been drawn up and used. Some ancient documents referred to such city plans. Although no original city plans made by the ancient governmental authority remain, except for a few manorial maps dating back to the eighth century and a few very small and mysterious fragments. There are naturally many later maps including medieval ones that have been used as bases for city plans over the years.[5]

We may also note that the formal city plans were of a very similar nature to the rural plans.

Maps in the medieval times

Through the ancient and medieval times, it was extremely uncommon for new maps to be commissioned; the formal maps created in an earlier age were persisted with by both the national and provincial governments, and these maps continued to serve as important bases for land registration and taxes. But maps themselves were made privately and used widely by various people. In the period spanning the end of the ancient times through the medieval times, the biggest map makers and map users were the manorial lords and their offices. Many of these manorial maps were large scale and pictorial maps.[6]

The earliest medieval manorial map that has survived was drawn to represent a hilly manor region in Kii province in 1143; this province at present falls within the Wakayama prefecture. This map was made to show the area of the manor when land to the right of the manor was established or enclosed. Another type of similar manorial map was made when the manor was developed. Figure 9.3 describes such a map that was drawn up at the behest of a manor in 1316 that was situated within the present-day Osaka prefecture. This map draws pictorially the boundary of the manor along surrounding ridges, a river and a main road, the Shinto shrines, Buddhism temples, various farm houses, many irrigation ponds, many paddies and wasteland. Such pictorial drawing was one of the main characters of large scale manorial maps in the medieval times. This method was especially effective in the expression of manors and lands not only in regions landscaped with well established *jori* grid patterns but also in places that were not covered with *jori* grid patterns. The pictorial method became a new tradition in the making of maps through the medieval and early modern times.[7]

Figure 9.3: Pictorial manorial-map of Hineno in Izumi province (1316).
Collection of Imperial Household Agency.

There is also a group of medieval maps that show using lines within the manorial territory to divide the area according to the spheres of influence of the manorial lord who lived mainly in Kyoto, known as Heian-*kyo* at that time, and local powerful stewards/farmers (see Figure 9.4). This map shows a manor around a lake along the coast of the Japan Sea with three dividing lines and several landmarks.

On the other hand, there are manorial maps that have very few pictorial elements. Some of them were made primarily based on traditional descriptions contained in ancient rural plans which were strongly based on the *jori* plan as the cadastral system. This method was still useful to indicate in detail the location of a plot of land. Among these maps, which mostly represented areas within the capital district, there were some that had not only section lines representing the *jori* grid patterns but also subdivided lines within it.[8]

Concerning city plans, the oldest complete ones that have been found relate to Kyoto. The map shown in Figure 9.5 draws the grid pattern of Heian-*kyo* with street names and locations of palaces and residences along with their names. This map is part of a volume of books that includes a study of certain ceremonial methods and an overview of the aristocracy in the late ancient and medieval times. The map itself is a revised one, but the original map was presumably made in the middle of the twelfth century. This type of city plan is thought to have been made on the basis of an ancient formal city plan that had been commissioned by the capital city government.[9]

These large scale maps are all extremely useful for representing landscapes of the time, although they inevitably have various biases of their own as already mentioned in reference to the ancient rural plans.

Small scale maps depicting the national territory or at a world level, all within a single sheet, were also created in the medieval times. The earliest map of Japan that has been found was known as the Gyogi-zu, and was made in 1305; Gyogi was the name the author of this map who was a very famous Buddhist priest. There were various versions of this map.

Although a part of this map that represented the Western parts of Japan has been lost, this map (Figure 9.6) contains drawings of provinces and the main highways of that period from the city of Heian-*kyo*. This map may presumably have served as an index map to the provincial and county maps that had been ordered by the national government in the eighth and ninth centuries.[10]

The world map made in the medieval times was a Buddhist map that expressed the Buddhist ideal world, which consisted of Japan, China and India, and all of their environs, around the imagined center of the world.[11]

Such small scale maps were mainly drawing the knowledge or expressing the cosmologies of the times, both concerning Japan and the world. While these are not directly effective in the analysis or reconstruction of past landscapes, these maps are nevertheless very useful as a source of information on the knowledge and thought of the period they were drawn in.[12]

(KINDA)

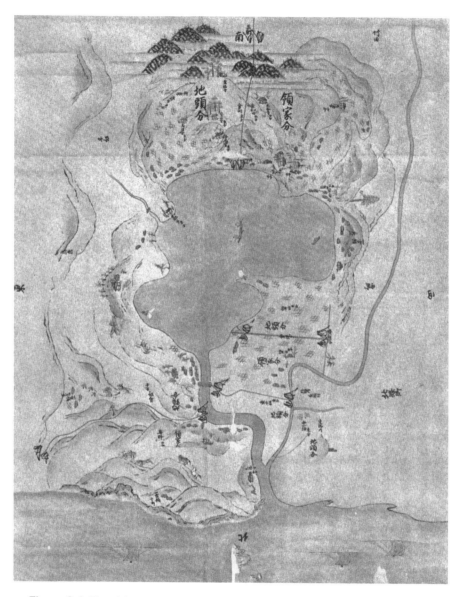

Figure 9.4: Pictorial manorial-map of Togo in Hoki province, with division lines (1258). Collection of Historiographical Institute, the University of Tokyo.

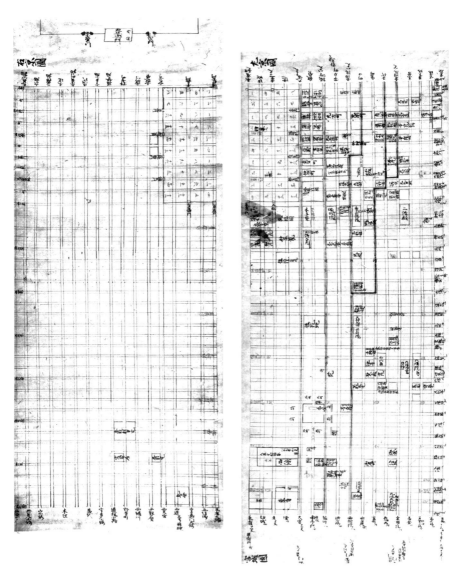

Figure 9.5: City plans of Heian-*kyo*, original drawn in the 12th century (National Treasure).
Collection of Tokyo National Museum.
Image: TMN Image Archives.
Source: http://TmnArchives.jp

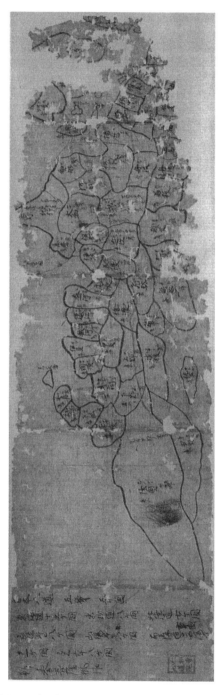

Figure 9.6: Map of Japan (a 'Gyogizu') (1305).
Collection of Ninna-ji Temple.

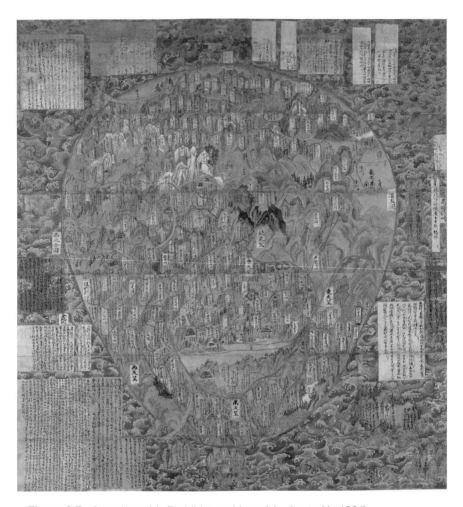

Figure 9.7: 'Gotenjikuzu' (a Buddhist world map) (estimated in 1364). Collection of Horyu-ji Temple.

Notes

1. A. Kinda, *Ancient Japan from Ancient Maps*, pp. 185–197, (Tokyo, 1999).
2. A. Kinda, *Ancient Manorial Maps and Landscapes*, pp. 60–98, (Tokyo,1998).
3. T. Kishi, Handenzu and *jori* plan, in Kishi, *Study on the Ancient registers in Japan*, (Tokyo, 1973), A. Kinda, *Geographical Study on the Jori Plan and the Rural Landscape*, pp. 44–46, (Tokyo, 1985), A. Kinda, *Landscapes of Ancient Japan*, pp. 1–40, 75–130, (Tokyo, 1993).
4. Kinda (1993), *op.cit.* pp. 170–184, Kinda (1999), *op.cit.* pp. 181–183.

5. Kinda (1993), *op.cit.* pp. 303–313. A. Kinda, Representation of *jori* and *jobo* plans on old maps related to Saidaiji temple, in M. Sato ed., *World of old maps related to Saidaiji temple*, (Tokyo,2005).

6. Y. Koyama, *The Medieval Village and Manorial Maps*, pp. 241–242, (Tokyo, 1987), Kinda (1993), *op.cit.* pp. 314–333.

7. N. Okuno, Establishment and development of manorial maps, in Study Group of Manorial Maps ed., *Basic studies of Manorial Maps*, (Tokyo, 1973), Kinda (1998), *op.cit.* pp. 318–322.

8. ibid.

9. A. Kinda, On city plans attached to the Kujoke's manuscript of Engi-shiki, in Kinda ed., *Heiankyo/Kyoto*, (Kyoto, 2007).

10. T. Oji, *World Image of Pictorial Maps*, (Tokyo, 1996), A. Kinda, *Views on the Earth*, pp. 290–295, (Kyoto, 2008).

11. Kinda (1998), *op.cit.* pp. 326–329.

12. Kinda (1998), *op.cit.* pp. 326–333.

Cartography in the Edo Era

Tokugawa Ieyasu (1542–1616) assumed power in 1603 and established the Tokugawa Shogunate. This Shogunate, the feudal military government of Tokugawa, is referred to as the Edo Era, after the name of the Shogunate's capital city. The Edo Era, which lasted for over 260 years, could be termed 'early modern.' Some features of the Edo Era are quite similar to those of early modern European history, while others are very different, so it is therefore possible to avoid using the term 'early modern' here as a translation for the Edo Era.

Once Oda (1973) revealed the history of Japanese cartography and Unno (1995) did the same in English, discussions about maps in the Edo Era have continued and been looked into more closely. Some important themes are introduced here regarding the politics of maps and about maps in the publishing culture.

Maps and politics

Kuniezu

In the Edo era the *Daimyo* (feudal lord) was required to draw and submit maps of their provinces, known as *Kuniezu* ('provincial maps'), to the Shogunate. Possession of such maps symbolized Tokugawa's control of the land as the leader of a unified nation. Tokugawa insisted that daimyo create provincial maps at least four times, the first of which was in 1604, just after Tokugawa unified the land. A recent study, however, raises the possibility that only the western parts of Japan received this order at that time (Kawamura 2005). It may therefore have been a political performance for the benefit of the Tokugawa Shogunate to show its power and authority to the daimyos in the western area who had recently bowed down to Tokugawa.

All lands controlled by the Shogunate were targeted by the second project, started in 1644 as the result of the firm establishment of the political system. Strict standards were set for the reduced scale and map symbols, in contrast to earlier projects that did not have a unified standard. This was the first time that all national lands were represented under the same codes and with a unified consciousness (Figure 9.8). The idea of unification followed in similar projects conducted in 1697 and 1835.

It was generally quite difficult to conduct research on the *Kuniezu* in detail due to quite large size of the map. However, the development of photo techniques and, more recently, digital engineering, has made it easier to access the *Kuniezu*. Some public institutes and libraries, such as the National Archives of Japan and Tokushima University Library, have added digital archives of the *Kuniezu* to their web pages. The research group for *Kuniezu*, established in 1996, and others, were founded to conduct detailed research works on the bibliographies and contents of the *Kuniezu*. It is now well known that the *Kuniezu* can be used to reconstruct the landscape and the changes it has undergone (Kuniezu Kenkyūkai 2005).

Figure 9.8: An example of Kuniezu in the second project.
Yamashiro province.
Collection of Uji City Historical Museum.

Silence of *Kuniezu*

As noted by Kawamura (1984), the contents of the *Kuniezu* were influenced by the political and social situations at the time. It is now possible to conduct research on the meaning of silence on the map, a concept first discussed by Harley (1988) before being applied by Yonemoto (2006) to recent discussions of *Kuniezu*.

As Toby (2001) pointed out, it is well known that the *Nihon sōzu* (map of All Japan), made by the compilation of the *Kuniezu* in the second project, did not contain Ryūkyū, the old name for Okinawa (Figure 9.9). After the invasion in 1609 of Satsuma (the old name for Kagoshima in the southern part of Kyūsyū island), Ryūkyū came under the control of both Japan and China. Satsuma controlled Ryūkyū on the Japanese side, and made the *Kuniezu* of Ryūkyū in the second project (Kuroda and Sugimoto, 1989). The Tokugawa Shogunate possessed the *Kuniezu* of Ryūkyū when it constructed a comprehensive map of Japan. The Shogunate, however, did not draw Ryūkyū on *Nihon sōzu*, and to understand the reason for this silence it is necessary to understand the history of the Japanese view of Ryūkyū.

Although Ryūkyū had been drawn on medieval maps of Japan (Figure 9.10), only part of the island was illustrated, on the fringe of the paper. Such representation was used for other areas, such as China, the Korean Peninsula and Ezo (the old name for Hokkaido), and for places in the non-real world, like Rasetsu Koku,

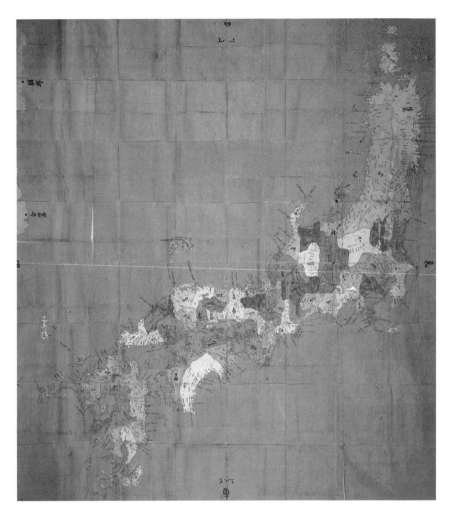

Figure 9.9: Shōhō Nihon Zu (Map of Japan made by the compilation of Kuniezu in the second project).
Collection of National Institute of Japanese Literature.

where it was believed that no males existed. Ryūkyū itself is explained in the map as a place where creatures with heads like birds lived. The Japanese people of medieval times identified these surrounding areas as 'Others,' and they became essential elements in the creation of a Japanese identity.

Toby (2001) discussed the ambiguous boundary of Japan by paying particular attention to Ryūkyū and Ezo among these 'Other' areas. Up until the late sixteenth and early seventeenth centuries, each area had been independent. Once Japan came to control them, however, the positions of Ryūkyū and Ezo in Japanese history became quite different. While the Tokugawa Shogunate established a new

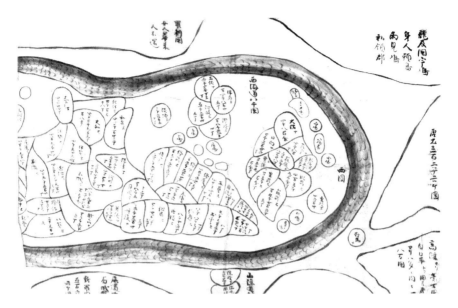

Figure 9.10: Nihon Zu (map of Japan) ca.1300.
Collection of Shomyo-ji Temple.

feudal domain and appointed new feudal lords for Ezo management, Ryūkyū maintained the country's previous political system, including its relationship with China. This act was, of course, only superficial, and Ryūkyū was actually and effectively under the rule of Satsuma. The Tokugawa Shogunate's political and diplomatic strategy was not to have Ryūkyū as part of Japan but to maintain it as a country in the Asian world that was ruled by China, in order to maintain its favorable position for trading Chinese commodities. This policy of keeping Ryūkyū among the 'Others' also served as a device for domestic control. When the messengers of Ryūkyū went to the capital Edo, they were strongly encouraged to dress in Chinese style, rather than in their original style, during their journey. Citizens watching their procession would feel the power of the Edo Shogunate being spread to a big foreign country across the sea.

The Tokugawa Shogunate at the time felt it was important not to identify Ryūkyū as part of Japan but to put it in the middle, between 'Self' and 'Others.' The dual position of the of Ryūkyū—partly 'Self' and partly 'Others'—was shown clearly in the representation of *Kuniezu* and *Nihon sōzu*, and the boundary of 'Japan' was, as Toby (2001) said, quite ragged and elastic.

Mapping authorities

The authority of the Shogunate guaranteed the contents in *Kuniezu* once it was submitted and agreed upon, so local feudal lords would often attempt to record the geographical information in such a way as to receive political merit. Numerous controversies and disputes between neighbors over territories and positions occurred throughout Japan when *Kuniezu* were drawn. For example, Fujita (2002) analyzed the conflict between the eight villages that comprised one district (Gou) in Settsu (the old name for northern Osaka and eastern Hyogo). Harada village had been the main settlement in the area and had a superior position to the other seven villages. The third *Kuniezu* project at the end of the seventeenth century presented the opportunity for the other seven villages to conspire to reduce the power of Harada village and obtain positions equal to it. The judgment, however, ruled against them, and consequently they were drawn clearly on the *Kuniezu* as low-ranking villages.

Conflicts over boundaries also arose in mountain areas, especially in the third project, for which the Tokugawa Shogunate gave instructions to draw all the boundaries of provinces or counties unambiguously (Sugimoto 1999). The dispute over the boundary between Settsu and Harima (the west province of Settsu), for example, started as a result of the residents of Settsu objecting to a report that insisted that some of Settsu's mountains belonged to Harima. Government officials conducted close examinations of the areas pertaining to the issue in the presence of the parties concerned, and finally decided that the boundaries should be based on definite ridgelines and rivers.

Two version of Settsu *Kuniezu* could now be seen; the draft map and the final version which were submitted to the Tokugawa Shogunate. While the former had some tags that showed disputed locations, the latter showed clear boundary lines, including place names used in the judgment to establish the lines (Figure 9.11).

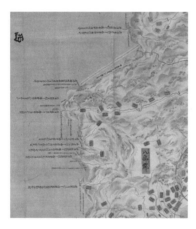 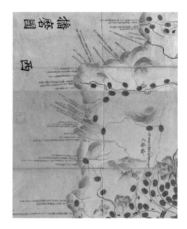

Figure 9.11: Representations of boundary disputes over Kuniezu.
Left: Draft version of Settsu Kuniezu. Collection of the Kyoto University Museum.
Right: A copy of final version submitted to the Tokugawa Shogunate. Collection of the National Archives of Japan.

Official on-site surveys and measurements also brought new measuring techniques to local areas (Narumi 2007). This new knowledge was applied to make village maps, which came to have official authority due to their accurate representation of the territories, and were used to resolve disputes among villages.

Maps and culture

Tourism culture and publishing maps

The historical origins of map-making in Japan may be ancient, but their publication only appeared with the advent of tourism and publishing in the seventeenth century. The end of the Age of the Japanese Civil Wars created an environment in which people were permitted to move freely and safely within the country. Accordingly, various styles of tourism, such as short trips and pilgrimages, became part of Japanese popular culture in the seventeenth century. It is clear that the production of city maps was related to the development of tourism.

The oldest published city map in Japan is *Miyako no Ki* of Kyoto (Figure 9.12), which was published in approximately 1626 (Ito 1994, Kinda 2007). It represented full streets with grid patterns and the names of neighborhoods but none of the suburbs in which most of the major sightseeing areas were located. The first published map of Kyoto was intended for the residents of that city, not for tourists, since the culture of tourism had only just begun and had not yet developed to the point where publishers thought of creating a tourism-related product. Kinda (2007) pointed out that the composition of the map followed the genealogy of the map of *Heiankyō* from the medieval period, and its purpose was to show figures or names in the present based on the medieval base map.

The drawing areas in the map of Kyoto spread to the suburbs during the first half of the seventeenth century (Figure 9.13), but the development of guide maps for tourists as well as for residents only dates from the latter half of the century. The most famous and typical map of the period, *Shinsen Zōho Kyō Ōezu*, was published in 1686 by the publisher Hayashi Yoshinaga (Figure 9.14). In addition to the large number of renowned spots represented in detail on this map, such as temples and shrines, it also contained detailed notes about the places. According to Yamachika (2007), Hayashi derived the map from previously published guidebooks, so it had the unique characteristic of being a map that also served as a guidebook. It was generally accepted by society, which came to be familiar with the development. However, *Shinsen Zōho Kyō Ōezu* was not necessarily convenient while traveling because of its large size—each side was more than one meter long. Publishers often made maps in several sizes for different purposes, and some publishers made portable maps that were only about 50 centimeters on each side. These were intended for tourists, and their contents were brief but sufficient for visiting the main sights. On the other hand, large maps like *Shinsen Zōho Kyō Ōezu* may have been examined while laid on tatami mats, rather than while traveling, in order to prepare for trips.

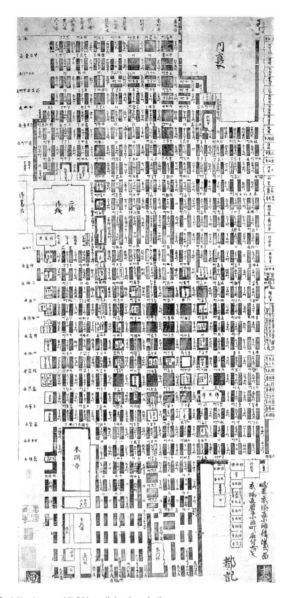

Figure 9.12: *Miyako no Ki* (Woodblock print).
Published c.1626.
Collection of the Kyoto University Library (Ōtsuka Collection).

Strategy for selling maps

Just after Hayashi's map of Kyoto grew in popularity, a famous map of Japan was published in Edo. Called now 'Ryūsen Zu,' it was drawn by Ishikawa Tomonobu (1661-c.1721) and first published by Sagamiya Tahei in 1687. Due

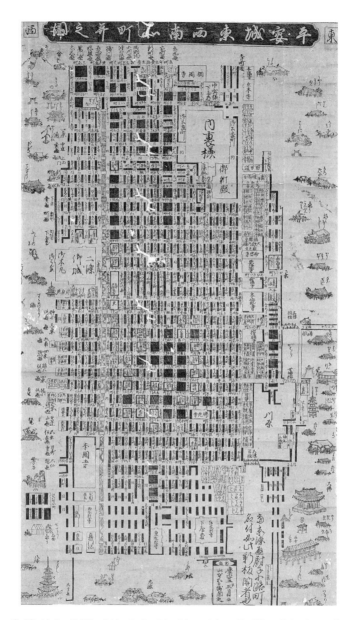

Figure 9.13: *Heianjō Tōzai Nanboku Machinarabi no Zu* (Woodblock print).
Published by Yamamoto Gohei in 1652.
Collection of the Kyoto University Museum.

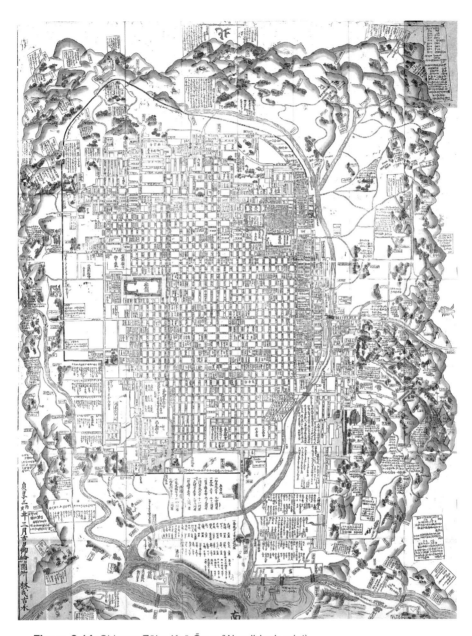

Figure 9.14: *Shinsen Zōho Kyō Ōezu* (Woodblock print).
Published by Hayashi Yoshinaga in 1686.
Collection of the Kyoto University Library (Ōtsuka Collection).

to its popularity, it was revised in a larger size four years later (Figure 9.15) and continued to be published for over 80 years (Miyoshi 1989). The figure of Japan in the map was distorted and in fact there were many published maps of Japan with better geographical information at that time, yet Ishikawa's map remained in popular demand from the 1680s to the 1770s. The strategy of the author and publisher with regard to society at that time can be examined.

The first characteristic feature of 'Ryūsen Zu' was that it was the first published map in Japan that clearly stated its author. The strategy was a great success because of Ishikawa Tomonobu's fame at the time as a *Ukiyoe* Painter and a pupil of Hishikawa Moronobu (?–1694), the founder of *Ukiyoe*. In other words, the publisher Sagamiya (and maybe Ishikawa himself) was less concerned with producing an accurate map than a beautiful picture of Japan for admirers of *Ukiyoe* (Uesugi 2007a). They did not, however, ignore the inherent function of a map. Miyoshi (1989) noted that 'Ryūsen Zu' had two praiseworthy features: its serviceableness and its usefulness. Although 'Ryūsen Zu' had enough information to make it useful for traveling in Japan, the information, on over 800 place names, had a clear geographical bias. Many famous places in eastern Japan, especially near Edo, were described in great detail, but the map contained very little information about the west. This was partly because it was assumed that the consumers of the map would be residents of Edo and the surrounding area. Furthermore, both Sagamiya's shop and Ishikawa himself were located in Edo as well, so they may not have been well acquainted with places outside that area.

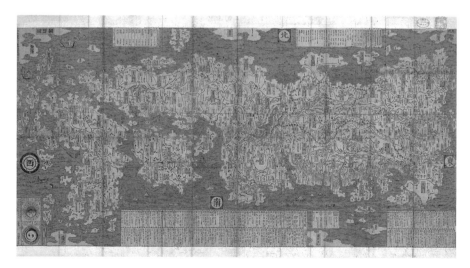

Figure 9.15: *Nihon Kaisan Chōriku Zu* (Woodblock print).
Original picture drawn by Ishikawa Tomonobu, Published by Sagamiya Tahei.
Collection of the Kyoto University Museum.

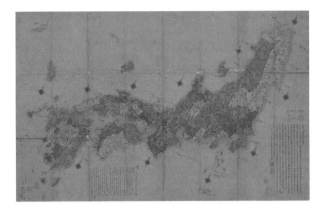

Figure 9.16: Kaisei Nihon Yochi Rotei Zenzu (Woodblock print). Drawn by Nagakubo Sekisui, Published by Asano Yahei in 1779. Collection of Kyoto University Library.

The publishers of 'Ryūsen Zu' changed four times. The three publishers after Sagamiya followed a strategy of increasing information based on developments. They changed the contents to coincide with changes to the daimyo or government officers in castle cities, and recommended that consumers who had already bought 'Ryūsen Zu' should buy a new map that had the latest information.

'Ryūsen Zu' remained the best-selling map of Japan until the 1770s, when popular culture became more concerned with the accuracy of maps than their beauty. After the age of 'Ryūsen Zu', map culture came to center around maps by geographers and surveyors (Figure 9.16), which basically led to the modern era.

View from the Sky

Viewing Landscapes from the Sky

After the latter half of the eighteenth century, greater demand for accuracy led to a corresponding decrease in aesthetics, although some still insisted on the importance of appealing to the senses. Bird's eye views had been drawn in Japan since ancient times, as can be seen, for example, in the pictures of Emaki (picture scrolls) in the ancient and medieval periods. In addition, as a sheet piece, *Ama no Hashidate Zu* (picture of Ama no Hashidate) (Figure 9.17) by the Zen priest Sessyū (1420–1506), is famous for its representation of the landscape of the sandbar and the environment in Tango (the old name for the northern part of the Kyoto Prefecture). In fact, its composition was just like as if viewed by a bird, and it was a combination of his scenic observations and his geographical imagination as influenced by Zen Buddhism (Tokyo Kokuritsu Hakubutsukan, etc. 2002, Fukushima, 2005). Designs of Byōbu ('folding screens') from the six-

Figure 9.17: *Ama no Hashidate Zu* (India-ink painting).
Painted by Sessyū 1501–1506 (National Treasure).
Collection of Kyoto National Museum.

teenth century onwards also used landscapes as seen from the sky, while drawings of cities such as *Rakuchū-Rakugai Zu Byōbu* (Kyoto) (Figure 9.18) and *Edo Zu Byōbu* (Edo) are also well known in the history of Japanese cartography (Yamori 1974, Ozawa 2002).

Such representation was applied to illustrations of guidebooks. At the onset of the culture of tourism, guidebook illustrations were naive and brief. However, a significant change took place in the 1780s with *Miyako Meisyo Zue* (Guidebook about Kyoto) written by Akisato Ritou. Akisato surveyed many places thoroughly with the help of painters, and collected geographical and historical information as well as landscape pictures. The illustrations of *Miyako Meisyo Zue* represented 'realistic' and detailed landscapes as though viewed from the sky (Figure 9.19), and enabled readers to take an imaginative journey. Many guidebooks published at the end of the eighteenth and nineteenth centuries followed this lead. Chiba (2001) pointed out that the illustrations in *Edo Meisyo Zue* (Guidebook about Edo) published in 1835 and 1837 were quite realistic because of their clear depiction of the landscape and the city structure.

The nineteenth century saw the publication of some interesting maps with unique bird's eye view compositions, most of which were drawn by painters. *Kyōraku Zu* (first half of the nineteenth century: Figure 9.20) by Yokoyama Kazan, *Tōkaidō Meisyo Ichiran* (1818) by Katsushika Hokusai, and *Edo Ichiranzu* (c.1803) and *Nihon Meisyo no E* (first half of the nineteenth century: Figure 9.21) by Kuwagata Keisai are representative of such maps (Yamori 1984). Onoda (2006) analyzed *Nihon Meisyo no E* and found that it included a substantial amount of geographical information—over 700 place names—derived from various *Meisyo*

Figure 9.18: *Rakuchū-Rakugai Zu Byōbu (Rekihaku Kōhon)* (Folding screen).
Painted c. 1530.
Collection of National Museum of Japanese History.

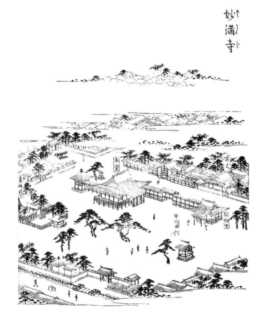

Figure 9.19: An illustration of *Miyako Meisyo Zue* (Woodblock print).
Written by Akisato Ritou, Published by Yoshinoya Tamehachi in 1780.
Collection of Kyoto University Library.

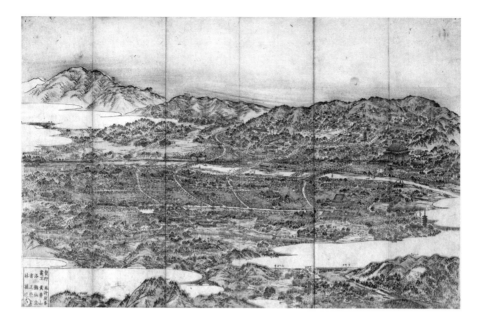

Figure 9.20: *Kyōraku Zu* (Woodblock print).
Painted by Yokoyama Kazan, published in the first half of the nineteenth century.
Collection of the Kobe City Museum.

Zue and the popular 'accurate' map of Japan made by Nagakubo Sekisui at that time (cf. Figure 9.16). These maps were not only beautiful and interesting but could also be reliably used as maps containing complete information.

Politics over the sky

Smith (2001) examined *Dainihon Kairiku Meisyo Zue* (Pictorial Map of Great Japan) (1864) by Utagawa Sadahide (1807–1879), a famous *Ukiyoe* painter active at the end of the Edo Era. According to Smith, this pictorial map (Figure 9.22) had three effects on the society that helped create the concept of 'National Territory.' These were the visual effect of images of various regions, the effect of the title, which declared Japan's national unity, and the effect of evoking the community of memory by describing historical locations.

Ukiyoe painters at that time generally drew landscape pictures and pictorial maps. Some of the works contained messages that were critical of the government in the form of caricatures, and some of them contained praise for the conditions at the time, but all had some degree of political influence on the community. Utagawa Sadahide can be singled out, however, because he was particularly conscious of the power of geographical imagination and, under the pseudonym

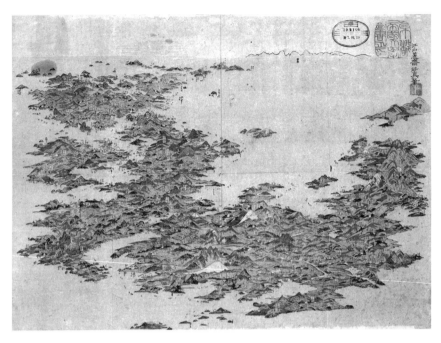

Figure 9.21: *Nihon Meisyo no E* (Woodblock print).
Painted by Kuwagata Keisai, published in the first half of the nineteenth century.
Collection of the Kyoto University Museum.

Figure 9.22: *Dainihon Kairiku Meisyo Zue* (Woodblock print).
Painted by Utagawa Sadahide, published by Iseya Shōnosuke in 1864.
Collection of the Kyoto University Library.

Hashimoto Gyokuransai, used not only the content of landscape pictures but also the map itself as a way of informing the imagination (Miyoshi 1999).

Kankyo Dainihon Shishin Zenzu (Official Map of Great Japan) (1871) was one of Hashimoto's typical works. More accurately, it was actually a cooperative work between Hashimoto and Utagawa (Figure 9.23) (Uesugi 2007b). *Dainihon Kairiku Meisyo Zue* did not depict all of Japan, despite the title referring to it as a map of Japan. As Smith said, it required readers to imagine the national territory based on the portion that was painted on it. On the other hand, Hashimoto's new

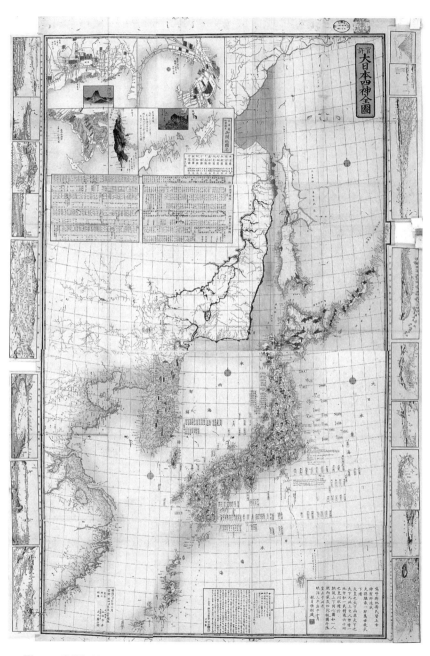

Figure 9.23: *Kankyo Dainihon Shishin Zenzu* (Woodblock print).
Painted by Hashimoto Gyokuransai (Utagawa Sadahide), published by Eikyū Dō
and Kinkō Dō in 1871.
Collection of the Kyoto University Museum.

work did show all of Japan, with numerous place-names. Anyone looking at the map could easily locate the most well known places, and the map would reinforce that their 'home' was in Japan. In addition, the authors used bird's eye pictures of famous cities arranged around the map, as well as recognizing many famous historical locations and new port towns. *Kankyo Dainihon Shishin Zenzu* therefore played a role in helping readers view Japan as historically continuous.

The map was made as an official publication, partly because the new government, created by the 1868 restoration, claimed that they could construct a modern society to succeed the political system of ancient Japan, which was regarded as the ideal society from Japanese history. Hashimoto's representation of historical continuity in the present map enabled the government to demonstrate their political considerations. This idea was reinforced by a verse on the map that was written by Akiduki Tanetatsu (1833–1904), an able politician and intellectual in the government both before and after 1868. The poetry celebrated Japan as an historical entity based on the authority of the Emperor and his lands, which had been maintained since ancient times.

Attention should be paid, however, to the fact that the map represented outer lands, such as China. In particular, the Korean Peninsula was shown in the same level of detail as the drawings of Japan. The latter part of Akiduki's verse described how the reputation and authority of the Emperor and the land would reach the surrounding countries. Such a graphic world and poetic representation allowed readers to imagine the extent of Japan's reach across the sea, and here we can see the early stages of the imagined community following imperialism.

Observations of imperialism

Utagawa observed the drastic changes in Japanese society that took place in the middle of the nineteenth century from the early modern era to the modern era. Another bird's eye painter, Yoshida Hatsusaburō (1884–1955), observed Japanese modernization and imperialism in the twentieth century. He and his pupils drew many bird's eye pictures of locations in Japan, most of which were published as guide maps or supplements in newspapers or magazines.

One of Yoshida's most important works, *Kyoto Meisyo Dai Chōkanzu* (Bird's-eye view of Kyoto) (Figure 9.24), was published by the Kyoto Prefecture in 1928 to celebrate the accession to the throne of Emperor Hirohito. Yoshida made a bold composition, as if viewed from the southwest, and located Mt. Hiei in the central background. From this picture it is possible to perceive the symbolic relationship between the mountain and the city; that is, the flourishing of Kyoto at the foot of Mt. Hiei, which citizens believed protected the capital city. For the representation of the flourish, he drew many sightseeing spots in and around Kyoto, some with English names, and the development of new transport networks, such as those for trains and trams. However, the range of Yoshida's gaze was not limited to the areas in and around Kyoto. Looking at the right-hand side of the picture, many

Figure 9.24: *Kyoto Meisyo Dai Chōkanzu* (printed picture).
Painted by Yoshida Hatsusaburō, published by Kyoto Prefecture in 1928.
Collection of Sakai City Museum.

distant places such as Lake Biwa (the largest lake in Japan), Mt. Fuji (the highest mountain in Japan), and Tokyo (the capital and the largest city) can be found.

A network of railway lines can also be found in *Kyoto Meisyo Dai Chōkanzu*; Yoshida preferred to paint railways and sea routes in his works as symbols of modernization. He actually traveled to various districts in Japan in order to sketch the newest forms of public transport, including those in colonial areas such as Sakhalin, Taiwan and Korea. He recognized the range of the Japan through his own experiences. With the development of transport systems, people were able to reach any part of Japan in only a few days, compared to the matter of weeks it had taken before modernization. Yoshida experienced both the expansion of the territory through colonization and the reduction of travel times caused by modernization. In fact, he expressed this dual structure of 'Japan' in his work. Place names such as Sakhalin, Taiwan and Korea can be found near the fringes of *Kyoto Meisyo Dai Chōkanzu*. Yoshida was just a painter of the times, and the bird's eye view technique was suitable for representing the modern era.

(UESUGI)

Bibliography

Chiba, Masaki (2001), *Edo Meisyo Zue no Sekai: Kinsei Kyodai Toshi no Jigazō* (The world of Edo Meisyo Zue: Self-Portrait of Megalopolis in Edo Era), Tokyo: Yoshikawa Kōbunkan.

Fukushima, Katsuhiko (2005), 'Ama no Hashidate Zu' to Tango Fuchū ("Ama no Hashidate Zu" and the landscape of Tango, Hasegawa, Koji (ed.), *Chizu no Shisou* (Ideas and Maps), Tokyo: Asakura Shoten, pp. 64–65.

Harley, J.B. (1988), Silences and Secrecy: the Hidden Agenda of Cartography in Early Modern Europe, *Imago Mundi* 40, pp.57–76. Reprinted in Harley, J.B. (edited by Laxton, Paul) (2002), *The New Nature of maps: Essays in the History of Cartography*, Baltimore: The Johns Hopkins University Press, pp. 83–108.

Ito, Munehiro (ed.), *Kyoto Kochizu Sanpo* (The Collection of Old Map of Kyoto), Tokyo: Heibonsya.

Kawamura, Hirotada (1984), *Edo Bakufu Sen Kuniezu no Kenkyū* (The study of Kuniezu compiled by the Tokugawa Shogunate), Tokyo: Kokon Syoin.

——— (2005), Edo Bakufu no Kuniezu Jigyō to Nihon Sōzu no Syūsei (the projects of Province maps and National maps by Edo shogunate), Kuniezu Kenkyūkai (ed.), *Kuniezu no Sekai* (World of Kuniezu), Tokyo: Kashiwa Shobō, pp. 7–23.

Kinda, Akihiro (1995), Ezu/Chizu to Rekishigaku (Old maps and history), Asao, Naohiro etc. (eds.) *Siryō Ron* (Study of historiography), Tokyo: Iwanami Syoten, pp. 307–326.

——— (2007), Kyoto Zu no Syuppan (the Publishing History of Maps of Kyoto), Kyoto Daigaku Daigakuin Bungaku Kenkyūka Chirigaku Kyōshitsu, and Kyoto Daigaku Sōgō Hakubutsukan (Department of geography, Kyoto University and the Kyoto University Museum) (eds.), *Chizu Syuppan no Yonhyaku Nen: Kyoto, Nihon, Sekai* (400 Years of Printed Maps: Kyoto, Japan and the World), Kyoto: Nakanishiya Syuppan, pp. 8–32.

Kuniezu Kenkyūkai (eds.) (2005), *Kuniezu no Sekai* (World of Kuniezu), Tokyo: Kashiwa Shobō.

Kuroda, Hideo and Sugimoto, Fumiko (1989), Simazu Ke Monjo Kuniezu Chōsa Houkoku (Research Report of the Document of Kuniezu in the Old Stock by Simazu), *Tokyo Daigaku Siryō Hensanjo Hou* (Report on the activities of the Historiographical Institute) 24, pp. 59–63.

Miyoshi, Tadayoshi (1989), Iwayuru Ryūsen Zu ni tsuite (the study about map of Japan by Ishikawa Tomonobu), *Chizu* (Magazine of Maps), 27–3, pp. 1–9.

——— (ed.) (1999), *Zusetsu Sekai Kochizu Collection* (Concise Illustrated Encyclopedia of World Maps), Tokyo: Kawade Shobō Shinsya.

——— (2000), E to Chizu no Aida wo Samayou (The Wandering Painter between Map and Picture), Kobe Shiritsu Hakubutsukan (ed.), *Ezu to Fūkei: E no youna Chizu, Chizu no youna E* (Pictorial Maps and Landscape: the Intersection of Pictures and Maps), Kobe: Kobe Shiritsu Hakubutsukan, pp. 110–114.

Miyoshi, Tadayoshi and Onoda Kazuyuki (eds.) (2004), *Zusetsu Nihon Kochizu Collection* (Concise Illustrated Encyclopedia of Maps of Japan), Tokyo; Kawade Shobō Shinsya.

Narumi, Kunitada (2007), *Kinsei Nihon no Chizu to Kenchi: Mura to 'Mawari Kenchi'* (Indigenous Land Surveying Techniques and Their Diffusion Process in Warly Modern Japan), Fukuoka: Kyūshū Daigaku Syuppankai.

Oda, Takeo (1973), *Chizu no Rekishi* (History of Maps), Tokyo: Kōdansya.

Onoda, Kazuyuki (2004), Kankō Sareta Nihon Zu (published maps of Japan), Miyoshi, Tadayoshi and Onoda Kazuyuki (eds.) (2004), *Zusetsu Nihon Kochizu Collection* (Concise Illustrated Encyclopedia of Maps of Japan), Tokyo; Kawade Shobō Shinsya, pp. 84–105.

——— (2006), Kuwagata Keisai 'Nihon Meisyo no E' wo Yomu (the study of "Nihon Meisyo no E" by Kuwagata Keisai), Kitani Yoshinobu Sensei Koki Kinen Ronsyū Kankōkai (ed.) *Kitani Yoshinobu Sensei Koki Kinen Ronsyū Kankōkai*, unknown: Kitani Yoshinobu Sensei Koki Kinen Ronsyū Kankōkai, pp. 547–559.

Ozawa, Hiromu (2002), *Toshizu no Keifu to Edo* (Genealogy of City Map and Edo), Tokyo: Yoshikawa Kōbunkan.

Sugimoto, Fumiko (1999), *Ryōiki Shihai no Tenkai to Kinsei* (the Development of Territory Managements and the Early Modern), Tokyo: Yamakawa Syuppansya.

Toby, Ronald (2001), Kinsei Ki no 'Nihon Zu' to 'Nihon' no Kyōkai (the Boundary of Japan and Japan Map in Edo Era), Kuroda, Hideo etc. (eds.), *Chizu to Ezu no Seiji Bunka Shi* (Mapping and politics in premodern Japan), Tokyo: Tokyo Daigaku Syuppankai, pp. 79–102.

Tokyo Kokuritsu Hakubutsukan and Kyoto Kokuritsu Hakubutsukan (eds.) (2002), *Sesshū: Botsugo 500 Nen Tokubetsu Ten* (Sesshū: Master of ink and brush (500th anniversary exhibition)), Tokyo: Mainichi Shinbunsya.

Uesugi, Kazuhiro (2007a), Nihon Zu no Syuppan (the Publishing History of Maps of Japan), Kyoto Daigaku Daigakuin Bungaku Kenkyūka Chirigaku Kyōshitsu, and Kyoto Daigaku Sōgō Hakubutsukan (Department of geography, Kyoto University and the Kyoto University Museum) (eds.), *Chizu Syuppan no Yonhyaku Nen: Kyoto, Nihon, Sekai* (400 Years of Printed Maps: Kyoto, Japan and the World), Kyoto: Nakanishiya Syuppan, pp. 33–67.

——— (2007b), Kindai Chizu to Academism (Maps and Academism in the Modern), Kyoto Daigaku Daigakuin Bungaku Kenkyūka Chirigaku Kyōshitsu, and Kyoto Daigaku Sōgō Hakubutsukan (Department of geography, Kyoto University and the Kyoto University Museum) (eds.), *Chizu Syuppan no Yonhyaku Nen: Kyoto, Nihon, Sekai* (400 Years of Printed Maps: Kyoto, Japan and the World), Kyoto: Nakanishiya Syuppan, pp. 104–125.

Unno, Kazutaka (1995), Cartography in Japan, Harley, J.B. and Woodward, David (eds.), *The History of Cartography: Cartography in the Traditional East and Southeast Asian Societies*, Chicago: University of Chicago Press, pp. 346–477.

Yamachika, Hiroyoshi (2007), Hayashi Yoshinaga Ban Kyō Ōezu no Tokuchō to sono Henka (Kyoto map published by Hayashi Yoshinaga: the characteristics and its transition), Kinda, Akihiro (ed.), *Heiankyō-Kyoto: Toshi Zu to Toshi Kōzō* (Heiankyō-Kyoto: Construction of the City and the Maps), Kyoto: Kyoto Daigaku Gakujutsu Syuppankai, pp. 75–97.

Yamori, Kazuhiko (1974), *Toshizu no Rekishi* (The History of City Map in Japan), Tokyo: Kōdansya.

CHAPTER 10

Landscapes in literature and painting

Taisaku KOMEIE

Representations of landscapes in literature and paintings have served as important historical resources for studying the landscapes' actual appearance, and for symbolic interpretations. Observing landscapes is more than just looking at what is on the ground; as art historians and historical geographers argue (for example, Seymour 2000), it is a way to construct social relations and political identities.

The purpose of this chapter is to provide an overview of the history of landscape interpretation in Japanese literature and paintings, making reference to typical examples of landscape imagery in social and political contexts. In particular, nineteenth century Japan has been a period of particular focus for studies concerning two issues. The first of these is the creation of the *modern self* and the conceptualization of landscapes, while the second is the relationship between landscape imagery and modern Japanese nationalism. Some art and literature historians have made note of the introduction of realism into landscape paintings and modern literature in the nineteenth century. As Karatani (1988: 24) declared, "Landscape is an epistemological constellation. Once it is set up, its origin is also covered." In Japan, landscapes started being viewed consciously by the modern self as objects during the nineteenth century. It can be assumed that Japanese people in ancient and medieval times did not view landscapes as we do today. Nonetheless, poems, paintings, and gardens indicate that landscapes were appreciated and loved in pre-modern Japan. Landscapes and the representation thereof were important elements in Japanese life, long before the modernist conceptualization of landscapes. So what, then, led to the discovery of new landscapes in Japan? In other words, what changed or did not change from pre-modern to modern times in terms of the ways of seeing landscapes? Drawing mainly on the studies of art and literary historians, this chapter sketches the history of landscape representation from ancient to modern times.

Landscapes in traditional poetry

In ancient *waka*, a traditional form of Japanese poetry that consisted of 31 or more syllables, the poet was inspired to write by the scene that surrounded them. The first imperial anthology of Japanese poetry, compiled in 905, was the *Kokin wakashū*. Its preface noted that what a poet sees and hears evokes literary representation:

> Japanese poetry has the human heart as seed and myriads of words as leaves. It comes into being when men use the seen and the heard to give voice to feelings aroused by the innumerable events in their lives. The song of the warbler among the blossoms, the voice of the form dwelling in the water—these teach us that every living creature sings.
>
> (translated by McCullough 1985: 3)

When external things are drawn into literature, the human heart is projected upon them. The depiction of landscapes was one of the most important aspects of ancient poetry. For example, in the early eighth century, a noble woman saw herself in a white flower in a pasture:

> *Natsu no no no, shigemi ni sakeru, himeyuri no,*
> *siraenu koi wa, kurushiki mono so.*
>
> By Sakanoue no Iratsume
> (*Man'yōshū*, Volume 8: #1500)

> Oh, the pain of my love that you know not –
> A love like the maiden-lily
> Blooming in the thicket of the summer moor!
>
> (translated by Taki 1965: 127)

Numerous landscape depictions can be found in *Man'yōshū*, the oldest anthology of Japanese poetry, compiled in the eighth century.

Landscapes were sometimes viewed in a political context. Some literary historians cite the earliest poetry, which depicted landscapes in a particular style, as *kunibome* or 'admiration for our country' by emperors or other rulers (Watanabe 2000). In the early seventh century, for example, after climbing Kagu Hill at the southern edge of the Nara Basin, Emperor Jomei, described the landscape of his country:

> *Yamato niwa murayama aredo, tori yorou Ame no Kagu-yama, nobori tachi kunimi o sureba, kunibara wa keburi tachi tatsu, unabara wa, kamome tachi tatsu, umashi kuni zo, Akizu-shima Yamato no kuni wa.*
>
> By Emperor Jomei
> (*Man'yōshū*, Volume 1: #2)

> Countless are the mountains in Yamato,
>   But perfect is the heavenly hill of Kagu;
> When I climb it and survey my realm,
> Over the wide plain the smoke-wreaths rise and rise,

Over the wide sea the gulls are on the wing,
A beautiful land it is, the Land of Yamato!

(translated by Taki 1965: 3)

With regard to *kuni-bome*, folklorists and literary historians have tended to stress the religious and agricultural aspects when referring to the earlier cultures of ordinary people. T. Uchida (1985), however, pointed out that, from a humanistic geographical viewpoint, emperors, noble people and their representatives conducted a ritual performance called *kuni-mi*, which meant viewing the country they ruled from certain vantage points. In the poem quoted above, according to Uchida's argument, Emperor Jomei viewed not only the Nara Basin but also an imagined ideal landscape of all of his lands and seas. As the ruler, the emperor had to admire and wish for prosperous lands containing many houses with 'smoke-wreaths,' and seas rich with natural resources, even though he could not actually see the sea from Kagu Hill. For rulers in ancient times, the viewing of landscapes was an inevitable duty that came with domination of the land. In the political context of ancient kingdoms, landscapes were represented from the viewpoint of the privileged classes.

Depicting countryside landscapes

Another important style for representing landscapes can be found in the poetry of lower officials, which developed from *kuni-bome*. Suzuki (2000) points out that several famous poets, such as Akahito Yamabe and Yakamochi Ōtomo, developed a style of *waka* from the eight century onward that depicted actual landscapes without using explicitly sentimental words. The following is one of Akahito's most famous *waka*, in which he describes seeing Mount Fuji from his ship while on an administrative visit to the Kantō region:

> *Tago-no-ura yu, uchi'idete mireba, mashiro niso,*
> *Fuji no takane ni, yuki wa furikeru.*

By Akahito Yamabe
(*Man'yōshū*, Volume 3: #318)

When going forth I look far from the shore of Tago,
    How white and glittering is
The lofty Peak of Fuji,
Crowned with snows!

(translated by Taki 1965: 188)

By shifting his gaze from the blue Pacific Ocean to the dominating, shining white peak of Mt. Fuji, Akahito presented a landscape whose central focus was the peak. How did these ancient poets, such as Akahito, acquire the views and styles that formed this new perspective? Watanabe (2000) reviewed the arguments of literary historians, and from this, he suggested that those lower-ranked official/poets following the emperors' travels were given the opportunity and the style with which to depict images of what they saw by the ritual admiration of landscape in *kuni-bome*. Acting as surrogates for the emperors, these literally able lower-ranked officials celebrated the local landscapes they saw. In ancient landscape poetry, admiration for the landscape was linked to the ideal of the emperors' governance (Suzuki 2000).

Compared with the earlier tradition of *kuni-bome*, Akahito and other landscape poets of the time made artful arrangements of words and acute observations about the natural environment. Suzuki (2000) praised Akahito's poetry as spatial and picturesque, and surmised that the construction of large capital cities, such as Fujiwara-kyō in 694 and Heijō-kyō in 710, created a distinct geographical contrast between urban and rural countrysides and prompted recognition from contemporaries of the natural environment as new and strange. Nobles and officials, traveling for the purpose of local governance, found something exotic about such journeys. The new way in which they viewed the landscape was from the perspective of an observer, an independent self apart or distanced from nature. Alternatively, they were independent individuals who found natural places that allowed them to represent their personal intellect and impressions. In the ancient times of the *Kokin wakashū*, landscape poetry represented a direct personal view combined with sentimental expressions. For example:

> *Toshi-goto ni, momiji-ba nagasu, Tatsuta-gawa,*
> *Minato ya aki no, tomari naru ramu.*

By Tsurayuki Ki
(*Kokin wakashū*: #311)

> Is its mouth the place
> where autumn finds a harbor –
> the Tatsuta River,
> which every year sends downstream
> leaves in a myriad hues?

(translated by McCullough 1985: 76)

In this case, the poet found not only the leaves' colorful glory but also their sorrowful end repeated in the autumn landscape of the Tatsuta River. Landscapes became a literary means of reflecting personal feelings.

Repeating the way of seeing

The development of landscape poetry, however, did not allow the free or independent depiction of a poet's impressions. The famous landscapes that were suitable for poetry were formulated as *uta-makura*, places about which so many poems had been written that the way of seeing the landscape had become firmly fixed. From late ancient times, poets could compose landscape poetry about a place without actually visiting it, simply by drawing on the intertextuality established by the corpus of preceding *waka* (Kamens 1997). For example, *Chikuen-shō*, a poetry guidebook compiled in the late thirteenth or early fourteenth century, supposedly in the poetry school of Sadaie Fujiwara, provides the following instructions (Nishida 2000: 158):

> A poem about Naniwa Bay should include the reeds on the shore unless you can see them. On Akashi or Sarashina, a luminous moon must be poeticized even on a cloudy night. In Yoshino or Shiga, cherry blossoms are a literary topic even in the off-season. Generally speaking, a famous thing or place should be poeticized unless you can see it.

This doctrine demonstrates the establishment of a fixed way of depicting landscapes at *uta-makura,* such as the reeds on the tidal flats at Naniwa Bay (now Osaka Bay), the moon at Akashi (Akashi City, Hyōgo Prefecture) and Sarashina (Nagano City, Nagano Prefecture), and the cherry blossoms at Yoshino (Yoshino Town, Nara Prefecture) and Shiga (west bank of Lake Biwa, Shiga Prefecture). The need to express their thoughts within the bounds of age-old traditions usually forced poets to reproduce those mannerisms. From the late medieval period until early modern times, poetry guidebooks such as *Chikuen-shō* and the multitude of *waka* regarding famous spots were compiled and copied. For example, when a local poet named Teitoku Matsunaga (1571–1654) attempted to depict the landscape of Sumiyoshi along the coast of Osaka Bay (Sumiyoshi Ward, Osaka City), he was able to refer to 200 or more poems from the compilations that were available during his time (Nishida 2000). His predecessors' poetry suggested to Teitoku that verses should focus on certain elements in the landscape, such as pine trees and forget-me-nots (*myosotis*) along the shore, sea breezes over the coast, or a market in front of Sumiyoshi Shrine. One of Teitoku's poems (Nishida 2000: 161) suggests that his verses came entirely from intertextuality:

> *Matsu-kage ya, chitose mo kokoni Sumiyoshi no,*
>   *Kishine no kusa no, natsu o wasurete*

> Under the shade of pine trees,
> Seems grass at the seaside of Sumiyoshi
> So comfortable for hundreds of years,
> Forgetting hot summer has come.

In this case, the poem consists of pine trees, forget-me-nots and Sumiyoshi (a place name) with the associated linguistic connotation of 'living comfortably.' The poet's attempts to write his own original *waka* were restricted by the traditional manner of observing this particular landscape. Therefore, Karatani (1988) questioned whether it was possible for pre-modern Japanese artists to discover *real* landscapes, as distinct from the traditional themes, in an original manner.

Reproducing the way of seeing

Nishida (2000) refutes Karatani's assertion by arguing that the mannerisms in Japanese poetry made it possible for poets to show deep sympathy with ancient or contemporary people in an intertextual manner. Viewing a landscape in the way that had been fixed by the existing literature was to share the manner of looking at a particular landscape. The establishment of intertextuality in landscape poetry incorporated certain landscapes into the culture and society. The case of Waka-no-ura Lagoon (Wakayama City, Wakayama Prefecture) shows the typical socialization of a landscape. When a Confucian scholar, Ekiken Kaibara, visited Waka-no-ura in 1698, it was already a seaside landscape that had been made famous in an ancient poem by Akahito Yamabe:

> *Waka-no-ura ni, shio michi kureba, kata o nami,*
>   *Ashibe o sashite, tazu naki wataru.*

By Akahito Yamabe
(*Man'yōshū*, Volume 4: #580)

> As the tide flows into Waka Bay,
> The cranes, with the lagoons lost in flood,
> Go crying towards the reedy shore.

(translated by Taki 1965: 191)

Ekiken discovered that the local lord of Ki'i Domain controlled the area, partly because Tōshōgū Shrine, sacred to the founder of Tokugawa Shogunate, was situated at the lagoon's innermost shore (Figure 10.1). Ekiken also learned of a recently established local custom of naming eight beautiful scenes, including the *Ashibe* Buddhist Temple and the *Kata-o-nami* sandbar (named after Akahito's poem). The text of this eighth century poem is clearly central to the composition of the landscape view. In comparing Waka-no-ura with other famous *uta-makura*, Ekiken observed that the landscape was well composed and controlled (Itasaka and Munemasa 1991: 141):

> Viewing from the hill, I found Wakayama Castle, Tōshōgū Shrine, Tenjin Shrine, Tamatsu Island, and Imose Hill in my perspective, a landscape of both the sea and the land with natural mist and smoke from the salt works. So many scenic spots come into sight. The landscape of the lagoon probably exceeds those of Japan's three most famous landscapes; I have not been to Matsushima but I have visited

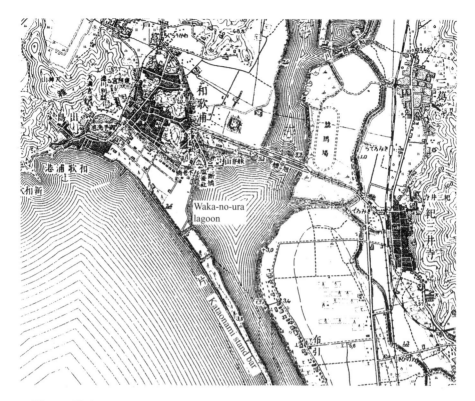

Figure 10.1: Waka-no-ura lagoon.
Source: Topographical map "Wakayama" (1: 50,000), 1934.

Itsuku-shima Island in Aki Province and Ama-no-hashidate in Tango Province. I have never seen such an extraordinary landscape in the other provinces I have visited. Besides, the mighty domain of Ki'i constructed brilliant and great shrines and temples and keeps them clean so as to be spectacles.

As Ekiken noted, the landscape had been well controlled since the establishment of the Ki'i Domain in the early seventeenth century (Hasegawa 1996). The lords regarded the lagoon as a part of the sanctuary attributed to Tōshōgū Shrine, within which new economic activities such as land reclamation and salt works were prohibited. However, *samurai* and other classes could visit shrines and temples and an official observation house from which they could enjoy the landscape. After the observation house was damaged by a storm in 1866, it was rebuilt not by the domain but by donations from ordinary people from the castle town of Wakayama who appreciated the landscape.

Visiting a poetry spot and viewing the landscape became a popular leisure activity in early modern Japan, enjoyed by various classes who shared the way of seeing same manner of seeing the sights. Landscapes became socialized among poets as well as among noble and ordinary people through a formulated, and therefore routine, way of seeing. They found it quite difficult to observe a well-known scene in a novel way or to discover new and unknown landscapes to appreciate. In order to achieve an original way of seeing, modernists in the nineteenth century needed to be isolated from tradition and to contemplate their own inner self.

Realistic way of seeing

Although many natural and cultural landscape paintings had been created in pre-modern Japan, they cannot be regarded, by today's definition, as 'landscape paintings.' For example, the tradition of *sansui-ga*, that of the Chinese-style paintings dominant in medieval times and in early modern Japan, had not represented a real landscape but rather an imaginary or ideal anchorite/anchoress or hermit in a mountainous environment. Artists depicted the type of relationship between man and nature developed by Chinese Taoism, Buddhism and the geomancy of *feng-shui* (Sullivan 1962). As Keiji Usami (1980: 172) declared, as a painter, 'a *topos* painted in *sansui-ga* subsists not in relationship to a person and objects but as an a priori and metaphysical model.' One of Sesshū Tōyō's most famous paintings, *Tōkei sansui zu* (A winter landscape of mountains and stream) (Figure 10.2), does not represent an actual material landscape but rather a thoroughly composed image of an ideal living space. These landscapes were fictional or imagined images that intellectuals could refer to as a cultural topic. For example, some early nineteenth century intellectuals sought out real scenes that they believed were similar to the landscapes in *sansu-ga*. They found a beautiful real landscape in Tsuki-ga-se (Nara City, Nara Prefecture) and described it in travel writings or Chinese style poetry, proving that they saw this countryside landscape through a veil of Chinoiserie and did not necessarily want to live there (Ōmuro 2002).

In contrast, *yamato-e*, or Japanese-style paintings developed during the late ancient and medieval periods, also had a tradition of representing landscapes. Painting a scene or landscape, especially as an illustration on a scroll, gave great pleasure to the aristocrats of the late ancient period. For example, one of Japan's oldest novels, *Genji monogatari* (Tale of Genji) written between the late tenth century and the early eleventh century, describes a royal competition to paint a scroll in the presence of the emperor. In this scene, the novel's protagonist, Prince Genji, defeats his rival by presenting a lonely landscape that represents the countryside where he hid during his political exile. But did those kinds of paintings accurately depict real landscapes? One early fourteenth century example, *Kasuga Gongen genki emaki* (Painting Hand Scroll of Miracle at Kasuga Shrine) (Figure 10.3), shows an artist trained in the landscape tradition of *yamato-e* composing a scene with stylized hills and trees. In this painting, although Mount Kasuga, a sanctuary behind the shrine (Nara City), is represented as a hill covered by thin snow, without a textual explanation it is not possible to identify the mountain. The elegant,

Figure 10.2: Toyō Sesshū, *Tōkei sansui zu* (fifteenth century, National Treasure).
Collection of the Tokyo National Museum.
Image: TMN Image Archives.
Source: http://TnmArchives.jp

Figure 10.3: *Kasuga Gougen genki emaki*, volume 9, (1309).
Collection of the Imperial Household Agency, Japan.

春
日
山
漆在
上大
郡和
　州

Figure 10.4: Bunchō Tani, 'Kasuga Yama' in *Nippon meizan zue* (1812).
Source: Tani (1970: 88–89).

rounded appearance of the forest has the symbolic sanctity of the hill but not the unique look. It was not until the early nineteenth century that Mount Kasuga was captured in a realistic way in Bunchō Tani's *Nippon meizan zue*, or an Illustration Album of Glorious Mountains in Japan (Tani [1804] 1970) (Figure 10.4).

Western painting techniques imported through restricted trade with the Netherlands had an influence on realist Japanese landscape paintings from the eighteenth century, which used the laws of perspective with shading and skiagraphy. The early pioneers of this new technique were Naotake Onoda (1746–1785), a representative of the Akita School of *Dutch Painting*, and Kōkan Shiba (1747–1818), the first Japanese oil and etching painter. They attempted to use their influence to introduce the stereographic style used in contemporary Western paintings to Japanese art. In traditional Japanese painting, Bunchō Tani (1763–1840) and others established *shinkei-zu*, or 'true landscape painting,' following a process of trial and error. So what was 'true' in Bunchō? Against the broad background of Japanese and Chinese paintings, at a time when traditional landscape painters were composing ideal or conventional scenes with stylized elements, he stressed the importance of sketching real and specific landscapes, especially mountain scenes. Bunchō's landscape album in woodblock printing, *Nippon meizan zue* (Tani [1812] 1970), included 90 illustrations of Japanese mountains, in which he tested the accuracy of his reproductions of stereographic geomorphology in drawings, as shown in Figure 10.4.

Bunchō's political connection with the Tokugawa government was one of the most important factors behind his desire to record 'real landscapes' (Kashiwagi 2003a). Born as a vassal in a kindred family of the Tokugawa, he was appointed in 1792 as a painter to serve Sadanobu Matsudaira, the highest government dignitary. Bunchō joined an official project that recorded local landscapes related to the defense of Tokyo Bay against foreign ships. He was ordered not to create artistic interpretations but, like a photographer, to record precisely what the project group observed along the seashore. The final 1793 version of his work, *Kōyo tanshō zukan* (Paintings of an Official Excursion), depicts real perspectives of the coastline, such as the complicated geomorphology shown in Figure 10.5). Although this work does not seem to have been appreciated as fine art within the conventional painting tradition of the time, Bunchō showed that 'real landscape' sketches were a valid alternative style of painting. His publication of *Nippon meizan zue* in 1812 heralded the arrival of a new school of landscape painting. In the preface he noted, "Since childhood, I have loved mountains and streams; in my journeys throughout Japan, I sketched every great mountain and stream I met." Natural geomorphology in reality was his teacher and his objective. It is worth noting that Bunchō traveled to colonial Hokkaidō to record some volcanoes that had hitherto never been the subject of conventional landscape poetry and painting (Figure 10.6). He discovered a new manner of viewing landscapes, not through a stylized or ideal model, but rather as a material object with a magnificent vista.

Figure 10.5: Bunchō Tani, 'Shimoda Minato' in *Kōyo tanshō zukan* (1793). (Important Cultural Property).
Collection of the Tokyo National Museum.
Image: TMN Image Archives.
Source: http://TmnArchives.jp

Figure 10.6: Bunchō, Tani, 'Usu Dake' in *Nippon meizan zue* (1812).
Source: Tani (1970: 116–117).

Vistas viewed from great heights presented opportunities for the next generation of 'true landscape' artists. The bird's-eye views (see chapter 9) created by
Bunchō's followers, including Keisai Kuwagata (1764–1828) and Kazan Watanabe
(1793–1841) were an important variation of *shinkei-zu*. Although they did not,
strictly speaking, look down from the sky, they did construct scenes from above.
Realist techniques of sketching material landscapes laid the groundwork for artificial compositions of realistic views in the artist's imagination. Keisai's *Edo hitome
zu byōbu* (A Look at Edo) (Figure 10.7) from 1809 targeted what was Japan's largest city at the time. The developing city was a spectacle that presented a popular
topic for the paintings of Sadahide Gountei (c.1807–?), an important successor
to Keisai. The depiction of actual landscapes became a new realm for nineteenth
century painting and visualization. Although inspired at first by the introduction
of Western perspective, the change took place as a part of artistic technical issues
and through the discovery of new scenes that could be represented as landscapes.

The modern self and external landscape

Painters looked for new landscapes in the early nineteenth century, but a similar
development was not present in literature, although some litterateurs began to

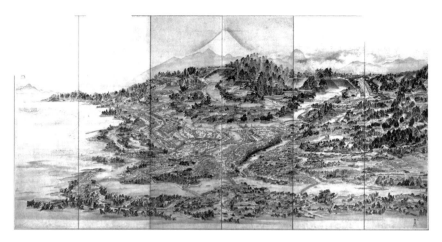

Figure 10.7: Keisai Kuwagata, *Edo hitome zu byōbu* (1809).
Collection of the Historical Museum of Tsuyama Region.

explore inland mountainous regions in search of unusual lifestyles. Within Japan, a politically and economically closed country, folklore in the deep mountains or peripheral areas was of interest to the urban population (Komeie 2005). For example, a lettered merchant named Bokushi Suzuki (1770–1842) ventured deep into the Echigo Mountain Range to visit Akiyama-go (Sakae Village, Nagano Prefecture) in 1828. Bokushi paid close attention to the traditional subsistence economy during his trip, such as swidden agriculture and the natural landscapes that surrounded settlements (Miya 1983: 325):

> Climbing up mountains and down to valleys, I often saw colorful scenes like baldachin in an old deep, green forest. Rolling up my trouser legs, I scraped my body against lianas and twigs. The dreamy landscape so interested me that I imagined Lord Madenokōji Fujifusa lived as a hermit on a mountain like this. Creeping under a thousand-year-old tree that lay across the path, I found mushrooms growing on deadfall, which no one gathers. There are no tourists or loggers on the trail. Only red-colored trees like baldachin are shining and darkening. Cold winds blow desolately, even during the day; sounds of streams echo idly.

Despite Bokushi's fascination with the landscape deep in the mountains, he recalled a famous historical drama in the fourteenth century about Madenokōji Fujifusa, who fell from power and died in obscurity. He sighed, "This landscape could have been a famous *utamakura* if poets like Saijō or Sōgi had visited here and made poetry (Miya 1983: 328)." Even confronted by such amazing nature, he believed that the only valuable landscapes were those that were poeticized within intertexuality. Bokushi was also one of the litterateurs who viewed landscapes only in traditional poetry.

In his argument regarding modern Japanese literature, Karatani (1988) pointed out that a lonely 'inner man' who is isolated from social relationships could see landscape in a material and objective manner and project his own identity on the landscape. According to Karatani, Doppo Kunikida (1871–1908) was one of the first Japanese writers to show landscape as a literary theme. For example, Doppo's 1898 short story 'Wasure'enu hitobito' (People I cannot forget) portrays a lonely man who tries to write a literary sketch about the people he had just seen on his journey. For example, the man recalled a landscape he had seen from his ship, of a fisherman on the shore of a small island (Kunikida 1949: 165):

> I saw a person on the shining seastrand at ebb tide. He is a man, not a child, who gathers something and drops it into a basket or a tub. He walks around again, squats down, and picks something up. I gazed at this beachcomber on the small seashore of a small island. As the ship went on, the figure shrank into a small black spot and the whole island, including the beach and the hill, vanished in the fog. In the ten years that followed, although I do not know his face, how many times did I recall him?

Paradoxically, it was not an intimate everyday environment but merely a distant landscape with which the main character in Doppo's story could sympathize or identify. As Karatani (1988) argues, realism in modern Japanese literature was established through the depiction of landscapes discovered as external scenes alienated from human life. Notably, reading the works of William Wordsworth and Ivan S. Turgenev provided Doppo with a window through which to appreciate natural landscapes. Referring to such Western literature, Doppo claims, "Originally, Japanese people did not know the beauty of deciduous trees, such as oaks. In terms of forests, only pine forests have been important in Japanese literature and painting. There is no poetry representing autumn rain in an oak forest" (Kunikida 1949: 13). The discovery of actual landscapes as a literary theme was part of the modernization of Japanese literature, influenced by imported Western literature.

Another important writer who 'discovered' landscape, and who also loved oak forests, is Roka Tokutomi (1868–1927) (Y. Uchida 2001). In 1898, on the recommendation of Doppo, Roka kept a natural observation diary, through which he became fascinated with the landscapes of deciduous forests and clouds. In his *Shizen to jinsei* (Nature and Life) (1900), Roka described an attachment to the natural landscape (Tokutomi 1933: 67):

> Walking in the woodlands, looking up at the misty sky, smelling the fragrance of the grass, listening to a gentle stream, and feeling the wind blowing on my skin, I found something stirring in my memory but I cannot grasp exactly what I feel. Does my soul suffer from nostalgia

for my home in the heavens? In spring, nature is my mother. When man is integrated with and enfolded in nature, he bemoans his finite life and yearns for eternity.

What was Roka trying to represent in his praise for nature? According to Yoshiaki Uchida (2001), Roka's natural landscape was an object that was independent from human beings, and he lived as a guest of nature. Recognizing nature as an external environment, he discovered that his life was animated in the natural world. A subject such as an anonymous quotidian landscape like an oak forest, which did not interest many of his contemporaries, became a basis for supporting human existence. To Roka, seeing landscape was to remind oneself of life.

The cases of Doppo Kunikida and Roka Tokutomi demonstrate that some modern writers tried to find the modern self in landscape or that a landscape could become a window through which to see one's identity. Their realist view of landscape paralleled the development of realist oil paintings of landscapes in the Meiji Period (1868–1912). The clear introduction of Western oil painting techniques enabled young Japanese painters to depict reality. In particular, Antonio Fontanesi (1818–1882), an Italian painter, was invited in 1876 by the Meiji government to be an art teacher and he taught his students to sketch quotidian landscapes (Kashiwagi 2003b). An early masterpiece by Chū Asai, *Shunpo* (Field in Spring) (Figure 10.8), is a good example of how an anonymous landscape that lacks poetry or any particular historical interest is still worthy subject matter for a painting. Not only the painter's acute observations about the actual landscape and agricultural work can be found in this rural landscape, but also his empathy

Figure 10.8: Chū Asai, *Shumpo* (1881) (Important Cultural Property).
Collection of the Tokyo National Museum.
Image: TMN Image Archives.
Source: http://TnmArchives.jp

for the coming of spring, as shown by the trees in full bloom. To oil painters like Asai, realistic sketching does not just mean the reconstruction of a material scene on a canvas but also finding the modernist himself who sees the external environment world in a sympathetic way. However, would many modern Japanese be able to see landscape in their own personal ways?

Nationalist mountain landscapes

As the modernist perspective was being developed, a geographic journalist named Shigetaka Shiga (1863–1927) published his influential work, *Nihon fūkei ron* (Discourse on Japanese Landscape), in 1894. This work is an important example of the amalgamation of scientific discourse, nationalism, and modernist landscape. In the preface, Shiga declared (Shiga [1894] 1976: 12–13):

> One cannot help admiring the beauty of one's home country. It is nothing but an ideation. However, is it just because it is one's home that Japanese people applaud Japanese rivers and mountains? It is because they are absolutely beautiful.

Shiga's argument depends on two realms: scientific physical geography and traditional literature, including traditional *waka* poetry. According to Shiga, Japan's natural environment has a wide variety of climates, flora and fauna, ample precipitation that creates impressive natural landscapes, great volcanic mountains, and strong erosion in valleys and along the coast. This explanation was notable for being the first time in Japan that the beauty of landscape was evaluated in scientific discourse. However, some geographers, including the first professor of geography at Kyoto University, Takuji Ogawa (1870–1941), criticized inaccuracies in Shiga's geological knowledge (Ogawa 1895: 192). Despite this, Shiga's discourse did play a role in landscape being viewed objectively from a geological perspective. Accordingly, an early alpinist in modern Japan, Usui Kojima, praised the book because it 'swept out' traditional landscapes associated with poetry (Kojima [1937] 1995: 371). Ogawa also expected that the book would encourage young people to observe the natural environment more objectively (Ogawa 1895: 192).

On the other hand, as part of an overtly academic explanation, Shiga quoted numerous Japanese poems regarding particular mountains and used Chinese poetic diction, suggesting that his perspective of landscape was similar to that of early modern writers and the tradition of *sansui-ga,* not to modernism (Ōmuro 2003). An illustration of 'ideal Japan' including pine trees, cherry blossoms, and Mount Fuji (Figure 10.9), which had been the most popular items in traditional early modern landscapes, shows Shiga's intention to extend the traditional scheme of landscape, rather than to invent a new concept of landscape like Doppo Kunikida and Roka Tokutomi had done. Published during the Sino-Japanese War of 1894–1895, *Nihon fūkei ron* was read in a kind of popular environmental determinism that admires beautiful Japanese in beautiful landscapes. Rather than discover a new personal landscape, Shiga instead added new poetics with an academic aura to traditional schemes of landscapes.

Shiga's discourse led to reproductions of a nationalist view of mountains in the early twentieth century. A typical example is Mount Fuji, the highest conic volcano on the Japanese mainland, which Shiga also extolled as the 'standard' for great mountains around the world. An illustration of Mount Fuji appeared in an early elementary school textbook (Figure 10.10), in which it was regarded as the greatest mountain in Japan. As Abe (1992) argues, admiration for Mount Fuji in school textbooks was intended to evoke nationalist empathy in students. The great Mount Fuji was supposed to represent the greatness of Japan, through which children could attain political identity as a member of the Japanese people. By using landscape as a form of national propaganda, was it possible for

Figure 10.9: 'Ideal Japan: What a beautiful country!' in *Nihon fūkei ron* (1894). Source: Shiga (1976:18).

Figure 10.10: An illustration of Mount Fuji in a Textbook.
Source: Yūzō (Shōzō) Tsubouchi, *Kokugo tokuhon* (Japanese Reader), 1900.
Text in the illustration: Section one. A great mountain. This is the highest mountain in Japan.

Japanese people to gaze at a natural landscape from an internal perspective as Doppo and Roka did? The history of landscape representation in Japan shows that a more powerful gaze has been generated in modern times than in pre-modern society.

Bibliography

Abe, Hajime (1992), Kindai Nippon no kyōkasho ni okeru Fuji-san no shōchō-sei (The symbolism of Mount Fuji in textbooks in modern Japan), *Chirigaku hyōron* (Geographical Review of Japan), 65A (3), pp. 238–249.

Hasegawa, Seiichi (1996), *Ushinawareta keikan: Meisho ga kataru Edo Jidai* (Lost landscapes: Edo period in the sights), Tokyo: Yoshikawa Kōbunkan.

Itasaka, Yōko and Munemasa, Iso'o (eds.) (1991), *Shin Nippon koten bungaku taikei* (New anthology of Japanese literature classics), Vol. 98, Tokyo: Iwanami Shoten.

Kamens, Edward (1997), *Utamakura, Allusion, and Intertextuality in Traditional Japanese Poetry*, New Haven: Yale University Press.

Kashiwagi, Tomo'o (2003a), 'Fūkei-ga eno mezame: Edo-kōki no Nippon (The rise of landscape: Japan in the late Edo period)', in Kashiwagi *et al.* (eds), *Akarui mado: Fūkei hyōgen no kindai* (Transparent windows: Politics of landscape), Tokyo: Taishūkan Shoten, pp. 27–62.

——— (2003b), 'Fūkei-ga no kaika: 19 seiki kōhan kara 20 seiki shotō no Nippon (Landscape in bloom: Japan from the latter half of the 19th century to the early 20th century)', in Kashiwagi *et al.* (eds), *Akarui mado: Fūkei hyōgen no kindai* (Transparent windows: Politics of landscape), Tokyo: Taishūkan Shoten, pp. 174–224.

Karatani, Kōjin (1988), *Kindai nippon bungaku no kigen* (The origin of modern Japanese literature), Tokyo: Kōdansha.

Kojima, Usui (1995), 'Kaisetsu (A comentary)', in Nobuyuki Kondō (ed.), *Nihon fūkei Ron* (Discourse on Japanese landscape), Tokyo: Iwanami Shoten, pp. 368–382.

Kokusho Kankō Kai (ed.) (1970), *Nippon meizan zue* (An illustration album of glorious mountains in Japan), Tokyo: Kokusho Kankō Kai.

Komeie, Taisaku (2005), '"Sanson" gainen no rekishi-sei: Sono shiten to hyōshō o megutte (Historicity in the concept of mountain village: On its perspective and representation)', *Minshū-shi kenkyū*, Vol. 69, pp. 3–20.

Kunikida, Doppo (1949), *Musashi-no*, Tokyo: Shinchō-sha.

McCullough, Helen Craig (ed.) (1985), *Kokin Wakashū: The First Imperial Anthology of Japanese Poetry*, Stanford: Stanford University Press.

Miya, Eiji (ed.) (1983), *Suzuki Bokushi zenshū: Chosaku-hen* (Collected edition of Suzuki Bokushi), Tokyo: Chūō Kōron Sha.

Nishida, Masahiro (2000), 'Dentō to jikkan to (Between tradition and reality)', in Yasuaki Watanabe and Teruo Kawamura (eds.), *Utawareta fūkei* (Poetized landscape), Tokyo: Kasama Shoin, pp. 155–173.

Ogawa, Takuji (1895), '*Nihon fūkei ron* o hyōsu (A review of Shiga's *Discourse on Japanese landscape*)', *Chishitsugaku zasshi* (Journal of the Geological Society of Japan), 2(17), pp. 190–193.

Ōmuro, Mikio (2002), *Getsurai gen'ei: Kindai Nippon fūkei hihyō-shi* (Visionary Tsuki-ga-se: A critical history of modern landscape in Japan), Tokyo: Chūō Kōron Shinsha.

——— (2003), Shiga Shigetaka *Nihon fūkei ron* seidoku (Critical reading of Shigetaka Shiga's *Discourse on Japanese landscape*), Tokyo: Iwanami Shoten.

Seymour, Susanne (2000), Historical geographies of landscape, in Brian Graham and Catherine Nash (eds.), *Modern Historical Geographies*, Harlow: Pearson Education Limited, pp. 193–217.

Shiga, Shigetaka (1976): *Nihon fūkei ron* (Discourse on Japanese landscape), Tokyo: Kōdansha.

Sullivan, Michael (1962), *The Birth of Landscape of Painting in China*, Berkeley and Los Angels: University of California Press.

Suzuki, Hideo (2000), 'Waka no busshō to fūkei (Natural object and landscape in Japanese poetry), in Yasuaki Watanabe and Teruo Kawamura (eds.), *Utawareta fūkei* (Poetized landscape), Tokyo: Kasama Shoin, pp. 1–26.

Taki, Seiichi *et al* (eds.) (1965), *The Manyōshū: The Nippon Gakujutsu Shinkōkai Translation of One Thousand Poems*, New York: Columbia University Press.

Tani, Bunchō (1970), *Nippon meizan zue* (Illustration album of glorious mountains in Japan), Tokyo: Kokusho Kankō Kai.

Tokutomi, Roka (1933), *Shizen to jinsei* (Nature and life), Tokyo: Iwanami Shoten.

Uchida, Tadayoshi (1985), 'Kodai Nippon no kunimi ni kansuru ichi-kōsatsu (A study about *kunimi* in ancient Japan), *Jimbun-chiri* (Japanese journal of human geography), 37 (4), pp. 77–85.

Uchida, Yoshiaki (2001), *Fūkei no hakken* (Discovery of Landscape), Tokyo: Asahi Shimbun-sha.

Usami, Keiji (1980), *Kaiga-ron: Egakukoto no fukken* (On painting: Restitution of depicture), Tokyo: Chikuma Shobō.

Watanabe, Yasuaki (2000), 'Fūkei hyōgen kenkyū no yukue (Where the study on landscape representation goes)', in Yasuaki Watanabe and Teruo Kawamura (eds.), *Utawareta fūkei* (Poetized landscape), Tokyo: Kasama Shoin, pp. 267–283.

CHAPTER 11

Monumental landscape

Kazuhiro UESUGI

Location of the global story

Monuments, heritage, memory, and commemoration: these are the key words for fashionable themes representing the past, and they attract many researchers from around the world. Various disciplines, including history, sociology, and geography, have identified with these key words in Japan too. For example, the Society of Historical Research, established by interdisciplinary researchers in 1908, adopted 'Monuments' as the theme of its annual meeting in 2007, and in January of 2008 published a special issue in its journal, *The Shirin* (Journal of History), entitled 'Monuments: An historical perspective.' Researches conducted on monuments has been, as Sugimoto (2008) said in the journal, trends not only for Western histories but also for Eastern and Japanese histories of Japan over the last 10 years.

These trends originated with discussions about nation-states. It is clear that translations of some of the 'Classics,' such as *Imagined Communities* by Anderson (1983) or *Les Lieux de Mémoire,* edited by Nora (1984–1992), influenced them to some degree. In fact, research on monuments tends to favor the modern period and to be on the scale of the nation, just as it was in the classics. This chapter, however, begins with the monuments of ancient and medieval Japan. One of the reasons of it is that motivations for this book are to obtain a general view of Japanese historical geographies. It is more important, however, that the inquiry into the monumental landscape in ancient and medieval periods is connected with a critique of the idea that monument and memory are possessions of the modern era. In Asia it has been common to build stone monuments commemorating historical events since the ancient period, especially under the Chinese influence. Therefore, Japanese monumental landscape cannot be discussed without first understanding the history and culture of stone monuments. Analysis of their epigraphs and the processes of building such structures takes us to an era with notably different cosmology and characteristics from those of the modern era.

The latter half of the chapter returns to the modern era and discusses the relationship between monumental landscapes and the creation of local identity. Although some local identities did connect easily to national identity, others did not. The chapter will visit famous Japanese places such as Kyoto, Hiroshima, and Okinawa. The reconstruction of Kyoto in the late nineteenth century, the preservation of a building destroyed by the atomic bomb in Hiroshima and the restoration of the site of the Battle of Okinawa are typical of modern monumental landscapes in Japan that help us to understand the differences and similarities between Japan and other countries.

Inscribed world

Geographical imagination in an ancient monument

Sixteen stone monuments created in ninth century Japan can now be seen (Table 11.1, Figure 11.1). These 16 monuments can be split into three categories according to their purpose: memorials of specific persons, celebrations of Buddhism, and commemorations of geographical events. *Tagajō hi* ('the monument of Tagajō'), located in the northeastern part of Japan, is typical of the latter category, and is one of best examples of ancient geographical imagination and cosmology.

Tagajō was the regional center of the Mutsu *koku* ('province') in northeastern Japan, which had administrative institutions and a military base directed at

Table 11.1: A list of stone monuments made by the 9th century.

ID	Name	Date of erection	Location	Subject of commemoration
1	Uji bashi danpi	(after 646)	Kyoto Pref.	bridge construction
2	Yamanoue no hi	681	Gunma Pref.	person (tombstone)
3	Nasu kokuzō hi	700	Tochigi Pref.	person (tombstone)
4	Tago hi	711	Gunma Pref.	setting of county
5	Genmei Tennōryō hi	721	Nara Pref.	person (tombstone)
6	Awa kokuzō hi	723	Tokushima Pref.	person (tombstone)
7	Kanaizawa no hi	726	Gunma Pref.	ancestors
8	Ryūfukuji sōtō	751	Nara Pref.	building of stupa
9	Bussokuseki	753	Nara Pref.	(Buddha icon)
10	Bussokuseki kahi	(753?)	Nara Pref.	Buddhism
11	Tagajō hi	762	Miyagi Pref.	improvement of Tagajō
12	Uchigawa magai hi	778	Nara Pref.	(Buddha icon)
13	Jōsuiji nandaimon hi	790	Kumamoto Pref.	building of temple
14	Jōsuiji tōrō saoishi	801	Kumamoto Pref.	votive lantern
15	Yamagami tajūtō	801	Gunma Pref.	building of stupa
16	Jōsuiji jiryō hi	826	Kumamoto Pref.	temple estate

Source: Kokuritsu Rekishi Minzoku Hakubutsukan (1997).

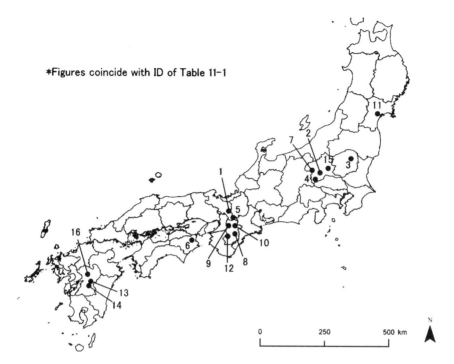

Figure 11.1: Distribution of ancient stone monuments.
Source: Kokuritsu Rekishi Minzoku Hakubutsukan (1997).

the Ezo, a distinct ethnic group living in an area further north. Archaeological research has determined that it was constructed in the early eighth century, and renovated three times by the mid-tenth century. It is clear that the main purpose of the *Tagajō hi* building was to commemorate the reconstruction of Tagajō in 762 by the provincial governor of the time, Fujiwara Asakari (?–764) (Table 11.2). The inscription on the monument indicates the location and origin of Tagajō. In particular, the explanation of its location, represented as the distance between Tagajō and other places, such as the capital (Nara at that time), Ezo, Hitachi, Shimotsuke and Makkatsu, provides an important consciousness of the outside world. Tagajō can be said to have represented its location in two ways: as the farthest area in the national order based on the relationship between the center and the periphery, or between the capital and the regions, and as the concept of frontiers between domestic areas and outer ones.

Hitachi *koku* and Shimotsuke *koku* were the provinces adjacent to Mutsu *koku* in the north. No commodities or information could be brought from the capital to Tagajō without passing through one of those provinces. For the people who lived in Tagajō, especially government officers, most of whom were born in the central capital, these provinces were not only neighboring areas but also functioned as a kind of device to remind and confirm the connection with the center of Japan.

Table 11.2: Contents of *Tagajō hi*.

Categories		Contents
1	location of Tagajō	1,500ri* from the Capital
		120ri from the border with Ezo-Koku
		412ri from the border with Hitachi-Koku
		274ri from the border with Simotsuke-Koku
		3,000ri from the border with Makkatsu-Koku
2	origin	Built in 724 by Ohno Azumahito
3	reconstruction	Reconstructed in 762 by Fujiwara Asakari
4	date of building monument	December 1, 762

* 1ri: about 640 m.

On the other hand, it should also be noted that, in the epigraph of the monument, distances from Ezo were inscribed before distances from these provinces. The land of Ezo did not belong to Japan, and the northern part of Mutsu *koku*, only 120*ri* (about 77 km) from Tagajō, was the frontier or contact zone with the Ezo. Emphasizing the proximity to a different ethnic group in the monument, rather than the relationship with the southern provinces, was an important strategy for the ruler of Tagajō to enhance the significance of his position in Japanese diplomatic policy and also to reconstruct the administrative and military base.

The last line that indicates the location of Tagajō in the monument shows the distance from the border of the Makkatsu ethnic group, who are believed to have had lived in the northeastern and maritime regions of China. The authentic historiography of the time, *Syoku Nihon Gi* ('The Sequel to Japanese History'), suggested that a number of bureaucrats in Mutsu were dispatched to Makkatsu, and it was also known that Makkatsu people came to Ezo or Mutsu several times. Mutsu was considered to be one of the entrances to the outer world that existed beyond the sea, as well as the frontier to Ezo on the same island, so the inscription about Makkatsu was essential to commemorate the meaning of Tagajō.

Buddhist monks and their irrigation engineering work

Irrigation equipment was essential to ancient Japanese agriculture; since ancient times, the Japanese have constructed ponds as a way of obtaining water for farming or everyday life. *Sayamaike* pond, on the southern part of Osaka plain, is the oldest of these artificial ponds still in use. Research conducted in the 1990s on excavations showed that the pond was constructed at the beginning of the seventh century. However, the oldest authentic Japanese-language historiographies—*Nihon Syoki* (Japanese History) and *Kojiki* (Old History), both written in the eighth century— represented the construction of *Sayamaike* pond as an event that took place during

Figure 11.2: *Tagajō hi.*
Left: Entire stone (photo by Miyagi Prefecture).
Right: Rubbed copy (Source: Tagajōshi 1986).

the reign of emperors between the first century BC and the first century AD. It is assumed that these emperors were residents of the world of mythology and, of course, that descriptions of them were created to establish their historical authenticity in the eighth century by authorities claiming to be their descendants.

After its construction in the seventh century, *Sayamaike* pond was repaired or reconstructed several times. In recent years, indications of 11 large reconstructions of the cross-section of the bank and the years in which they took place have been validated by historical research (Table 11.3, Figure 11.3). A stone monument found in the water of the pond in the 1990s, known as *Chōgen Sayamaike Kaisyū hi* ('monument of repair work of *Sayamaike* pond by Chōgen'), helped to determine the age of the pond. The monument (Figure 11.4) was erected in 1202 to commemorate the repair (layer 9 in Figure 11.3) by Chōgen (1121–1206), a famous Buddhist monk known for the construction and reconstruction of many temples, especially of the *Tōdaiji* temple in Nara.

According to the monument, people at that time believed that *Sayamaike* pond was constructed by Gyōki (668–749), who was regarded as a Buddhist saint and who helped build *Tōdaiji* temple along with many other temples, roads, bridges, and ponds. In fact, Chōgen practiced his own work with a strong awareness of Gyōki (Kinda 2008: 289–295), and *Sayamaike* pond and *Tōdaiji* temple were typical examples of his actions. The monument served not only to commemorate the repair work but also to declare the close relationship between the ancient saint and the medieval monk. However, these functions may not have been displayed

Table 11.3: The major layers of the bank of *Sayamaike* pond and date of (re)construction.

Layer	Date of (re)construction
1	1964
2	1927
3	1886
4	18C–19C
5	18C–19C
6	1741
7	1608
8	1558–1569
9	1202 by Monk *Chōgen*
10	762
11	713 by Monk *Gyoki*
12	c. 616
13	(original soil)

Source: Sayamaike Chōsa Jimusyo (1998).

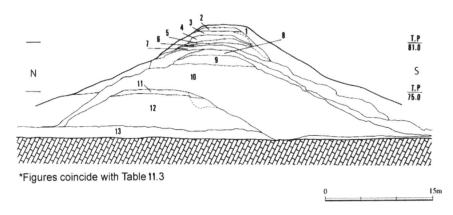

*Figures coincide with Table 11.3

0   15m

Figure 11.3: Cross section of the bank of *Sayamaike* pond.
Source: Sayamaike Chōsa Jimusyo (1998).

to the people at all, because the inscription on the monument was very clear and without abrasion, despite being made on soft stone. This indicates that it was not built on the land but was buried in the bank right after the construction (Sayamaike Chōsa Jimusyo 1998). This raises the question of whether the stone can be considered as a real 'monument' without having any audience.

Such a question arises from modern conceptions regarding commemoration and monuments. These filters should be discounted and the written inscription

Figure 11.4: *Chōgen Sayamaike Kaisyū hi* (monument of repair work of *Sayamaike* pond by Chōgen).
Source: Osaka Furitsu Sayamaike Hakubutsukan (Osaka Pref. Sayamaike Museum) (2006).

regarded as an invocation of the gods of the Buddha. It was important for Chōgen to aim his announcement of the completion of the pond repair not at the people but at the world of the gods, because of his desire to achieve a sense of identification with an old saint. It was popular in medieval Japan to bury sutras and statues of the Buddha. Chōgen's burial of the monument was, therefore, not surprising when viewed in such a cultural context.

A long period passed before the buried stone came back into public view. It was discovered when *Sayamaike* pond underwent large-scale reconstruction at the beginning of the seventeenth century (layer 7 in Figure 11.3). Even then, however, the stone did not obtain the status of a 'monument.' It was placed at the bottom of the pond and reused as part of a stone-built sluice gate. The first time it was regarded as a 'monument' was when an archaeological research team chanced upon the letters on a stone of the sluice gate in the 1990s. Following this discovery, it transformed dramatically from simply being a stone in the pond into an important reminder of historical events related to the pond in the medieval (with a longing for the ancient) and early modern eras. A museum dedicated to the pond's history was built close to the pond in 2001, and the 'monument' has been displayed publicly as one of the most important exhibitions recounting the history of the pond.

Device connecting the past and the present: Commemoration in the eighteenth century

Uji bashi danpi ('fragmental monument of the Uji bridge') (Figure 11.5) was constructed to commemorate the bridging of the Uji river. Uji was very important

Figure 11.5: *Uji bashi danpi* (fragmental monument of Uji bridge).
The upper quarter of the monument was originally created in ancient times, and the rest was added during repair work in the eighteenth century.
Photo: Kazuhiro UESUGI.

area, both politically and strategically, as a distribution center located at the intersection of a principal road and river in *Kinai* (the capital region). The epigraph initially stressed the rapidity of the river, and then commemorated the construction of the bridge by the Buddhist monk Dōtō in 646. The inscribed year shows that it is the oldest stone monument in Japan (cf. Table 11.1), yet some historians doubt the contents on the basis of other documents, which claim the Uji Bridge was built by Dōshō in the 660s.

The monument's disappearance had gone unnoticed, probably because of the river's flooding, and a copied epigraph in the fourteenth century was the only evidence of the monument's existence. Centuries later, in 1791, it was rediscovered on the riverside, though it was only the upper quarter of the stone. When Kobayashi Kōsetsu (1755–1820), a doctor recognized for his sophisticated taste, and his intellectual colleagues received the information, they decided to conduct repair work and establish it into a temple near the river (cf. Figure 11.5).

The culture of reminiscence was widespread in eighteenth century Japan. For example, many satirical *Ukiyoe* pictures have been found with subject matter based on historical events. Viewers were expected to have a certain degree of knowledge about the history if they enjoyed looking at them. While many published texts provided outlines of the history, they were often inaccurate and contained exaggeration and dramatization. The historical knowledge of ordinary people was made by these media. Meanwhile, the educated classes required more sophisticated means for the preservation of their identity, and thoroughly investigated the 'accurate' and 'detailed' knowledge of history and historical geography. Accordingly, to know the historical truth was to be an intellectual authority in that time, and this was the atmosphere in which Kobayashi lived. An understanding of the history of the Uji Bridge and commemoration of discovered monuments were natural and genuine actions for him.

Some intellectuals of the age constructed new monuments to commemorate the history discovered through their own research works, as explained, for example, in the research works of Nabika Seisyo (1668–1738), a Confucian famous for being the editor of *Go Kinai shi* (Topography of Kinai) in 1735. To determine the topography, Nabika and his colleagues frequently visited towns and villages in Kinai to conduct field surveys, and verified the locations of various institutions and graves mentioned in historical documents (Shirai 2004). From a modern perspective, the results of their work cannot be seen as correct, but the attitudes and practices they adopted are admirably similar to modern historical geographers. *Go Kinai shi* was, as Muroga (1936) described it, 'a concrete work produced by empirical studies' before the birth of academic geography in Japan.

In addition to the topography, Nabika also planned the construction of monuments on the historical heritages found through his own investigations. He was particularly enthusiastic about the commemoration of important ancient shrines in a statute book, *Engi shiki*, some of which were lost or whose names had been changed. He considered ancient institutions and society to be ideal, and believed

Figure 11.6: Monument of ancient shrine in northern Osaka plains by Nabika Seisyo. Photo: Kazuhiro UESUGI.

that the reconstruction of an ideal society was essential in order to commemorate aspects of ancient political heritage, such as imperial mausoleums and shrines. The plan to build monuments into the shrines in the northern Osaka plains became a reality in 1736, and 20 stone monuments inscribed with the original shrine names were set in each of the shrines (Figure 11.6).

According to Inoue (2000), the responses of local residents to his commemorative acts were varied. The conflict between those local people with strong traditional sentiments and religious beliefs and the intellectual class, who wanted 'accurate' and 'detailed' knowledge of the past, is clearly visible. Shrine halls were reconstructed in some villages and the shrines' names restored to the original ones based on Nabika's study. Despite this, they did not accept his views on ancient society. They considered their shrines to have miraculous properties, and Nabika's opinion did nothing more than provide legitimacy to their religious power. That is, their reactions to the shrines were based on their own religious beliefs and traditional knowledge. On the other hand, some villages attempted to reject

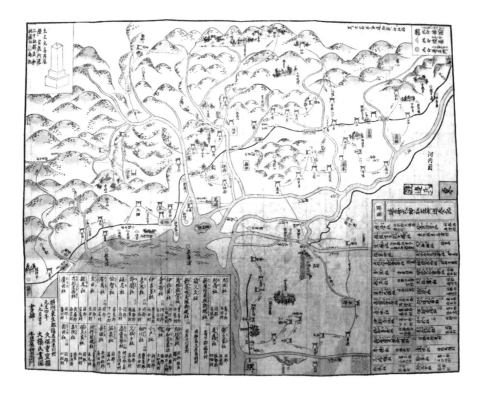

Figure 11.7: *Setsuyō Engishiki jinja Zaisyo Junsan Ki* (Route map of ancient shrines with the monuments in northern Osaka plains).
Source: Kobe City Museum.

his proposals regarding the construction of monuments. For them, the names given in their own time were the right ones, and had long been familiar, while the ancient names revealed by Nabika were new and the villagers felt no connection to or knowledge about them. Nevertheless, the villagers were unable to reject the project because it was supported by the Edo Shogunate—'absolute power'—so they reluctantly accepted the construction of the monuments. In this way, structures connecting the past and present emerged in the local landscape.

In 1739, the monuments were marked on a published map with an excursion route (Figure 11.7), which was produced by one of Nabika's pupils, who had devoted himself to the construction of the monuments. The explanation on the map stressed the fact that the monuments were authorized by the Edo Shogunate.

Commemoration in the modern era

Anniversaries of the capital

The Edo Shogunate was overthrown and a new centralized government was established under the Emperor in 1868. The term *Kindai* ('modern'), when used in Japanese history, commonly refers to the period from 1868 to 1945. As the political landscape changed, the imperial families and court nobles left Kyoto and moved to Tokyo. Kyoto had managed the city as *Miyako* ('capital') under the Emperor since 794, the year of the construction of *Heiankyō*—the old name for Kyoto. The loss of the Emperor meant *Miyako's* loss of identity, as well as the loss of economic and political power.

For the citizens of Kyoto, searching for a way to overcome this crisis, the year 1894—the 1100th anniversary of *Heiankyō*—was a great opportunity to revive the city and reconfirm its identity. Two national events were held that year: the National Industrial Exhibition and the 1100th anniversary festival in Kyoto, for which Okazaki, an eastern suburban area of Kyoto, was developed as the site. The rural landscape was changed drastically into a center of commemoration with an exhibition hall, amusement parks and so on. Among these new establishments, the Heian Jingū Shrine was constructed as the most important monument to commemorate the 1100th anniversary (Figure 11.8, Kobayashi 2007). The shrine was erected with a strong sense of *Heiankyō*. For example, the dedicated deity was Emperor Kanmu, the first emperor of *Heiankyō*, and the shape of the center hall was based on the palace of *Heiankyō*. Furthermore, a parade with historical commemoration—*Jidai Gyōretsu*—was also included as part of the anniversary festival. Participants in the parade clothed each historical cloth in *Miyako* and lined up in historical order. It was presented to audiences as the chronicle of Kyoto, depicted over 1100 years, and Kyoto portrayed as the 'eternal' *Miyako* and the center and source of Japan's national identity. The parade was regarded

Figure 11.8: Heian Jingū shrine.
Photo: Kazuhiro UESUGI.

as the religious event of the shrine after the festival, and became an annual event. The date for the parade was established as October 22nd, the day when Emperor Kanmu entered the capital, and was therefore suitable for commemoration of the city's origin (Figure 11.9).

Some historians made contributions to the commemoration by way of historical investigations (Kobayashi 2005). For example, Yumoto Fumihiko (1843–1921), a member of the festival committee, surveyed the city with his colleagues and settled on the exact location of *Heiankyō*. They also constructed monuments at the site of important ancient institutions such as the Palace and the Main Gate (Figure 11.10). The construction date was October 22, the same as the parade. Yumoto and his team also wrote the first detailed history of Kyoto, considered today to be the keystone of modern historical research on the city.

It should be noted that these exhibitions and anniversary festivals were held with new technology clearly being a major factor at the time. In 1890 Kyoto had a hydroelectric power station near Okazaki that used water from Biwa Lake, and a tram was built between Port Fushimi and Okazaki that passed through Kyoto Station. People could travel on the latest form of public transport to the exhibition grounds, at 10 kilometers per hour, visit the Industry Pavilion, the Agriculture Pavilion and Technology Pavilion and be dazzled by a variety of never-before-seen

Figure 11.9: Parade of Jidai Matsuri (festival commemorating the city's history) on October 22nd.
Photo: Heian Jingū.

Figure 11.10: The monument of the ruins of the ancient Palace.
Photo: Kazuhiro UESUGI.

exhibits created using new techniques. Over one million people attended the exhibition and were fascinated with Kyoto, both in terms of commemorating the past and with an eye on the future.

The age of anniversary festivals

The Constitution of the Japanese Empire—modern Japan's first Constitution— was promulgated in 1889. Two major wars shortly thereafter, against the Qing dynasty (1894) and against Russia (1904), led to national conscription and also a sense of national identity. In such social circumstances, many places in Japan planned various anniversary festivals to coincide with Kyoto's 1100th anniversary, in order to create a sense of belonging to the nation. The commemoration of local history within the wider national history was regarded as the best way to connect a traditional local identity with the newly formed national identity in the modern era. Takagi (2005) said that the period around the late nineteenth and early twentieth centuries could be called 'the age of the anniversary festival.'

The first anniversary festival to be held in this period was Tokyo city's 300th anniversary in 1889, commemorating the development of the city under the Tokugawa Shogunate and the new government. Prior to that, it had not been common to commemorate the Tokugawa Shogunate because it had been the enemy of the new government. Nevertheless, the Imperial Household Agency cooperated with the festival, and some members of the Imperial Family even participated in it. Citizens developed a sense of feeling of obligation from the Emperor toward his former enemy, and began to associate veneration of the Emperor with commemoration of the Tokugawa Shogunate. This celebration was followed by 300th anniversaries being held by other former castle cities, commemorating the construction of castles or the first entry to the cities of the first domanial loads. The promotion of the obligation of the Emperor was also emphasized in these local festivals. The 'age of anniversary festivals' served to create local identities by commemorating local histories, and also to establish a national identity under the authority of the Emperor.

The anniversary festival of Kyoto did not, of course, commemorate the Edo era itself; rather, it was more directly connected to the Emperor. It is known, however, that the person who promoted Tokyo city's 300th anniversary also advised on the festival in Kyoto, and it is clear that the historical theme of 'the age of anniversary festivals' became one of the important contexts of Kyoto's 1100th anniversary.

Second commemoration for the old capital

A hundred years later, Kyoto welcomed its 1200th anniversary. Five key themes were attached to the celebrations (Table 11.4), and many related commemorative events were planned. For example, Tozai subway line was constructed under key theme 2, and the promotion of the Kansai Science City plan was supported under key theme 1. These projects also formed part of the city's plan for the twenty-first

Table 11.4: Five key themes for the 1200th anniversary of *Heiankyō*.

1	City planning for the Twenty-first century
2	Construction of new traffic and information network
3	Industrial development
4	Improvement of society and environment
5	Inheritence and development of culture

Figure 11.11: Reconstructed 1/1,000 scale model of *Heiankyō*.
Now exhibited at Kyotoshi Heiankyō Sōseikan (public exhibition hall for Heiankyō) near the ruins of the Palace of *Heiankyō*.
Photo: Kyoto City Library of Historical Documents.

century. As well as looking to the future the construction of a cultural city center based on the past was also presented forward, especially under key theme 5. One of the most symbolic events of the 1200th anniversary was the construction of the Museum of Kyoto, intended to exhibit the city's 1200 years of history and culture. The museum itself functions as a monument that embodies the history of Kyoto, as it is located on Sanjō Street, derived from *Heiankyō*, and incorporates a modern building as a part of the museum.

Some academic research works on Kyoto's history were published to commemorate the anniversary, along with the building of a 1/1000 scale model of *Heiankyō* (Figure 11.11). The largest model of the historical city took two-and-a-half years to build and required research from many fields, including archaeology, Japanese history, architectural history, and historical geography (Kinda 2002). It became a monument of research history, not just a commemoration of the anniversary.

War Heritage

Memory of Hiroshima

Hiroshima, Nagasaki, and Okinawa are well-known Japanese battle sites of the Asia-Pacific war. Hiroshima and Nagasaki, the cities struck by atomic bombs, have public memorial parks with monuments located at each hypocenter. In addition, after 2000, National Peace Memorial Halls for Atomic Bomb Victims were constructed in each of these cities. The victims of the atomic bombs are now commemorated by the nation with a message of peace.

The most famous monument in Hiroshima is the Genbaku Dome. Originally built as an exhibition hall for local products by a Czech architect in 1915, it has been preserved as a symbol of the bombed landscape, and was registered as a World Cultural Heritage site as the Hiroshima Peace Memorial (*Genbaku Dome*) in 1996.

This 'modern' European architecture was a famous pre-war landmark of Hiroshima, a symbol of the promotion of industry. On August 6, 1945, this symbol was destroyed in a flash, and the definitive damage it suffered did not allow it to be reconstructed. The ruins of the architecture have, however, served as a landmark up to now; it is a symbol not of the modern era but of a bombed landscape.

Some important times are noted for the process of memorializing the ruin. Yoneyama (1999; 2005) pointed out that once Hiroshima began talking about protection of the Dome in 1966, a range of opinions from various perspectives were expressed, resulting in heated debate. A nationwide fund-raising campaign for the preservation was developed, although the idea of preserving such a reminder of misery was distasteful to the survivors. And, in the 1970s, some survivors tried to protest the spatial hegemony of Hiroshima city in enclosing the memory of the Atomic Bomb in and around Genbaku Dome. Yoneyama (1994) referred to the hegemony as the 'taming of memoryscape,' which had an impact on city plans and tourism development.

Abe (2006) discussed the history of the 'taming of memoryscape,' and concluded that it was older than Yoneyama had assumed. Hiroshima city had established a reconstruction project using the icon of 'Peace City' and planned the memorial park as far back as the late 1940s. According to Abe, Genbaku Dome was an element of this plan right from the beginning, and the position of Genbaku Dome was announced on August 6, 1951 more explicitly in the *Report of the Hiroshima Peace City Plan* as an important element of the memorial park and 'only one' legacy of the Atomic Bomb. The 'taming of memoryscape' in Hiroshima had started once Hiroshima city considered itself as the future Peace City, and Genbaku Dome was given its symbolic role from the beginning.

The memoryscape of 'Peace City' spread worldwide with the slogan 'No more Hiroshima.' The registration of the World Heritage site as the second War Heritage site, after Auschwitz, helped to strengthen the spatial hegemony. It must be remembered, however, that this registration was not unconditionally accepted by the rest of the world. The United States opposed the registration at the meeting and China abstained in objection to insufficient war responsibility. In addition, as mentioned above there was a lack of consensus even within Japan. Genbaku Dome itself was given protection, but the significance of the monument has always been a source of conflict, and will probably remain so.

Monuments and tourism

As well as being famous as a tourist resort with a subtropical environment, Okinawa prefecture, located in the South China Sea, is also known as a memorial space of the Asia-Pacific war. Okinawa, the site of a three-month battle in 1945 that cost over 200,000 lives, was the only prefecture in Japan that was the site of a ground battle in the war. The fiercest battlegrounds were the southern part of Okinawa Island. Today, the prefectural peace memorial museum and park with many monuments stand in the center of this area (Figure 11.12), and many tourists make a pilgrimage to the southern part of Okinawa Island.

Figure 11.12: Okinawa Prefectural Peace Memorial Museum.
Photo: Kazuhiro UESUGI.

Table 11.5: Tourism Course Model for a half-day trip in Okinawa 1963.

	Route	Sightseeing Spots
1	Naha City	Administrative district; Kokusai-dōri St.; Sūgenji Temple; Naminouegū Shrine; *Gokokuji Temple*
2	Tomigusuku Village	*Remains of Japanese Navy headquarters*
3	Itoman Town	Hakugindō; Tomb of Kōchi kin group; *the Memorial of Gen. Simon Bolivar Buckner Jr.; Shiraume Monument;* Nashiro Beach; *Himeyuri Monument; Konpaku Monument; Kenji Monument; Shimamori Monument; Reimei Monument; Kōgyō-Kenji Monument*
4	Gushikami Village	Shizenkyō Bridge; *Hakusui monument;* Minatogawa area
5	Tamagusuku Village	Kannon-dō temple in Ohjima; Ukinju-hainju ponds; Tamagusukujō Castle Site; the site of Military Government
6	Chinen Village	Chinenjō Castle Site; Seifā-utaki Sacred Site
7	Sashiki Village	Tsukishironomiya Shrine; Landing Monument of Imperial Prince Yoshihisa
8	Ōzato Village	Ōzatojō catsle Site
9	Yonabaru Town	Oyakawa Sacred Site; Landing Monument of Emperor Hirohito
10	Haebaru village	*the Site of Army hospital*

Italics: Heritage or monument about the Battle of Okinawa.
Source: Okinawa Tourist Agency (1963).

The connection between the pilgrimage to the battle site and the tropical resort was, from the beginning, an essential part of Okinawa's post-war tourism strategy (Uesugi 2006). In the 1950s the Ryukyu (Okinawa) government, under the control of the United States until 1972, discussed the reconstruction policies. There were few basic industries in Okinawa because of the prefectureship of the islands, so the development of tourism was indispensable to the reconstruction plans. The prospectus of the Okinawa Tourist Agency, founded in 1954, said that it was necessary to make sightseeing spots based on the war, as 'there are many potential tourists who would like to go to Okinawa to commemorate the dead, not only from Japan but from all countries of the world' (Yamashiro 1964: p.11). The legislative branch of the Ryukyu government discussed the importance of the battle sites in the southern part of the island as a tourism resource, and in 1957 enacted the Governmental Park Law (the equivalent of the National Parks Law in Japan) for the preservation of important landscapes. The battle sites were envisioned in the discussions as reminders to avoid war and ensure world peace. Changing the battle sites to sightseeing locations created international goodwill and led to the acquisition of foreign exchange (Official Report, extra, September 16, 1957).

The Okinawa Tourist Agency published guidebooks with tourism course models. The first guidebook after the war in 1954 recommended a simple four-course model, the shortest of which was a half-day tour of certain battle sites in the southern part of the island. Another edition, published in 1963, contained the same course models with more details recommending tourists to visit the war heritage just after starting from Naha, the central city of Okinawa (Table 11.5). The other three models also used the first model at the beginning of the tour. The memory of the war became a profitable resource for Okinawa tourism in the 1950s and 1960s (Uesugi 2006).

The landscape of the southern part of the island changed gradually with the development of the tourism policies. The Ryukyu government and Okinawa Tourist Agency did not wish to memorialize the war throughout the entire area, but they did promote some memorial centers for the sake of facilitating effective and efficient pilgrimage. The government began to consolidate monuments and cineraria in the area because of the difficulty in managing all of them in the various places, and to avoid any confusion among tourists regarding a suitable commemoration site.

Guidebooks listed some of the monuments that had been accepted as suitable sightseeing spots and some tourism facilities were installed, including toilets and parking lots. As tourism increased, souvenir stores and dining halls were built near the monuments. In the rest places, on the other hand, almost all monuments and cineraria were reduced, and all traces of the battle were removed completely from the landscape, so people gradually forgot the local history of the construction of monuments. After more than 60 years, few residents were aware of the places of monuments set in the past. The wind blowing through the sugar cane fields has carried away the memory of commemoration.

Bibliography

Abe, Ryogo (2006), Heiwa Kinen Toshi Hiroshima to Hibaku Kenzōbutsu no Ronsō: Genbaku Dome no Isō ni Chakumoku shite (Hiroshima, the Peace Commemorating City, and Conflict over the A-bombed Building: Focus on the Positioning of the Atomic Bomb Dome), *Jinbun Chiri* (Japanese Journal of Human Geography), 58(2), pp. 197–213.

Anderson, Benedict (1983), *Imagined communities: reflections on the origin and spread of nationalism*, London: Verso. (Japanese translation) Shiraishi, Takashi and Shiraishi, Saya (trs.) (1987), *Souzō no kyōdōtai: Nashonarizumu no kigen to ryūkou*, Tokyo: Libroport.

Inoue, Tomokatsu (2000), Nabika Seisyo no Shikinaisya Kensyō to Chiiki: Seetsu Koku Shikinaisyagō Hyōseki no Konryū wo Chūshin ni (Commemoration of ancient shrines by Nabika Seisyo and local correspondence: a case study about constructions of the monuments in northern Osaka plains), *Osaka Shiritsu Hakubutsukan Kiyō* (The Bulletin of Osaka City Museum), 32, pp. 1–12.

Kinda, Akihiro (2002), *Kodai Keikanshi no Tankyū* (Landscape History of Ancient Japan), Tokyo: Yoshikawa Kōbunkan.

——— (2008), *Daichi eno Manazashi: Rekishichirigaku no Sanpomichi* (Gaze Round Lands: Promenades of Historical Geography), Kyoto: Shibunkaku Syuppan.

Kobayashi, Takehiro (2005), "Heian Tsūshi" no Hensan to Yumoto Fumihiko: Jū-kyū Seiki Matsu Kyoto ni okeru 'Chi' no Kōsaku (The Compiling "Heian Tsūshi" and Yumoto Fumihiko: the Mitures of Knowledge in the end of the nineteenth century), Meiji Ishin Shi Gakkai (eds.), *Meiji Ishin to Rekishi Ishiki* (Historical Knowledge and the Restoration), Tokyo: Yoshikawa Kōbunkan, pp. 109–144.

——— (2007), Heian Sento Senhyakunen Kinensai to Heian Jiugū no Sōken (The 11th centenary of the transfer of the capital to *Heian-kyo* and the foundation of the *Heian* Shrine), *Nihonshi Kenkyū* (Journal of Japanese Hisotry), 538, pp. 1–28.

Kokuritsu Rekishi Minzoku Hakubutsukan (National Museum of Japanese History) (1997), *Kodai no Hi: Ishi ni Kizamareta Message* (Ancient Monuments: Messages Inscribed on Stones), Sakura: National Museum of Japanese History.

Muroga, Nobuo (1936a), '*Go Kinai Shi* by Nabika Seisyo 1', *The Shirin* (Journal of History), 21(3), pp. 169–192.

——— (1936b), '*Go Kinai Shi* by Nabika Seisyo 2', *The Shirin* (Journal of History), 21(4), pp. 133–145.

Nora, Pierre (ed.) (1984, 1986, 1992), *Les Lieux de Mémoire*. Paris: Gallimard. (F) (Japanese translation) Tanigawa, Minoru et al. (trs.) (2002, 2003), *Kioku no Ba: France Kokumin Isiki no Bunka-Syakai Shi*, Tokyo: Iwanami Shoten.

Okinawa Tourist Agency (1963), *Kankō Okinawa* (Guidebook of Okinawa), Okinawa Tourist Agency.

Osaka Furitsu Sayamaike Hakubutsukan (Osaka Pref. Sayamaike Museum) (2006), *Jōsetsu Tenji Annai* (Guidebook for Permanent Exhibition), Osakasayama: Sayamaike Museum.

Sayamaike Chōsa Jimusyo (1998), *Sayamaike: Maizōbunkazai hen* (Sayamaike Pond: buried Cultural Properties), Osakasayama: Sayamaike Chōsa Jimusyo.

Shirai, Tetsuya (2004), *Nihon Kinsei Chishi Hensan Shi Kenkyu* (Study of the History of Topographies in Early Modern Japan), Kyoto: Shibunkaku Syuppan.

Sugimoto, Yoshihiko (2008), 'Monument kenkyū no shin chihei (New trends in research on monuments)', *The Shirin* (Journal of History), 91(1), pp. 256–263.

Takagi, Hiroshi (2005), Kinensai no Jidai: Kyūhan to Koto no Kensyō (The Age of Anniversary Festival: Commemoration in the Old Clans and the Old Capital), Sasaki, Suguru (ed.), *Meiji Ishinki no Seiji to Bunka* (The politics and Culture in the Age of the Restration), Kyoto: Shibunkaku Syuppan, pp. 303–344.

Tagajōshi (Tagajō city) (1986), *Tagajōshi Shi* (History of Tagajōshi), volume 3, Tagajō: Tagajōshi.

Uesugi, Kazuhiro (2006), Naha kara Mabuni he: Fukkimae Okinawa ni okeru 'Irei Kūkan no Chūshin' (From Naha to Mabuni: the centre of commemoration of the war dead 1945–1972), *Nijusseiki Kenkyū* (Twentieth Century Studies), 7, pp. 29–52.

Yamashiro, Zenzō (ed.) (1964), *Okinawa Kankō Kyōkai shi* (History of Okinawa tourist agency), Naha: Okinawa Kankō Kyōkai (Okinawa tourist agency).

Yoneyama, Lisa (1994), Taming the memoryscape: Hiroshima's urban renewal, Boyarin, Jonathan (ed.) Remapping memory: the Politics of Timespace, Minneapolis: The University of Minnesota Press, pp. 99–135.

——— (1999), *Hiroshima traces: time, Space, and the Dialectics of memory*, Berkeley: University of California Press. (Japanese version) Ozawa, Hiroaki etc. (translations) (2005), *Hiroshima: Kioku no Politics*, Tokyo: Iwanami Shoten.

PART 5

Cultural landscapes

CHAPTER 12

Characteristics of the Japanese landscape history

Akihiro KINDA

Foundations and transformations of town planning

The Japanese Islands are located at the eastern fringe of the Eurasian Continent. Traditional Japanese cultures have been variously influenced by the continental cultures. For example, around the tenth century BC, during the *yayoi* period, activities such as the cultivation of rice paddies and the manufacturing of bronze tools were adopted. Similarly, the ritual of burying mirrors with dead bodies inside great tombs known as *kohun* was absorbed and practiced in the later centuries. This influence was also observed in the manufacturing of iron tools from the third century AD. The ancient kingdom called *Yamato-chyotei* was established during the fourth and fifth centuries AD and transformed into an imperial state in the first half of the seventh century, accommodating palaces, policies of land planning and a bureaucratic system. Buddhism reached the state via the continental countries and was soon practiced in addition to the traditional Shintoism during the sixth century.

The second half of the seventh century saw the rise of several formal systems such as *ritsuryo* within the Japanese ancient society under the strong influence of China, and these systems became the bases of the Japanese traditional culture; these systems were also applied to a few modern cultural landscapes. During the sixth and the first half of the seventh centuries, each of the emperors who came in power set up their own imperial palace at a location of choice. However, the first Chinese-style capital city was constructed in 684 AD with considerable modifications from the archetype. The construction of several capital cities followed until the end of the eighth century.

The last ancient-style imperial capital was Heian-kyo, now known as Kyoto, which was established in 794 AD. The city plan was prepared such that Heian-kyo would be in the shape of a perfect rectangle, 5.2 kilometers long from north to south and 4.5 kilometers wide east to west between two rivers on the alluvial fan in the northern part of the Kyoto Basin. The capital was divided into the east and west capital cities by an 84-meters-wide principal street and the two cities were controlled by separate capital-city governments. The plan of each capital city comprised nine east-west belts, which were referred to as *jo*, controlled by a principal; each *jo* contained four *bo*—one *bo* spanning approximately 500 meters on one side. Each *jo* and *bo* was separated by major streets, approximately 24 to 51 meters wide. Each *bo* was again divided into sixteen sections called *cho* by minor streets that were 12 meters wide.

The imperial palace district was situated at the north-central region of the capital area. Two market places were set up and managed by the market masters. The allocation of housing lots was carried out in a style similar to that in the former capitals.

The *jo* and *bo*, and the sections within each *bo* were numbered. This numerical place indication system was implemented in the eighth century. It is worth noting that the Chinese capital cities in the eighth and ninth centuries did not boast of such numerical indication systems; on the contrary, each *bo* was given a particular name. The Japanese numerical system for the city plan was originally established in the eighth century, and although it was a modification of the Chinese style of planning, the system was designed to cater to Japanese special conditions.

The population of Heian-kyo was around 100,000, of which nearly 90% was constituted by common people and the rest comprised the royal and aristocrat families, the higher bureaucrats and their servants. The government facilities focused on the imperial palace district and the surrounding areas, and many of the noble men and higher bureaucrats' residences were also located near this area. In the ninth and tenth centuries, the buildings or facilities were widely distributed, except in several of the south-western sections of the city. On the other hand, in the eleventh and the twelfth centuries, the buildings were mainly distributed in the east capital. It is important to note that the west capital was relatively unpopulated and the residential districts expanded to both the northern and eastern suburbs outside the original capital area. The north-eastern part of the original capital area and its nearest suburbs were the most favored and expensive residential districts for aristocrats and higher bureaucrats, since the imperial palace had moved from its original region to this location in the early part of the eleventh century after it was burnt down. In the case of the eastern suburbs across the Kamo River, from the original capital to the east bank, several large temples were established in the second half of the eleventh century, and these were the areas where the new breed of aristocrats and warriors established their residences in the twelfth century.

The pattern of the surface remains of the grid street is a reflection of the process of planning and transformation of the above mentioned city. The grid street patterns were well maintained within the east capital city; however, this was not the case in the west capital city. In particular, the south-western part of the west capital city had no surface and did not yield any archeological remains of the grid street pattern described above. A document issued in 828 AD reported that the region, at that time, included around 580 urbanized sections, not considering the imperial palace and governmental districts; as for the rest of the region, which spanned across approximately 400 sections, very little was known.

Another document revealed that in 1086 AD, around 300 sections were under cultivation in the west capital.

Heian-kyo, along with the former capitals, was the hub of the imperial highways and the transport destination for various products from all provinces. The imperial highways, with relay posts in six different directions with each road district, were first constructed from the main gate at the southern end of the principal street. Since the tenth century, many major streets in the capital had extended into the suburbs and further since long, and there had been a concerted drive toward urbanization and the development of villas in the nearby resort areas. The market place in each capital city had access to water via an artificial canal. Through these canals and connected rivers, the market places were further connected with the Seto-naikai Inland Sea in the west and south and with Lake Biwa toward the east and north. These transportation networks were maintained throughout history, even after the government's transport system became largely ineffectual in the tenth century. All these were important infrastructures for Heian-kyo, which became the largest home city for the manorial lords in the eleventh century; the city also became popular as the biggest handicraft centre until the Industrial Revolution.

Besides the imperial capitals, the regional and provincial capitals were also constructed as district centers in the ancient times. In fact, a few regional and provincial capitals tended to adopt processes similar to those in the capital city while creating grid patterns, although they were mostly incomplete or only imagined, and others were weakened or obliterated as new cities emerged.

The administrative districts in ancient Japan included the districts that surrounded the capital and seven other road districts that consisted of several provinces each, culminating in a total of around 70 provinces. Each province was divided into several counties and each county consisted of a number of primary administrative units that were called *go*. A basic law system, *ritsuryo*, and other laws, including family register systems and land cadastral systems based on the *jori* plan, were either completed separately or connected with each other from the late seventh century to the middle of the eighth century.

Although the administrative system of the Japanese ancient state included both the political and cosmological structure of the ancient territory, the spatial structure of the territory has basically been maintained and passed on to form the present prefectures. Within a province, the registration and allocation of cultivated lands was carried out according to the *jori* plan, and the boundary lines of the local governments were planned in straight lines on the plains as well along the imperial highways.

Since medieval times, lots of towns related to the market, port, relay post, shrines, temples and castles were developed. The national highway system had not been maintained, although local transportation itself became quite active with the rapid growth in markets and in the monetary economy. Out of the many medieval and early modern towns, castle towns are regarded as being the most characteristic of their time and have become one of the most important subjects in historical geography. A large number of castle towns were built as military, political and economic centers for approximately 200 *daimyo* districts or *han* territories all over Japan between the latter half of the sixteenth century and the first half of the seventeenth century.

A castle town included the following districts: a castle, typically like the Himeji Castle; residential districts of the upper and lower class warriors; townsmen; trade and handicraft workers; a few moats and embankments surrounding the castle and the town; and streets. It is important to note that there were several types of castle towns that incorporated such elements. In most general variety of the castle town, only the upper class warriors' residential districts near the castle and the district housing the important townsmen were enclosed by the moat and embankment.

The shape of the castle town was usually irregular, depending on the landforms and the main routes of the highways. Despite this, the basic pattern of the residential blocks for both warriors and townsmen was rectangular. The major styles of these blocks were the Kyoto and Edo styles; housing lots constructed in the Kyoto style had their fronts on the two opposite sides of the block and were situated back to back with each other. On the other hand, the lots built in the Edo style had their fronts on all sides of a block and an open space at the center of the block.

The urban network in early modern Japan was primarily centered on three metropolises, Edo, Osaka and Kyoto. Most castle towns that were secondary class in hierarchy were connected to Edo via national or sub-national highways; water transportation, too, was an extremely significant mode at that time. Other towns like Nagasaki, which was a port town, were also considered as second class towns, while many others—particularly those that housed markets, postal services and temples/shrines—were usually regarded as third class towns.

Formation and transformation of rural landscapes

The *jori* plan in the ancient state was a basic system—effective in overcoming troublesome bureaucratic procedures—that was gradually implemented by the middle of the eighth century. It was a uniform system that indicated locations through a numerical method based on the unit of *cho* (approximately 1.2 hectares, 109 meters on each side) in a grid pattern, and a cadastral system. Thus, it was originally not necessary to visually construct the grid pattern into paths and ditches, although it was represented and characterized by an interlacing network of paths and ditches in the later period. The *jori* plan, in other words, originally contained two components: the *jori* location system as a cadastral method and the *jori* grid pattern on the ground.

The land administration system was persisted with as the basic system of provincial administration despite the break-down of the allocation system of arable land at the beginning of the tenth century. All lands for cultivation were generally indicated by the *jori* plan for the purposes of registration and taxation, and the section was the basic unit for all permissions and grants. Compared to the original *ritsuryo* system of the eighth and ninth centuries, the *jori* plan indicated more important boundaries with regard to land ownership, and rights and responsibilities toward the payment of taxes to both provincial governors and land owners (such as the manor lords and the big temples/shrines) in the tenth and eleventh centuries.

In the eleventh century, a new custom was established, which enabled a land owner to expand his rights within a basic section. In other words, the grid lines of the *jori* plan gained an additional function: these lines now served as boundaries of rights, interests and duties for parties who intended to expand and control them. Thus the basic section came to be an important unit in the actual operation of the Japanese agricultural economy and society. Even after the breakdown of the provincial-level use of the *jori* plan, within a manor, a system like the *jori* plan that could be used to identify lands for managing a manor was still necessary. The methods that were adopted in such a situation, in the absence of a provincial-level *jori* plan, were often standardized within a manor.

A great number of remains of paths and ditches, coinciding with *jori* grid patterns on the ground, have been found as a result of the progress in archaeological excavations. While the earliest example of an underground *jori* grid pattern has been dated back to the second half of the eighth century, most others have been dated to a much later period through the use of archaeological methods. It is particularly noteworthy that such paths and ditches were identified to be constructed in and around the twelfth century, and have continued to be built or reconstructed until very recently, facilitating modern land divisions on the ground; this, despite intervals of abandonment that have caused by repeated floods and natural calamities.

However, by the end of the sixteenth century, the location-indication system of the *jori* plan, as a whole, was replaced by a village name system and a minor location-name system within it. The minor location-names were used to identify locations of lands in detail, but they continued to correspond to grid patterns that were manifest as actual land divisions on the ground. This location-indication style continued, in many cases, into the modern times and the grid pattern became a basic factor in cultural landscapes.

A vast number of *jori* grid patterns were widely found on the ground until a drastic change caused by land consolidation took over with a view to modernizing agriculture. The grid patterns that remained on the ground were, in many cases, fitted to a standardized plan within a plain as a whole, making it possible for us to reconstruct the original plan on the basis of these grid patterns.

In the beginning of the eighth century, the distribution pattern of arable lands was selective and the rural settlements were dispersed as same as arable lands. Both these patterns expanded throughout the major plains of central Japan, although most of the arable lands were still undergoing extensive land utilization. Since the twelfth century, land utilization began to gradually intensify, and some dispersed settlements transformed into nucleated types in or near the capital district. This trend became quite popular and eventually, by the end of the sixteenth century, was the chosen way of life for great segments of the Japanese population, although the dispersed settlements and selective distribution of arable lands, such as in the case of the Tonami Plain located quite far from the capital district, were still popular.

Confusion of the landscape

The traditional houses were made of wood; the walls were made of clay and had wooden doors and windows, both of which often consisted of paper screens. The materials used to construct the roof included tiles, straws, and boards, and these choices varied from place to place or depended on the social status of the occupants. One- or two-storied buildings were quite popular, except in some mountainous regions, and were usually made harmonious with the landscape through social or administrative control. However, brick buildings with glass windows and other western-style buildings, most of which were incomplete imitations, began to be constructed at the end of the nineteenth century and quickly spread from the major cities to the towns and even to the rural areas. Furthermore, concrete and tinplate and many other substances were added to list of building materials, especially after World War II. As a result, the traditional landscapes were broken down and various confused landscapes emerged.

Such confusion spread throughout Japan and this became quite a serious issue. Of the major changes that were induced by such confusion was the change in lifestyle from the traditional living rooms, where the occupants sat directly on the *tatami* mat, to western style rooms where chairs were used. This drastic change was not only observed in business/industrial buildings but also seen in ordinary households. The Japanese more often than not accepted such changes without much hesitation. This could be due to their traditional beliefs that held new buildings as desirable for a new stage of life or to welcome an important guest. One such instance that may be cited as a traditional validation of the renewal of buildings is the time-honored ritual of re-building the 'Ise' Shrine once every twenty years. The combination of Japanese and Western styles might have resulted in new styles, and the confusion was often a consequence of such combination and may continue for a while. For example, many traditional style houses or shops in Kyoto, which were built nearly a hundred years ago, require fundamental repair work or re-building today; however, many building owners who are unable to spend the required money for the repairs may choose to live in new-style buildings. Furthermore, since 1850, a regulation has been in place that forbids the re-building of traditional wooden houses owing to the greater risk of such buildings catching fire.

Industrialization and urbanization have greatly encroached upon the rural areas causing serious landscape-confusion all over Japan. Land consolidation in rural areas was carried out in the first half of the last century and again, with the intention of achieving more mechanization, since the late 1960s. Industrialization was effective in improving and consolidating the paddy for the purpose of a better rural economy. The land consolidation process has involved the mechanization of agriculture so as to save labor, who can then be employed in manufacturing industries. Such intervention may lead to the destruction of sustainable rural economies and the end, for instance, of traditional landscapes of terrace paddies that are largely dependent on labor-intensive cultivation.

No effective policy or comprehensive agreement has been reached across society to maintain or form desirable rural and urban landscapes in Japan. While some instances of preserving the historic or natural landscapes exist, these are restricted to limited areas. The only step taken to spread awareness of the importance of traditional landscapes has been the introduction of new laws since 2006 to preserve traditional cultural landscapes and improve them.

Expected and unexpected changes in both spatial organization and the landscape

Industrialization in Japan resulted in the creation of four major industrial regions in and around Tokyo, Nagoya and Osaka, and in northern Kyushu before World War II. This process revealed, at the same time, a new regional gap between the Japan Sea coastal region and the Pacific coastal region, owing to differences in the levels of industrialization. The former was often called "Ura-Nihon" (The back of Japan), for it was industrially underdeveloped and was plagued by an undesirable image on account of a large amount of snowfall and a rather bleak industrial climate. The latter, by contrast, was called "Omote-Nihon" (the front of Japan) and had a bright image as a result of its winter sunshine and well-developed industry.

Immediately after World War II, the preservation of the exhausted country was an urgent political/economic task, especially with regard to developing its natural resources and improving the infrastructure for the manufacturing industry. The Comprehensive National Development Act was enacted in 1950 and the National Income Doubling Plan was rolled out in 1960. The Comprehensive National Development Plan (CNDP) was instituted in 1962, which tried to develop many new industrial areas both as New Industrial Cities and Special Areas for Industrial Consolidation, besides the four major industrial areas.

However, a number of these were concentrated along the Pacific-Setouchi coastal belt, which was similar to Front Japan, and the regional gap was not mitigated. People moved to the metropolitan areas on the Pacific-Setouchi coastal belt. Outside the area, on the other hand, the net migration flows became negative. The drift of population away from the countryside, especially from the mountainous regions, revealed the existence of many depopulated areas, where rural communities could not be maintained; soon, a number of deserted villages were found. On the other hand, metropolitan areas (MA) like Tokyo and Osaka that were already overpopulated were expanding outward such that both rural and urban landscapes were fragmented and the improvement of social infrastructure was often delayed.

A new CNDP was introduced in 1969 and the CNDP III was instated in 1973. Both these programs aimed to achieve well-balanced development in the country, and launched determined efforts in that direction. However, the regional structure could not be revised. A scheme for producing many regional units, each of which would have a medium-sized city, was planned as part of CNDP III; however, the trend toward larger metropolitan areas continued. CNDP IV, in 1987, expanded this concept and proposed a Dispersed Multi-nuclear Structure for the country, while CNDP V, in 1997, presented the concept of the Multi-Country Axes, both of which tried or are still trying to form other cores of regional life/economy besides Tokyo MA.

The centralization of net migration flows focused on metropolitan areas, especially on Tokyo, is still progress. Several metropolitan areas, including Tokyo MA and Osaka MA, continue to grow, but the ratio of the increase in Tokyo MA is much higher than those in other metropolitan areas. Economic activity, especially of the tertiary sector, has remained concentrated on Tokyo MA, and the erstwhile twin-centered structure, focused on Tokyo and Osaka, has been transformed almost entirely to a Tokyo-centered structure.

Traditional spatial organizations at the national level, which have traditionally had a multi-centered structure based on Tokyo, Osaka and Kyoto, are, at present, changing their focus to a single base in Tokyo, although the nation is still administratively organized on a prefectural and provincial level. The changing spatial organization is now facing a globalizing economy and culture, and its reformation is being discussed at the national level. These circumstances tending to focus to Tokyo may strengthen the changes in the hierarchical structure of spatial organizations as well as influence the eventual situation with regard to the confusion of landscapes.

Subject index

A

afforestation 155, 157, 158, 164, 179, 180, 182
Age of the Japanese Civil Wars 207
Agriculture Pavilion 254
Ainu 164
Akashi 227
Akita School of Datch Painting 232
Akiyama-go 235
allocation 24, 116–119, 122, 124, 176, 189, 268–270
Ama no Hashidate Zu 212
ancient 3–9, 12, 13, 21–26, 28, 30, 37, 38, 41, 13, 44, 48, 56–58, 61, 65, 67, 70, 71–73, 75, 78–80, 93, 95, 115, 116, 122, 128, 130, 131, 154, 176, 189, 192, 194, 196, 207, 212, 218, 223–228, 230, 243, 244, 246, 247, 249, 251, 252–254, 267, 269, 270
arable land 7, 24, 25, 115–119, 122, 124–126, 131, 137, 143, 144, 146, 148, 151, 152, 157, 158, 168, 176, 177, 270–272
Arbor Day 180
Asia-Pacifi c war 258, 259
atomic bomb 244, 258
Auschwitz 258
Azuchi 26, 90–93
Azuchi castle 90–92

B

Back Japan 32
bald mountains 156, 164, 179, 181, 182
Battle of Okinawa 244
behavioral approach 11

bird's eye 213, 218, 219
Biwa Lake 254
bo 9, 24, 25, 41, 43–45, 120, 124, 125, 268
British 4, 107
Buddhism 21, 37, 75–77, 194, 212, 230, 244, 267
Buddhist 21, 24, 37, 58, 65, 67, 72, 80, 163, 196, 228, 247, 250
Buddhist temple 24, 37, 58
Bungo-Funai 85
Bureau of Forestry 180, 181
Byōbu 212, 213

C

Cadastral map 10
cadastral system 24, 118, 126, 196, 269, 270
capital 3–5, 8, 9, 11, 13, 22, 23, 25, 28, 40, 41–50, 52–60, 62, 67, 70, 72, 75, 77, 95, 99, 104, 109, 115, 122–125, 128, 132, 133, 144–146, 151, 196, 202, 205, 218, 219, 226, 245, 250, 253, 254, 268–269
castle 4, 7, 8, 25–27, 49, 50, 83, 89–93, 96, 101, 103–105, 109, 110, 256, 269
castle town 7, 8, 11, 27, 28, 89–93, 95, 96, 98, 99, 101–106, 229, 270
castle vista plan 93, 95
centralization 33, 274
Chikuen-shō 227
China/Chinese 4, 5, 9, 21, 23, 24, 27, 37, 41, 44, 45, 48, 71, 79, 80, 107–109, 117, 124, 125, 196, 203, 205, 249, 230, 232, 238, 243, 259, 267, 268
Chinese characters 21, 37
Chinese merchant 80

Chinese quarter 109
Chinese town 9
Chinoiserie 230
cho 24, 44, 54, 67, 117, 119, 120, 140,
    146–148, 150, 151, 169, 171, 174, 177,
    180, 190, 192, 268, 270
Chōgen Sayamaike Kaisyū hi 247
Christianity 26, 27, 85, 107
church 107
city plan 8, 43, 52, 196, 256, 258, 267, 268
colonial grid pattern 167, 168
Colonial Grid Plans 168
colonization 163–166, 219
commemoration 243, 248, 251, 253, 254,
    256, 257, 261
commons 137, 155, 156, 158, 171, 179, 180
Comprehensive National Development
    Plan 32, 273
confusion 6, 31, 33, 119, 125, 261, 272, 274
confusion of the landscape 31, 33, 272, 274
contextual approach 14, 15
cosmology 12, 243, 244
county 6, 28, 30, 40, 45, 53, 54, 56–58,
    120–122, 127–129, 158, 190, 196, 269
county seat 6, 54, 57, 58
cross-sectional 5, 6
cultural landscape 13–15, 21, 26, 32, 159,
    230, 267, 271, 273

D
daimyo 26–28, 202, 212, 270
Dainihon Kairiku Meisyo Zue 215, 216
Dazaifu 23, 48–54, 56, 60–62
Dejima 108–109
dispersed settlements 167, 168, 182, 272
do 12, 22, 52, 54, 74, 105, 117, 122, 130,
    156, 179, 236
downtown 67, 68, 104–106
Dutch 107, 108, 232

E
early modern 3, 5–9, 11–13, 89, 91–93, 95,
    96, 98, 99, 104, 106, 107, 109, 110, 137,
    138, 141, 144, 146, 148, 152, 154, 155,
    157, 158, 163, 170, 175, 179, 194, 202,
    218, 227, 229, 230, 238, 249, 269, 270
East Asia 26, 79

Edo 9, 28, 29, 99, 104–106, 143–147, 158,
    202, 205, 208, 211, 213, 215, 234, 253,
    256, 270
Edo castle 104, 106
Edo era 99, 202, 256
Edo Hitome Zu Byōbu 234
Edo Ichiranzu 213
Edo Meisyo Zue 213
Edo Shogunate 205, 253
Edo Zu Byōbu 213
Emaki 212, 230
Emperor 25, 26, 28, 29, 38, 41–44, 56, 58,
    65, 67, 68, 70, 99, 124, 163, 180, 189,
    218, 224–226, 230, 247, 253–256, 267
Engi shiki 251
environmental determinism 238
Ezo 203–205, 245, 246

F
farmer-soldiers 166
feng-shui 230
feudal domain 99, 157, 205
feudal lord 77, 80–83, 85, 89, 93, 96, 98, 99,
    101–104, 106, 109, 143, 157, 169, 202, 205
feudal system 6, 83–84
fish fertilizer 144
Forestry Agency 181
Front Japan 32, 273
Fujiwara-kyō 23, 41, 226
fukei 6, 238
Fushimi 92, 254

G
Genbaku Dome 258–259
Genji Monogatari 230
geographical imagination 212, 215, 244
geomancy 230
Gion festival 70
Gion shrine 68, 70
go 4, 21, 25, 40, 45, 56, 57, 89, 93, 99, 192,
    228, 235, 251, 260, 269
Go Kinai shi 251
gobanme-shugi 178
Gou 206
Governmental Park Law 260
governor 23, 25, 40, 49, 53, 54, 56, 57, 116,
    117, 125–127, 171, 192, 245, 271

green manure 143, 144, 152, 153, 155, 179, 180
grid pattern 4, 6–10, 12, 13, 24, 25, 28, 47,
    48, 50, 52, 100, 118–126, 128–130, 132,
    167, 168, 189, 190, 192, 194, 196, 207,
    267, 270, 271
grid street pattern 5, 12, 23, 41, 44, 46, 49,
    52, 54, 124, 268
gridism 178
Ground map 74
Gyogi-zu 196

H
Hachijoin-cho 67
Hakata 26, 48, 49, 79, 80
hamlet-type 133
han 27–29, 99, 100, 270
handen-zu 190, 192
Harima 206
Heian Jingū Shrine 253
Heian-kyo 23, 25, 30, 43–46, 48, 52, 56, 58,
    65, 67, 70, 95, 196, 267, 268, 269
Heijo-kyo 23, 41–45, 124, 125, 226
Heisenji 75–77
Hell Valley 72
heritage 58, 243, 251, 252, 258, 261
highway 22, 28, 29, 51, 53, 54, 57, 101, 107,
    122, 147, 171, 269
highway system 22, 28, 53, 54, 269
Hiragishi 166
Hiroshima 33, 101, 243, 244, 258
Hiroshima Peace Memorial 258
Hitachi 245
Hojujidono 65
Hokaido Colonization Bureau, 165
Hokkaidō 29, 146, 163–169, 176, 182,
    203, 233
Hokkaidō Kaitaku-shi 165
Hokke 77
Home Ministry 171
Honganji 77, 92
Honsyu Island 58, 83, 99
Hōrai Corporation 173
horizontal cross-sections 5
Horyuji temple 58
Hossho-ji temple 65
housing lots 43, 44, 123, 268, 270
Hyogo 206, 277

I
Ichijo street Ichijodani 70
Ikko 77
Imagined Communities 243
Iminomiya 73, 74
imperial capital 22, 23, 41–43, 48, 49, 53,
    54, 58, 115, 124, 267, 269
imperial highway 48, 269
Imperial Household Agency 256
imperial palace 41, 43–45, 47, 267, 268
imperialism 218
Industrial Revolution 30, 140, 163,
    173, 269
industrialization 31, 32, 109, 110, 143,
    272, 273
Industry Pavilion 254
intensify 271
iriai 155, 156, 179
irrigation 6–8, 11, 26, 117, 130–132, 140,
    143, 144, 146, 148, 151, 157, 176, 192,
    194, 246
Ishikari plain 166
Ishiyama-Honganji 77, 92

J
Japan 26, 28–33, 37–39, 44, 45, 48, 56–58,
    61, 68, 70, 75, 77, 79–81, 89, 95, 96,
    99, 100, 102–109, 115, 122, 124, 125,
    131, 137, 143, 144, 146, 148, 152, 153,
    155, 158–208, 211, 212, 215, 216, 218,
    219, 223, 228–230, 232–235, 238–240,
    243–246, 249–251, 253, 256, 259, 260,
    269–273
Japan Sea 23, 32, 80, 81, 96, 196, 273
Japanese cedar 158
Japanese cypress 157
Japanese Empire 181, 256
Japanese mulberry 173
Ji 80
Jidai Gyōretsu 253
Jinai-machi 77, 86, 87
jo 24, 43, 44, 49, 59–62, 120–122, 124, 125,
    131, 267, 268
Jodo-shin sect 77–80
jori 4, 6–8, 10, 12, 13, 24, 25, 28,
    118–132, 176, 189, 190, 192, 194, 196,
    269–271

jori grid pattern 7, 8, 10, 12, 13, 25, 28, 120–124, 128–130, 132, 189, 190, 192, 194, 196, 270, 271
jori indication system 120, 121, 124, 125, 192
jori numbering system 190
jori plan 24, 118–131
jori style indication system 128
Jurakudai 93

K

Kagoshima 203
Kagu Hill 224, 225
Kaihotsu 137, 159
Kaiho-type 99
Kamakura 25, 67, 70, 72
Kamakura government 25, 65, 67, 70, 72
Kamigyo 68, 70
Kankyo Dainihon Shishin Zenzu 216, 218
Kansai Science City 256
Karaku Ichiranzu 213
Kasuga Gongen Genki Emaki 230
Kasuga Shrine 230
keikan vii, 6
Keisai Kuwagata 234
Ki'i Domain 228, 229
Kibe Village 176
Kinai 22, 250, 251
Kindai 253
Kino (Yoshino) River 158
kiri-zoe 151
Kitano 67
kōchi seiri 176
Kojiki 37, 246
Kokin Wakashû 224, 226
kokufu 5, 23
Komaki 4–6, 89–91, 95
Komaki castle 89, 91
Kōnosu 176
Korea/Korean 21, 24, 27, 37, 38, 49, 50, 79, 107, 181, 203, 218, 219
Korean Peninsula 37, 38, 203, 218
Kōyo Tanshō Zukan 233
Kubiki Hill 151
kuni-bome 225, 226
Kuniezu 202, 203, 205, 206
Kushida Shrine 80
Kyo 25–29, 31, 65, 67, 207

Kyoto 4, 9, 11, 25, 29, 31, 33, 44, 45, 67, 68, 70, 77, 80, 82, 83, 89, 92, 93, 99, 100, 104, 154, 158, 196, 207, 208, 212, 213, 218, 219, 238, 243, 244, 253, 254, 256, 257, 267, 270, 272, 274
Kyoto Meisyo Dai Chōkanzu 218, 219
Kyoto Station 254
Kyushu Island 107

L

lagoon 79–82, 107, 137, 147, 148, 177, 228, 229
Lake Biwa 23, 38, 48, 91, 219, 227, 269
Land consolidation 31, 128–130, 271, 272
Land division 18, 46, 122, 123, 125, 126, 128, 130, 271
Land Improvement Act 178
Land Readjustment Act 176, 178
land readjustments 175, 176
land registration 23, 40, 118–119, 189, 190, 194
land tax 116, 119, 141, 180
Land Tax Revision 180
Landscape 3–6, 8–15, 21, 26, 28, 29, 31, 32, 52, 62, 65, 68, 71, 72–75, 77, 78, 80–83, 85, 89, 90–93, 95, 96, 98, 99, 102, 109, 120, 131, 137, 144–149, 151, 152, 154, 157–159, 163, 164, 167, 171, 173–176, 179, 181, 182, 190, 192, 194, 196, 202, 212, 213, 215, 216, 223–230, 232–240, 243, 244, 253, 258, 260, 261, 267, 271–274
landscape history 3, 14
Landschaft 6
large families 21, 40
large scale map 46, 129, 189, 190, 196
laws of perspective 232
Lieux de Mémoire 243
love for forest 180, 181

M

Machi 67, 68
Machi street 67
Machi-gaikaku-type 102
Machiya-Kakugai-type 102
Makeup Women's Slope 72
Makkatsu 245, 246

manor 4, 24, 25, 28, 39, 56, 57, 123,
126–128, 131, 133, 170, 190, 192, 194,
196, 271
manorial map 190, 194
Manyōshū 242
market town 6, 8, 12, 27
marketplace 12, 43, 44, 48, 54, 107
medieval 3–5, 7–13, 24–26, 28, 31, 48,
49, 65, 67, 68, 70, 72–95, 77–81,
83–85, 89, 91–93, 95, 96, 98, 99,
102, 103, 107, 130–132, 140, 154,
155, 164, 176, 189, 194, 196, 203,
204, 207, 212, 223, 227, 230, 243,
247, 249, 269
Meiji Restoration 27, 147, 163
Meisyo Zue 213, 215, 216
memory 215, 236, 243, 258, 261
metropolis 270
metropolitan area 32, 33, 273, 274
military base 23, 50, 53, 60–62, 244, 246
Minamoto clan 65
minor place-name 118, 119, 128
Mishima Farm 171
Miyako 207, 213, 253
Miyako Meisyo Zue 213
Miyako no Ki 207
Mizuki 48–51
mochi-zoe 151
modern 3–9, 11–13, 21, 26, 29, 49, 89,
91–93, 95, 96, 98, 99, 104, 106, 107,
109, 110, 128–130, 137, 138, 143,
144, 146, 148, 152-155, 157, 158,
163, 164, 168-171, 173–177, 179,
180, 182, 192, 194, 202, 212, 218,
219, 223, 227–230, 236–240, 243,
244, 248, 249, 251, 253, 254,
256–253, 267, 269–271
modern self 223, 237
modernization 110, 129, 163, 170, 173,
179, 218, 219, 236
monument 243–250, 253, 257, 258
monumental landscape 243, 244
morphologies 99
Mount Fuji 225, 238, 239
Mount Hiei 218
Mount Kasuga 230, 232
Mount Nasu 171

mountain castle 49, 50
mulberry plantations 174, 182
multi-centered structure 274
Muromachi era 67, 68
Muromachi government 67, 68, 89
Muromachi street 70
Musashino terrace 144, 146
Museum of Kyoto 257
Mutsu 58, 60, 244, 245, 246

N
Nagasaki 27, 29, 107–109, 258, 270
Nagato 72, 73
Nagoya, 32, 33, 157, 158, 273
Naha 261
Nakasen-do 105
Nanao 96, 98
Naniwa Bay 227
Nara 9, 41, 42, 131, 158, 192, 224, 225,
227, 230, 245, 247
Nasu Canal 171
Nasu Farm 171, 172
Nasuno-ga-hara 171, 172
National Archives of Japan 202
national chronicle 37, 41
National Industrial Exhibition 253
National Parks Law 260
National Peace Memorial Halls for Atomic
Bomb Victims 258
National Territory 196, 215, 216
Ngato 73
Nichiren 77, 80
Nihonbashi 105
Nihon Fûkei Ron 238
Nihon Meisyo no E 213
Nihon Sōzu 203, 205
Nihon-shoki 41, 48
Nihon Syoki 37, 246
Niigata dune 148
Nijo street 65
Nikkō 145
Nippon Meizan Zue 232, 233
No more Hiroshima 258
nōjō 170
Nopporo village 166
Noto-Nanao 96
numerical indication system 44, 268

O

Obama 80, 81
Odoi 95
Ogawa Village 146
Okazaki 253, 254
Okinawa 146, 203, 244, 258–261
Okinawa Tourist Agency 260, 261
Okinohama 80
Onin war 68, 70, 82
Ordinance Survey 174
Osaka 9, 11, 28, 29, 32, 33, 38, 77, 78, 92,
    93, 99, 100, 104, 143, 149, 158, 194,
    206, 227, 246, 252, 270, 273, 274
Osaka plain 246, 252
Osaka temple town 78
Others 119, 204, 205
Owari (Nagoya) Domain 157

P

Pacific Ocean 70, 225
palace 11, 23, 27, 38, 40, 41, 43–45, 47, 68,
    93, 253, 254, 267, 268
parade 60, 253, 254
pasturing 163, 170
Pax Tokugawa 137
Peace City 258
perceived worlds of the past 11
pine forests 153, 236
place-identifying system 9
plantation forestry 158
population 10, 28, 32, 43, 45, 61, 68, 70,
    71, 77, 82, 99, 106, 110, 137, 141, 143,
    144, 146, 151, 152, 157, 163, 164, 175,
    235, 268, 272, 273
population explosion 141, 144
port 27, 48, 49, 72, 78–81, 91, 95, 96, 98,
    107, 110, 218, 254, 269, 270
Port Fushimi 254
port town 27, 79–82, 95, 96, 98, 107, 110,
    218, 270
Portugal/ Portuguese 26, 85, 107, 108, 144
post town 28
prefecture 4, 10, 21, 29
prehistoric 3–6
pre-jori minor place name 190
province 4, 7, 21–25, 27, 28, 39, 40, 43, 45,
    48, 49, 53, 54, 56–61, 115, 120, 121, 123,
    124, 126, 128, 131, 189, 190, 192, 194,
    196, 202, 206, 229, 244–246, 269
provincial capital 5, 13, 22, 50, 53, 54, 57,
    58, 60, 62, 72
provincial constable 25–27, 68, 82, 83
provincial government 23, 25, 41, 49, 53,
    56–58, 60, 115, 116, 122, 124, 126, 127,
    167, 189, 194

Q

Qing dynasty 256

R

railroad 110
Rakuchū-Rakugai Zu Byōbu 213
Rasetsu Koku 203
re-building 203
reclaimed paddies 117
reclamation corporation 165
rectangular plan 62
red pine 154, 180
regional capital 23, 33, 48–50, 60, 62
regional kingdoms 21, 40
relay post 6, 48, 54, 269
rent 116, 119, 123, 127, 147
Report of the Hiroshima Peace
    City Plan 258
research group for Kuniezu 202
residential district 45, 268, 270
retrospective 5
rice paddy stairs 146, 151
Riku'u Highway 171
Ritsu 72
ritsu-ryo 115–119, 127, 131, 189
River Ishikari 167
River Kiso 157
River Sakai 148
road district 22, 49, 50, 269
road villages 166
Rokuhara 65, 66
Rokujo street 67
roll plans 124
royal highway 22, 28
royal palace 38, 41, 93
rural landscape 8, 10, 168, 169, 176, 182,
    190, 237, 253
rural plan 194

rural settlement 3
Russia 29, 164, 166, 256
Ryūkyū 203–205, 260, 261
Ryukyu government 260, 261
Ryūsen Zu 208, 211, 212

S
Saga 25, 67, 70
Sakhalin 219
sandbank 79, 80
Sanjo 67, 257
Sanjō Street 257
sansui-ga, 230, 238
Sapporo 33, 166
Sarashina 227
satellite town 67, 70
sato-yama 179
Satsuma 203, 205
Sayamaike pond 246, 247, 249
Self 205, 223, 226, 230, 237
Sembonmatsu Farm 171, 173
Sendai 33, 166, 103
Sendai domain 166
Sengoku era 68
Sericulture 174
Seto inland sea 77
settlement pattern 167
Settsu 148, 192, 206
Settsu-Kawaguchi Shinden 148
Shichijo street 148
shifting cultivation 10, 151, 158
Shiga 67
Shijo-Machi 68, 70
Shimogyo 68, 70
Shimo-hiramaru 151
Shimotsuke 245
shinden 137, 143, 144, 146–148, 150, 151
Shingon 75
shinkei-zu 232, 234
Shinsen Zōho Kyō Ōezu 207
Shinto 75, 194
Shin-totsukawa 168
Shiobara Tracks 171
Shirakawa 65
Shitenno-ji 93
Shiunji-gata 147
Shiwa-jo 147

Shizen to Jinsei 236
Shogunate 202–206, 228, 253, 256
Shokuminchi kukaku zu 168
shokusan kōgyō 163
Shirin (Journal of History) 243
Shrine Grounds Map of Iminomiya 73
Shunpo 237
silk filature industry 163, 174
Sino-Japanese War 238
Small scale map 189, 196
Society of Historical Research 243
Society of Jesus 85, 107
Sokaku-type 99–101
Sotomachi 109
Spanish 26, 107
spatial organization 7, 26, 29, 33, 274
spatial pattern 67, 68, 71, 85, 91
spatial structure vii, 67, 71, 77, 78, 84, 269
state guesthouse 48, 51
stock breeding 170
straight lines 122, 269
street 5, 12, 23, 25, 41, 43–45, 48, 49, 52, 54, 65, 67, 70–73, 80, 85, 90, 93, 95, 103, 104, 106, 107, 109, 124, 196, 257, 267–269
Sumiyoshi 227
swidden 151, 152, 158, 181, 235
swidden agriculture 158, 181, 235
Syoku Nihon Gi 246
Syugaisyo 3
Syugo 68

T
Tagajō 244–246
Tagajō hi 244, 245
Taiho-ritsuryo 38
Taiwan 219
Tale of Genji 230
Tamagawa Canal, 144, 147
tanada 151
Tango 212, 229
Taoism 230
tatami mat 31, 207, 272
Tatemachi-type 103–105
Tatsuta River 226
tax 22, 23, 57, 116, 119, 126, 143, 180, 189

Technology Pavilion 254
temple town 77–79, 92, 95
Tendai 75
Tenryu-ji temple 70
Tera-machi 95
thick cross-sections 3, 5, 9, 12, 15
thin cross-sections 5, 9
Title deeds 8, 123
Toba 65
Tōdaiji temple 43, 192, 247
Tōhoku railway 171
Tokai-do 22, 105
Tokaidō Meisyo Ichiran 213
Tōkei Sansui Zu 230
Tokugawa government 27–29, 99–102, 106,
    107, 109, 137, 143, 144, 148, 149, 163, 233
Tokugawa regime 104, 106, 109, 140
Tokugawa Shogunate 202–206, 228, 256
Tokushima University Library 202
Tokyo 9, 28, 29, 32, 33, 99, 109, 143, 145,
    146, 174, 176, 180, 212, 219, 233, 253,
    256, 273, 274
Tokyo Bay 233
Tomioka 174
tonden-hei, 166
Toshogu shrine 103, 228, 229
town wall 68, 77, 78, 82, 85, 95, 100
township system 167
Tozai subway 256
tragedy of the commons 155
tsubo 24, 85, 120–123, 125, 127, 131, 165,
    166, 168, 190
Tsuki-ga-se 230
Tsurugaoka-Hachiman 71

U
Uchimachi 99–101, 109
Uchimachi-Sotomachi-type 99–101

Uchino 93
Uemachi terrace 149
Uesugi clan 102
Uji bashi danpi 249
Uji Bridge 249–251
Ukiyoe 211, 215, 250
United States 167, 171, 176,
    259, 260
uptown 104
uta-makura 227, 228

V
vertical themes 5
village registry system 40

W
waka 223, 225, 227, 228, 238
Wakamiya street 71, 72
Waka-no-ura 228
warrior 3, 7, 8, 25–27, 56, 106, 110
Wasure'enu hitobito 236
water channel 106
World Cultural Heritage site 258
World Heritage 58, 258
World War II 3, 30–32, 109, 272, 273

Y
Yamashina 77, 78
Yamato dynasty 23, 37–40
yamato-e 230
Yodo River 77, 148
Yokomachi-type 103–105
Yonezawa 102
Yoshino 158, 227

Z
Zen 80, 212
Zushi 70, 72

Author index

A

Abe 239, 258
Akiduki, Tanetatsu 218
Akisato, Ritou 213
Arizono 174, 179
Asai, Chū 237, 238
Ashikaga, Kenryo ix, 8, 11, 67
Ashikaga, Takauji 67

B

Baker, Alan 7
Bird, Isabella 145

C

Chiba 154, 155, 180, 181, 213
Chōgen 247, 249

D

Darby, H.C. 15
De Rijke, Johannis 179, 180
Dōshō 250
Dōtō 250

F

Fontanesi, Antonio 237
Fujioka, K. 5, 15
Fujita, Yoshihisa 152, 157
Fujiwara, Asakari 245
Fujiwara, Sadaie 227

G

Gountei, Sadahide 234

H

Harada 146
Harley 203
Hashimoto, Gyokuransai 216
Hayashi, Yoshinaga 207
Hettner, A. 4
Hirohito (Emperor) 218
Hisatake 157
Hishikawa, Moronobu 211
Honda, Seiroku 180
Hoskins, W. 6

I

Igarashi, Tsutomu 151
Ishikawa, Tomonobu 208, 211
Izawa, Yasobē 148

J

Jimmu (Emperor) 180
Jomei (Emperor) 224, 225
Jones, D.W. 171

K

Kaibara, Ekiken 157, 228
Kanmu (Emperor) 253
Karatani 223, 228, 236
Kawamura 202, 203
Kawase, Zentarō 180
Kimura, Motoi 144
Kinda, Akihiro 167, 207, 247, 257
Kishi, T. 8, 146
Kitō, Hiroshi 143

Kobayashi, Kōsetsu 250
Kojima, Usui 238
Komaki, S. 4
Komeie, Taisaku vii, x, 137, 163, 223
Kumazawa, Banzan 155
Kunikida, Doppo 236–238
Kuwagata, Keisai 213, 234

M
Mackinder, H. 4
Madenokōji, Fujifusa 235
Matsudaira, Sadanobu 233
Matsukata, Masayoshi 171
Matsunaga, Teitoku 227
Meiji (Emperor) 163
Meitzen, August 7
Minami 157
Minamoto, Yoritomo 70
Mishima, Michitsune 171

N
Nabika, Seisyo 251
Nagakubo, Sekisui 215
Nakashima 180
Nishida 227, 228

O
Oda, Nobunaga 27, 89
Oda, Takeo ix
Ogawa, Krobē 146
Ogawa, Takuji 238
Onoda, Naotake 232
Ōtomo, Yakamochi 225

P
Passarge, S. 4
Perry 107

R
von Richthofen, Ferdinand 179
Rodrigues, João 144

S
Sagamiya, Tahei 208
Sakanoue no Iratsume 224

Sauer, C. 6
Schluter, O. 4
Senda, M. 12, 83
Sesshū Tōyō 230
Shiba, Kōkan 232
Shiga, Shigetaka 238
Smith 215
Suizu, Ichiro ix
Suzuki 225, 226
Suzuki, Bokushi 235

T
Taishō (Emperor) 163
Takahashi, Yuich 70
Takemae, Gonbē 148
Tani, Bunchō 232
Toby 203–205
Tokugawa, Ieyasu 202
Tokutomi, Roka 236
Toyotomi, Hideyoshi 11, 27
Tsubaki 169–171
Tsuji, Morimitsu 143
Turgenev, Ivan S. 236

U
Uchida, T. 225
Uchida, Yoshiaki 236
Ueno, Eizaburō 178
Uesugi, Kazuhiro x
Usami, Keiji 230
Utagawa, Sadahide 215

W
Watanabe, Kazan 234
Wordsworth, William 236

Y
Yamabe, Akahito 225, 228
Yamamura, Aki x, 65, 72, 75
Yamori, K. 7, 99, 100, 103, 109, 110, 213
Yokoi, Tokiyoshi 178
Yonekura, J. 4
Yonemoto 203
Yoshida, Hatsusaburō 218, 219
Yumoto, Fumihiko 254